Reduce Your Tax Bite

Reduce Your Tax Bite

as reported in

The Wall Street Journal

Edited by HENRY F. MYERS

DOW JONES BOOKS
PRINCETON, NEW JERSEY

Published by Dow Jones Books
P.O. Box 300, Princeton, NJ 08540

Copyright 1980 by Dow Jones & Company, Inc.

Printed and bound in the United States of America
10 9 8 7 6 5 4 3 2 1

Library of Congress Cataloging in Publication Data

Main entry under title:

Reduce your tax bite.

   Drawn from the Wall Street Journal's Tax Report column.

   1. Tax planning—United States. I. Myers, Henry, 1929-
KF6297.R4   343'.73'04   79-21653
ISBN 0-87128-583-5

Introduction

This book is designed to save you money on federal taxes. It can do so by explaining, quickly and concisely, many of the latest developments in tax law as they have been applied to all kinds of people—the famous and the infamous, the rich and the poor, the sophisticated and the naive. In some cases, the tax problems of people that you will read about will closely parallel your own tax problems.

Included among the many topics discussed in this book are a wide range of problems concerning marriage and divorce, disputes with the Internal Revenue Service, property cases and capital gains, tax-exempt situations, payroll taxes and pay levels, many business entanglements for (both corporations and individuals), numerous different kinds of tax deductions, gambling and even living abroad. You will learn the latest decisions on what kinds of fringe benefits are taxable income to you; what kinds of educational expenses have been ruled deductible; what can and cannot be considered medical-expense deductions; what kinds of gifts are deductible; where the IRS and the courts draw the line between business-travel expenses and commuting costs; and the tax impact of accidents and various other misfortunes.

This book isn't a comprehensive guide to personal tax planning. However, it will bring you up to date on many important developments in tax law over the past few years, because it comprises the timeliest items that have appeared weekly in The Wall Street Journal's front-page "Tax Report" by Sanford L. Jacobs.

Dealing largely with legislative changes, Tax Court and other court decisions and IRS rulings and announcements, the "Tax Report" offers both tax practitioners and laymen a running commentary on the continually changing tax scene. To make this collection of "Tax Report" items more useful, court decisions and IRS rulings are cited at the end of each item. However, no case reported here should be relied upon as definitive until you or your tax expert has consulted the original opinion or ruling and determined that it has not been superseded.

In the citations, the abbreviations "T.C." and "T.C. Memo" refer to regular and memorandum decisions of the U.S. Tax Court. The full texts of these decisions are available in *Tax Court Reporter* and *Tax Court Memorandum Decisions,* published by Commerce Clearing House Inc. Decisions of other federal courts appear in *U.S. Tax Cases,* also published by Commerce Clearing House. IRS rulings are available at IRS offices and from several legal publishers.

—HENRY F. MYERS
Editor

Table of Contents

Family, Marriage and Divorce

He ran off to Uruguay, so the IRS ran after his wife—for her money, of course.

Bertha Zimler grabbed $20,000 from a joint account with her husband, Dr. Victor Zimler, when their marriage was headed for the rocks. He demanded the money; she refused. He sued for divorce; a Nassau County, N.Y., court refused. But the court set up a property settlement. He was to give her some assets and pay some expenses; she was to give him the $20,000.

He gave her nothing. He got a divorce elsewhere, remarried and was living in Uruguay. He owed the Internal Revenue Service for taxes, interest and penalties. The IRS tried to grab the $20,000 Bertha grabbed from the joint account. Victor had a right to the money, so the IRS had a right to take it, the agency said. But Victor had thumbed his nose at the property settlement, so Bertha didn't have to give him the money, a federal court said. The IRS claim "is no greater than Victor's," the court noted.

If the IRS gives Bertha everything Victor was supposed to give her, then she would have to give the money to the IRS, the court asserted. That, of course, means Bertha got to keep the dough.

Zimler v. U.S., U.S. Dist. Ct., East. Dist. N.Y., 1979
6/20/79

For her sake he should have stayed on the island and paid her alimony.

Residents of Puerto Rico normally don't pay U.S. tax on income derived from sources within the island commonwealth, whose citizens, of course, are also U.S. citizens. Elinor W. Manning lived in Puerto Rico when her husband Richard deY. Manning moved to New York City and filed for divorce. A Puerto Rico court, acting on her counter suit, granted a divorce decree.

Richard paid Elinor $17,000 a year alimony. She figured it wasn't taxable. The IRS said it was, as it came from outside Puerto Rico, from Richard in New York. He owned property in Puerto Rico that paid him more than the alimony, so her alimony could be considered coming from that source in Puerto Rico, Elinor asserted. However, the "source" of alimony is the ex-husband, the Tax Court reminded Elinor.

And Richard lived outside Puerto Rico, so her alimony came from outside and was taxable, the court concluded.

Manning v. Commissioner, T.C. Memo 1979-146
5/2/79

∽

He was a dependent, but neither parent could claim him as one.

Betty and Thomas Jones separated in July. Their son stayed with Betty in Mesquite, Texas, when Thomas moved to Dallas. They were divorced the next year. But the year of the separation they filed tax returns as married filing separately. Both claimed their son as their dependent.

A parent normally must provide *more than* 50% of a child's support to claim him as a dependent. Under Texas community-property law, half of Thomas's income belonged to Betty. For federal income tax purposes, she also was entitled to 50% of their deductions. But neither one could claim their son as a dependent because each was considered to have "provided exactly one-half of the child's support," the Tax Court said, meaning neither parent met the more-than-50% support requirement.

Jones v. Commissioner, T.C. Memo 1979-136
4/18/79

〜

He earned it all, but she was entitled to half of it.

While employed by the U.S. government in Guatemala, William L. Binford was married to a Guatemalan. Under Guatemala law, one-half his income belonged to his wife. She was a nonresident alien as far as the IRS was concerned and she didn't have to pay U.S. taxes; Binford had to pay, as he was a U.S. citizen.

Despite the community property law, Binford's employer (Uncle Sam) withheld income taxes on his *entire* salary. That meant an overpayment, which he tried to have refunded to him. But the IRS said his wife was entitled to half his withholding so she must apply for the refund. Alas, by then she and Binford had split. So he sued the U.S. for her unclaimed refund.

But a federal court said it was the ex-wife's money and only she could apply for it. In effect, Binford wanted "to be regarded as the recipient of half his salary when his tax is computed" and all of it when the withholding refund is counted, the court observed.

Binford v. U.S., U.S. Dist. Ct., Oregon, 1979
4/4/79

〜

He kept Polly on the farm. But then there was the farmhand, and the IRS.

When Polly came into his life, George Hanhauser built a love nest. He set up a corporation with her as president and had it buy a 145-acre farm. She moved into the farm house. It was close to George's Simpson, Pa., business, and he could make it to the farm for lunch or dinner with Polly. But his wife Marjorie was active in his business, and he had to hide his spending on Polly.

So George got some of his suppliers to make kickbacks to his paramour's company. It raked in about $38,000 one year. But Polly ran off and married the farmhand Barrows. George ousted her as president of their love-nest company. But her marriage with Barrows failed; she returned; George reinstated her in the company. Then the IRS came around and said the kickbacks counted as George's taxable income.

This tale of an affair of some years ago was spun out recently in a Tax Court decision, which said George owed nearly $40,000 in tax and penalty on the funds diverted to pay for his paramour. The decision discloses that George's business went through bankruptcy proceedings. It doesn't say what has become of Polly.

Hanhauser v. Commissioner, T.C. Memo 1979-504
1/17/79

◠

Did a daughter-in-law mess things up by filing with their son?

Denise lived with husband Alvin's parents, the William J. Martinos, in Middletown, Conn. They provided nearly all her support; she hadn't a job, and Alvin was in the Army. The Martinos claimed their daughter-in-law as a dependent. But the IRS said they couldn't claim her because she had filed a joint return with Alvin. Normally you can't claim someone as a dependent if he files a joint return with his spouse.

Actually Denise and Alvin didn't have to file jointly. He had made only $1,800 that year, so little that a joint return wasn't mandatory, nor was a separate return required for either of them. But he wanted to get back $28 of withholding, and he did when they filed the joint return. And the Tax Court said the joint return wouldn't spoil the Martinos' claiming Denise.

In effect, the joint return was "a claim for refund rather than a return," the court said. So it was as if Denise hadn't filed a joint "return," and thus the Martinos could claim her as a dependent, the court concluded.

Martino v. Commissioner, 71 T.C. 43
1/17/79

∽

A claim of alimony was just baloney to the tax collectors.

The divorce decree called for Thomas I. Swendseen to pay his ex-wife Jacquelyn $550-a-month child support, $900-a-month permanent alimony and $10-0,000 when he sold property he alone inherited from his father. If the property brought less than $1 million, she got 10%, and if he hadn't sold the real estate in 10 years, he had to pay her $100,000. Later, he sold a piece of the property and paid her 10%, $11,538, and deducted it as alimony.

But the IRS said he had paid her a nondeductible property settlement. The IRS argued that the divorce decree called for monthly alimony, so her share of the real estate, which the decree didn't label, wasn't alimony. However, the decree didn't rule out additional alimony, the Tax Court declared. The payment met some tests as alimony.

And because state law didn't give a wife rights to property her husband alone inherited, the payment couldn't have been a property settlement, the court asserted. So it was alimony, deductible by Swendseen (an Edina, Minn., resident) and taxable income to Jacquelyn, the court concluded.

Swendseen v. Commissioner, T.C. Memo 1978-501
12/27/78

⌒

The wife got the house. Because she did, he owed tax.

You can be in thrall to the tax collector when you make a divorce settlement that gives your half of the family home to your wife. That happened to Nelson A. Murray, a Jacksonville, Fla., pathologist when he divorced Mary after 35 years of marriage. Dr. Murray didn't pay her alimony; he gave her his half interest in their home, which she sold later for $303,000.

The IRS figured that Dr. Murray bought his wife's right to alimony and her other "marital rights" with his interest in the home. It was as if he had sold his half and given her the proceeds. So, the IRS said he owed tax on his "gain" on the deal based on his cost and the value of the home at the time of the divorce settlement. The Tax Court agreed with the IRS.

Dr. Murray's half of the house cost him $44,200; the house was worth $250,000 at the time of the divorce pact, so he had a taxable gain of $80,800 ($125,000 minus $44,200).

Murray v. Commissioner, T.C. Memo 1978-352
10/4/78

Divorce, it seems, is a haven for loving couples who hate taxes.

The tax tables don't favor married couples if both partners work. They would pay less if they weren't married. A married couple with $40,000 of combined taxable income—$20,000 from each spouse—pays the IRS $10,700, whether filing separate returns or a joint one. But two single people with like incomes have a total tax bill of $8,884, or $1,816 less than the marrieds.

Some married folks used to get divorced near the end of the year and file as singles, then remarry the first of the next year only to divorce again for tax avoidance. The IRS stopped this marriage-divorce merry-go-round some years ago. But the agency recently ruled that a married couple getting divorced but planning to stay together without remarrying will qualify as single taxpayers. Prentice Hall, tax publisher, reported the ruling with this comment:

"We won't presume to offer any advice on this one."

IRS letter ruling 7835076
9/20/78

⌒

The ex-wife of the owner of Harrah's Club wanted to ignore their divorce pact.

Scherry and William F. Harrah, the Reno and Lake Tahoe, Nev., casino owner, were divorced nine years ago. Their lawyers negotiated a community property settlement that gave her stock in two Harrah firms. That was in addition to $250,000 cash, a Rolls-Royce, a Ferrari, a Plymouth station wagon, furs, jewels and $90,000 a year alimony.

She sold the stock back to the Harrah firms—leaving him the sole owner—for about $4.5 million. When she figured her profit on the sale, she didn't treat the stock as community property. But the IRS did and wanted her to ante up $250,000 in added tax. The crux of matter was whether the stock came to her as community property. She said it didn't; the settlement should be ignored.

She was trying to "prove that the agreement didn't mean what it said," the Tax Court said, and she failed. The ex-Mrs. Harrah could beat the IRS yet, for she has more disputes with the agency before the court.

Harrah v. Commissioner, 70 T.C. 72
9/6/78

⁓

Another wife fights to avoid a tax trap in Louisiana's marriage laws.

The state's community property law makes a wife owner of half her husband's income—even if they're separated and she never gets any of the money. Naturally, the IRS dutifully chases estranged wives to see that they pay tax on their half—even if they don't see a dime of it. A new twist in this marital morass involved the period between when Dr. Walter H. Brent, an orthopedic surgeon, filed a petition to divorce Mary Ellen Brent and a final divorce was granted.

For that year, the doctor paid tax on only half the $75,000 he made, figuring half his earnings were his estranged wife's. But Louisiana law says a divorce ends community ownership retroactively to the date the divorce petition was *filed*. So she argued that she didn't own any of his income after he filed the petition. The IRS took the doctor's side and said she had to pay despite the state law's retroactive provision.

She was saved by the Tax Court, which said

*the retroactivity clause made all Dr. Brent's in-
come that year his own—and so, too, the tax
liability.*

Brent v. Commissioner, 70 T.C. 75
9/6/78

⌒

A promise: The IRS tried to rustle money from
two ranchers.

Two brothers promised their father before he died
that they would share with their mother proceeds from
steers sold at their Brocton, Mont., ranch after he died.
He died more than 20 years ago and the sons kept their
word: Their mother got 20% of yearly steer sale receipts.
The brothers operated the ranch as partners and excluded from their partnership income sums paid their
mother. She counted the amounts, roughly $6,000 a
year, as taxable income.

Yet the IRS attacked this familial arrangement,
claiming the sons must pay tax on the payments because they hadn't a legal obligation to split the steer
sales with their mother. But the Tax Court put the ki-
bosh on that. Montana law made the sons' verbal promise binding on them. Their mother had a legal right to
20% of the sales receipts, so her share was excluded
from the sons' partnership income, the court determined.

Schmitz v. Commissioner, T.C. Memo 1978-317
8/30/78

⌒

A divorced father trounces the IRS on a child-sup-
port deduction.

Federal tax law generally says that a child of divorced parents is the tax dependent of the parent who
provides more than half of the child's support. That's

usually assumed to be the parent who has custody of the child. But there are many exceptions: if the noncustodial parent provides $1,200 or more annually, that parent gets the dependency deduction, unless the other one proves that he or she provided a larger share.

Francis Schmitz met the $1,200 test and in fact contributed slightly more to his three children than did his former wife, Patricia, who had custody. But she claimed that she also provided lodging, the value of which enlarged her contribution beyond 50%. The IRS agreed with Patricia; she had exclusive use of the home. But the Tax Court upheld Francis. He and Patricia owned the house jointly. That meant each contributed half the kids' lodging, leaving his overall share of the support larger than hers.

Schmitz v. Commissioner, T.C. Memo 1978-282
8/23/78

Learn about "Lester," a case that every divorcee with kids should know.

Carol Ann Zettlemoyer, sad to say, wasn't aware of the Lester case, which set a rule on taxing support payments. When she and Ronald split up, they signed a court order for him to pay support for her and their son. The order was on a printed form and said Ronald would pay $70 a week "for the support of his wife Carol and XXXX for the support of" their child.

The IRS said the entire sum was alimony and thus taxable income for Carol. But she argued that part of it was child support, which wasn't taxable income. The support decree, though, didn't designate a specific part as child support; the place on the printed form where that could be spelled out had been x-ed out. And the Supreme Court said some time ago in the Lester case that if a court order for support for a wife and child doesn't fix any part as child support, the whole amount counts as the wife's taxable income. So Carol got stuck with the entire sum.

"It is regrettable that taxpayers . . . only learn about Lester after it is too late to do anything about it, thus adding tax grief to domestic grief," the Tax Court asserted.

Zettlemoyer v. Commissioner, T.C. Memo 1978-246
7/26/78

⌒

House mates: A separated couple can be apart under the same roof, a court finds.

Support payments during marital separation usually are deductible. But the Tax Court denied Richard Sydnes a support deduction because he continued to live in the same house with his wife Lugene. He argued that they had separate rooms, ate meals apart and seldom saw each other. But the court said the deduction was available only if a separated couple lived apart.

The Tax Court declared that it shouldn't be required "to delve into intimate questions of whether husband and wife are in fact living apart while residing in the same house." But that prim assertion was rejected by an appeals court. A deduction for support isn't automatically barred if a separated couple live under the same roof, the higher court asserted.

Delving into Richard and Lugene's living arrangements, the appeals court determined that in fact they were living apart in the same house. Thus Richard could deduct some $1,200 for support.

Sydnes v. Commissioner, U.S. Ct. of Appeals, 8th Circ., 1978
6/28/78

Did Marianna intend to return to David the year she left him?

That year, in July she took their child and moved into her parents' home. By September she had divorced David H. Rotroff, who didn't contest the divorce, though he hoped she would return to him. And she did, in October. And they stayed together all the years after that but without remarrying. The year of the divorce David filed as head of a household.

But the IRS said he didn't qualify as head of a household that year because the couple's home wasn't Marianna's principal place of abode the *entire* year: Part of the year she was at her parents' home. David argued that her parents' home wasn't her principal abode at all for she was there only temporarily and intended to return to him. But she didn't intend that when she left: She took her child, some of her belongings, and got a divorce, the Tax Court noted.

From July to October David's home wasn't Marianna's principal abode, so that year he "isn't entitled to calculate his tax as a head of household," the court concluded.

Rotroff v. Commissioner, T.C. Memo 1978-46
2/8/78

～

Hell hath no fury . . . She turned him in to the IRS after he divorced her.

Mary and Julian Parker were separated for two years, then divorced. During the separation he filed joint returns, but she didn't sign them. After the divorce she learned someone signed her name to the returns and she told the IRS. The IRS told Julian his tax must be based on married, filing separately, so he owed

$6,700 more tax plus a 5% penalty. (Mary owed nothing for she earned nothing in the years involved.)

A joint return isn't always void if a spouse hasn't signed it. The crucial thing is whether both spouses intended to file jointly. Mary testified that she would have refused to sign if she had been asked. But that alone "doesn't preclude" finding she intended to file jointly, the Tax Court asserted, and went on to find she intended to file jointly: She hadn't tried to stop Julian from filing jointly; indeed, she mistakenly believed the law required them to file jointly.

She didn't protest the joint filing; she objected to someone else signing her name, the court said.

Mary wasn't trying to protect herself from a joint tax liability when she went to the IRS; she was trying to find out who signed her name and "possibly to cause trouble" for her ex-husband, the court observed.

Parker v. Commissioner, T.C. Memo 1978-23
2/1/78

⌒

She wouldn't sign, but her husband put her name to a joint return, anyway.

A wife needn't sign a joint return for it to be valid: Often it's enough if she intended to file jointly with her husband. Tom and Mary Garland lived apart for some years pending a divorce. While separated they filed two joint tax returns. When Tom asked Mary to sign a third joint return, she had learned she would be liable for any taxes due on his income, even though she hadn't any taxable income, and she refused to sign.

Tom wrote her name on the return and put his initials beside it. A few years later, Mary discovered what Tom did when the IRS attached her bank account for taxes due on the return. She told the IRS she hadn't signed the return. If the return wasn't valid, Tom owed about $8,000. He had to pay, the Tax Court said. Mary didn't intend filing jointly, she refused to sign and when she found out he signed her name, she promptly protested to the IRS, the court noted.

And as a lawyer Tom should have known better, the court asserted, and it ordered him to pay a $388 fine.

Garland v. Commissioner, T.C. Memo 1977-373
11/9/77

⌒

The man pays: His ex-wives abroad owed taxes on alimony.

Foreigners often should pay U.S. tax on money they received from American taxpayers, even though the foreigners don't live here. To assure payment, the law obliges the payer to withhold the tax. But, A. Uno Lamm, a Swede living in California, hadn't withheld taxes on alimony paid his two ex-wives, neither Americans and both living out of the U.S.

The IRS dunned Lamm for some $8,200 of taxes and penalties on about $20,000 alimony paid the women. The harassed husband had deducted the payments on his U.S. tax return, but argued that the payments were from funds he had in Sweden and shouldn't be taxed by the U.S.

However, alimony from an alien resident in the U.S. paid to a nonresident alien is "U.S. source income" regardless of the source of the funds from which the alimony is paid, the Tax Court reminded Lamm, and told him to pay the women's tax bills.

Lamm v. Commissioner, T.C. Memo 1977-336
10/19/77

It's unfair how the tax laws treat divorced men, one of them argued.

A husband normally can file a separate return, claim his wife as a dependent and get a $750 exemption if she hasn't any income and isn't anyone else's dependent. He can claim her for the full year even if she dies before year-end. But if they're divorced, he loses the exemption for the year. To Raleigh Hamilton, that seemed unfair, especially as he had provided more than half his ex-wife's support the year they were divorced and exemption for relatives other than spouses is based on supplying half their support.

In Tax Court, he claimed the law violated the 14th Amendment's "equal protection" and the Fifth Amendment's "due process" clauses. But the 14th Amendment generally doesn't apply to U.S. tax laws, the court told Hamilton, who was his own lawyer.

The Fifth Amendment applies, but he failed to show that the law was arbitrary or capricious, the court said. So, he must pay the $990 added tax the IRS assessed him.

Hamilton v. Commissioner, 68 T.C. 49
10/5/77

～

She was dependent. But did that mean he could claim her as a dependent?

An unmarried woman shared Nevett F. Ensminger's four-room house. She got over half her support from Ensminger and earned less than $750 a year herself. Ensminger figured that made her his dependent, so he claimed her as one and filed as single, head of a household, lessening his tax bill. But the IRS said she wasn't his dependent and he wasn't head of a household.

The tax code barred her qualifying as a member of Ensminger's household because their relationship violated a local law where they lived, the IRS argued. Ensminger didn't argue about his relationship with the woman. Instead, he claimed the law was unconstitutional, and his right to privacy barred applying a law on sexual conduct to conduct in the privacy of his home. However, he had the burden of showing the relationship didn't violate local law, the Tax Court observed, and he failed to do so.

He also was barred from claiming her as a dependent, the court added, under a provision of tax law that denies dependency status to someone who qualifies only because the person is a household member. (They must qualify for another reason, such as being a relative.)

Ensminger v. Commissioner, T.C. Memo 1977-224
8/31/77

⌒

He forged her name on their joint refund check and created this mess:

Both husband and wife are supposed to endorse a refund check based on a joint return. Irving and Virginia were separated pending divorce when their refund came, and he had a pal forge Virginia's name. His bank honored the check and stamped it "PEG," meaning "prior endorsements guaranteed." The couple owed the IRS back taxes, and Irving used part of the $3,300 check to buy a $1,200 money order at the bank. The bank made it in both their names, but the IRS accepted it with only Irving's endorsement.

Eventually, Virginia asked the IRS for her half of the $3,300 refund. The IRS asked the Comptroller General to sort out the mess. The Comptroller said the bank owed the U.S. $3,300 because the bank guaranteed the forged endorsement. (The bank could pursue Irving for the money.) However, the IRS owed the bank $1,200 for accepting the bank's joint money order without a proper endorsement. The IRS should pay itself the $1,200 back taxes the couple owed out of the $3,300 the bank owed the IRS, and hold the balance for Irving and Virginia, who must agree on how the remainder should be split between them, the Comptroller ruled.

U.S. Comptroller General Opinion B-18795
8/3/77

⌒

The IRS loses again in fight to count Medicare as support for the elderly.

To claim elderly parents as dependents, taxpayers must provide more than half their support. Social Security benefits and other welfare payments count as support the aged provide themselves. The IRS also wants to count the often-large amounts Medicare pays hospitals on behalf of the elderly. The Tax Court, though, rejected that notion in 1975 in the case of a $10,000 Medicare payment to a hospital for care of an 81-year-old woman whose daughter claimed her as a dependent.

The IRS appealed to the Second Circuit. The agency argued that Medicare benefits amount to welfare and should be treated as support like Social Security payments. However, the appeals court rejected the IRS argument. Medicare benefits are more like payments by private insurance companies, the court said. Private health insurance benefits don't count as support, and Medicare shouldn't be either.

Medicare benefits aren't like Social Security,
the court said: Social Security makes regular pay-

ments directly to the aged, but Medicare only pays during an illness and then directly to the hospital.
Turecamo v. Commissioner, U.S. Ct. of Appeals, 2nd Circ., 1977
5/25/77

◠

Unjust deserts: Kurt walked out on his wife and the court ordered him to pay her temporary alimony. He can deduct the money and she pays tax on it, the tax code says. But she says that isn't fair. "A man shouldn't be rewarded financially for deserting his wife," she complains, arguing that Kurt couldn't deduct the cost of supporting her if they were still together. Fair or not, she owes the tax, the Tax Court told Kurt's wife.
Jean C. Rosenbaum v. Commissioner, T.C. Memo 1979-22
7/18/19

◠

Now that's cruel: A separate maintenance decree issued in New Jersey to a woman on grounds of her husband's "extreme cruelty" doesn't mean the couple's legally separated for federal tax purposes. So they can't file as "unmarried," to save taxes, the Tax Court decreed.
Capadanno v. Commissioner, 69 T.C. 51
2/15/78

◠

Married? A couple asked the IRS to recognize their signed pact to continue "as fully independent, single individuals" despite the pair's getting married. In a private ruling the IRS told them to file as married taxpayers; state law counted them as married and that fixed their status for filing U.S. tax returns.
IRS private ruling 7719014
5/25/77

Trusts and Children

Two lawyers paid rent to their kids' trusts and avoided some taxes.

They are brothers, Richard and Roger Quinlivan, of St. Cloud, Minn. They owned the building their law firm occupied. But to cut their taxes and put money aside for their kids, they put their interests in the building into trusts lasting 10 years and six months (Clifford trusts) for their children; a bank acted as trustee. Their law firm deducted the $1,000-a-month rent paid to the trusts.

Such transactions keep IRS loyalists awake nights, and the brothers Quinlivan were "lawing" with the IRS over the rent deduction. The IRS said there wasn't a bona fide "business purpose" for the transfer to the trusts and lease back to the law firm, so the firm couldn't deduct the rent. But an appeals court rejected the IRS's argument. The rent was reasonable, the firm needed office space and the trust wasn't under the brothers' control, the Eighth Circuit said.

So this tax dodge was perfectly legal, the court concluded. "The law permits (this) method of tax minimization."

Quinlivan v. Commissioner, U.S. Ct. of Appeals, 8th Circ., 1979
6/27/79

⌣

Did she wait too long to give up $10 million from her dad's trust fund?

When her mother died at age 100, Lois P. Cottrell

was 74 years old. She was to get $10 million from a trust her father set up 33 years earlier; if she didn't take the money the trust would give it to her kids. If she got the money and bequeathed it to them at her death, it would be subject to estate tax. The Stonington, Conn., woman disclaimed the money, believing it could go from the trust to her children tax-free.

But the IRS said she made a $10 million gift when she renounced the money and owed gift tax of $4.6 million. She argued that a disclaimer within a "reasonable time" isn't considered a gift and she had disclaimed the money soon after her mother's death. Alas! The time tolled from when her father set up the trust 33 years earlier rather than from her mother's death, the Tax Court determined.

Thirty-three years wasn't a reasonable time to wait before renouncing the money, the court said, and it concluded that the gift tax must be paid.

Cottrell v. Commissioner, 72 T.C. 46
6/20/79

⌒

One man knew how to work a legal stock sale dodge, but another one didn't.

Clair E. Roberts was in on the ground floor of Sambo's Restaurants and ended up with a potful of its stock. If he sold it outright, he would owe an indigestible tax bill. So he set up a trust for his kids and made a series of "sales" of Sambo stock to the trust. The trust signed $1 million of notes for the shares, then sold them. But it kept the proceeds, paying Roberts only interest and some principal on the debt each year.

Thus, he was able to spread out reporting his profit on the stock. But the IRS said the setup was a sham and Roberts owed $344,000 tax. The IRS argued that it was as if he had used the trust as his conduit to sell the stock. But the Tax Court saved his bacon. He hadn't any control over the trust, nor did he have access to the proceeds the trust got from selling the shares, the court observed.

Paul G. Lustgarten of Miami Beach, Fla., tried a similar deal with $1 million of Cooper Laboratories stock and his son Bruce. And he failed. He set it up so he retained too much control, the Tax Court said, and thus he owed $346,000 tax.

Roberts v. Commissioner, 71 T.C. 26, and Lustgarten v. Commissioner, 71
T.C. 25
12/20/78

⌢

An eye man looked to beat taxes, but the IRS wanted to look past his trust.

Ophthalmologist Hobart A. Lerner incorporated his practice, at the same time giving his equipment to a trust for his kids. The trust rented the equipment to the Rochester, N.Y., physician's corporation for $650 a month. Thus, $7,800 a year was split off his income to his kids, who, of course, were in a much lower tax bracket than he. The IRS said the deal was a sham and the $7,800 of rent should be taxed to the doctor.

The IRS argued that there wasn't any business purpose for the arrangement. But the Tax Court didn't see it that way. The corporation couldn't use the equipment rent-free as the doctor, not the firm, owned it originally. The trust was valid, the court said. The doctor hadn't any control over it; the trustee, though his friend and attorney, acted independently on behalf of the kids. And the rent was reasonable.

The court totally rejected the IRS's conten-

tions and observed that the tax code recognizes that "valid trusts can be created which result in . . . minimizing taxes."

Lerner v. Commissioner 71 T.C. 24
12/6/78

❧

An $18 million "gift" isn't one that the IRS can tax.

Three wealthy sons of Chicago financier Henry Crown had their partnership lend $18 million interest-free to trusts for their children and other relatives. The IRS figured the use of $18 million at 6% a year was worth $1 million annually and told the Crown boys to pay gift tax on $1 million. But Lester Crown resisted paying his $46,000 share of the tax.

He argued, and the Tax Court agreed in 1977, that interest-free loans among family members aren't taxable gifts. The IRS appealed the Tax Court decision. The agency argued in an appeals court that the gift-tax laws are broad enough to cover such transactions. But the Seventh Circuit disagreed. The appeals court said that this "may be a significant loophole," but declined to fill it in by "judicial construction." Crown didn't have to pay.

Moreover, the appeals court said it wasn't ruling whether the IRS could close the loophole by issuing a regulation or whether Congress had to do it.

Crown v. Commissioner, U.S. Ct. of Appeals, 7th Circ., 1978
10/4/78

❧

The IRS assaulted a trusty way to increase a man's income, spare him tax.

William D. Pityo couldn't work due to an injury.

He needed more income, but his chief asset was Arvin Industries stock, which paid a small dividend. If he sold the shares outright, he would incur a huge capital gains tax. So he set up trusts for his wife and kids and sold the stock to the trusts in an "installment sale." The trusts were to pay him about $50,000 a year for 20 years for 21,500 shares of Arvin stock.

To meet the payments, the trusts sold 15,400 of the shares and put the proceeds in mutual funds. Pityo reported his gain on the sale a little at a time as he was paid by the trusts because he had made an installment sale. But the IRS said the trusts were merely conduits for Pityo and should be ignored. The agency wanted to tax him at once on a $445,000 gain on sales the trust had sold, as if he had sold them himself.

But the Tax Court rejected the IRS's contention. Pityo hadn't any control over the trusts; they weren't conduits for him. Though devised to save taxes, the sales to the trusts were valid, the court ruled.

Pityo v. Commissioner, 70 T.C. 21
5/24/78

⌒

Repeated losses don't stop the IRS from pursuing this gift-tax issue.

Sometimes recipients pay gift tax rather than givers of a gift who normally are liable for the tax. The IRS contends that givers realize taxable income when recipients pay the tax. But the Tax Court and some appeals courts repeatedly have rejected this argument. Yet, the IRS pressed it against a woman who gave $6.7 million of stock to trusts for her eight grandchildren. The trusts paid $2.1 million gift tax.

She realized income because the trusts paid her

gift-tax liability for her, the IRS contended. It said she owed $635,000 tax. In another case the agency wanted $502,000 from a couple who gave $5.3 million to trusts for five grandchildren and the trusts paid $1.6 million gift tax. In both cases the Tax Court spurned the IRS, and ruled in effect, the givers made "net gifts," the value of the stock minus the gift taxes, and they didn't realize any taxable income.

Despite "overwhelming precedent to the contrary," the IRS "continues to urge that we change our long-established position," the court noted.

Estate of Douglas Henry etc. v. Commissioner, 69 T.C. 53; Owen v. Commissioner, T.C. Memo 1978-51; and Hirst v. Commissioner, U.S. Ct. of Appeals, 4th Circ., 1978

2/15/78

∽

It's a sham, the Tax Court agreed, but disagreed on how to strike it down.

The tax-avoidance scheme involved five trusts for the children that owned 90% of a partnership; a corporation the father controlled owned 10%. However, the partnership's earnings resulted only from the enormous amounts of borrowed money father and his corporation were able to supply the partnership. The object was to split the profits among the trusts to reduce the tax bite. The IRS contended the whole thing was a tax-avoidance gimmick and father's corporation should be taxed on all the partnership's earnings.

The Tax Court agreed it was a sham; but how to attack it created dissension. A majority opinion said the partnership didn't meet the test as a partnership in which capital is a "material income-producing factor" because so much of its capital was borrowed. Ruling that borrowed capital doesn't count creates a new concept of tax law, nine judges asserted, in attacking the majority opinion's reasoning but supporting its result.

The court should have found other reasons to void the partnership and avoided setting a questionable precedent, the disagreeing judges declared.

Carriage Square Inc. v. Commissioner, 69 T.C. 10
11/16/77

⌒

Chicken feed? The kids owned part of the firm but Dad took the profits.

Giving children a share of a family firm is one way to split income and thus cut taxes on their parents, who usually retain controlling interest in the company. However, the IRS is suspicious of such situations. The agency told a poultry and egg operator to pay $58,000 tax due because his kids' ownership of the business was a sham.

His case would be judged on four criteria: Did the custodian, in this instance the mother, actively protect the kids' interest? Did the father have complete dominion over the business despite the children's ownership? Did he get all the economic benefits of ownership, depriving the kids of theirs? Did he deal at arm's length in getting advances from the firm or paying them back? While the chicken man got most of the earnings, he used the funds to build up the business, signed notes for the sums and borrowed at the bank to pay interest due his kids. And his wife was an active custodian, the Tax Court determined.

The father "has never attempted to control" the children's ownership, the court asserted, and rejected the IRS contentions.

Kirkpatrick v. Commissioner, T.C. Memo 1977-281
8/31/77

Estates and Trusts

Interest piled up after death, but the IRS struck down a deduction for it.

William M. Wheless left an estate with sizable assets and debts. The late Houston, Texas, resident's holdings couldn't readily be turned into cash. So his estate paid interest on his debts, interest that accrued after he died. The estate deducted $150,000 in interest as an administrative expense. The IRS barred the deduction.

The IRS said the interest was a claim against the estate, which, because it accrued after his death, wasn't deductible. The Tax Court said the IRS was wrong. The interest was an obligation of the estate's executors and thus was an administrative expense.

The interest was deductible, the court concluded, after reminding the IRS that qualifying as a deduction as a claim against the estate and qualifying as an administrative-expense deduction were two different things.

Estate of Wm. N. Wheless v. Commissioner, 72 T.C. 44
6/27/79

⌣

What about filing an amended return if you sold assets inherited after 1976?

Late in 1978, Congress changed the effective date of "carry-over basis" to Jan. 1, 1980—retroactively killing it until then. But that way for heirs to report gains or losses on inherited property was effective with property inherited from people who died after 1976. So thousands of heirs already have reported gains or losses using carry-over basis.

Some had to pay more tax than they would have paid if carry-over basis didn't exist; some paid less. They will need to file amended returns because carry-over basis doesn't apply to those prior years. Some will be getting tax refunds, and can file quickly to get their money. But some should wait, says Bernard Barnett, national tax partner at Seidman & Seidman, a CPA firm. "You shouldn't jump too fast," he says, because Congress may enact relief for heirs caught by the retroactive change.

If relief comes, added taxes won't be due. And if it doesn't come, only 6% interest annually is added to the tax that will be due. "That isn't bad considering today's bank interest rates," Mr. Barnett remarks.

1/24/79

◇

It cost her $552,000 to get a hunk of her rich, dead husband's estate.

Merl C. Kelce, chairman of Peabody Coal Co., married Dorothy Sivley Kelce three years after he divorced Dorothy's sister, Shirley, his second wife. Less than two years later, Kelce died. Dorothy wasn't named in the will, and she retained a lawyer to get her piece of the estate, which was valued at $20.4 million. State law said a wife left out of her husband's will was entitled to a third of his estate.

But the executor, Kelce's adopted son, figured Dorothy's sister Shirley was the legal spouse because her Mexican divorce from Kelce wasn't valid, meaning Dorothy's marriage wasn't valid. And a Hong Kong woman to whom Kelce had given money claimed to be his legal spouse. Dorothy's attorney got her to withdraw for 4% of whatever Dorothy got in excess of $750,000. Eventually, Dorothy got $3.1 million cash and $800,000 of real estate. She paid her lawyer $552,000 and deducted it.

Dorothy claimed the legal fee was to "conserve and maintain her property." But the Tax Court told her that costs to protect or assert rights as an heir aren't deductible.

Kelce v. Commissioner, T.C. Memo 1978-506
1/17/79

⌒

These things take time, the lawyer said. The IRS said $10,000 for being late.

Constance, a housewife married for 35 years, hadn't any business experience. When she was made executrix of her mother's estate, she hired a lawyer to handle it. Only five of the six children were named beneficiaries in the will. The sixth, Florence, was left out. But she possessed some of her mother's securities and was co-owner of a joint bank account.

Florence refused to turn over these assets. The dispute with Florence ran on, and Constance kept asking the attorney about winding up the estate. These things take time, he said, assuring her he would take care of it. But the estate's tax return was filed three years late, and the IRS imposed a $10,000 late penalty. The IRS said relying on an attorney doesn't excuse an executrix for filing so late. Sometimes it does and sometimes it doesn't, the Tax Court said.

Constance "didn't sit supinely by and leave everything to" the lawyer, the court noted. "She made inquiry of him." He led her to believe erro-

neously that the dispute with Florence justified the delay. She was inexperienced and justified in relying on him, the court said, and concluded that the penalty shouldn't be imposed.

Estate of Agness DiPalma v. Commissioner, 71 T.C. 27
1/3/79

⌢

A dead husband didn't pay taxes for 10 years. What can the IRS do to his widow?

A New York State man died without having filed a return or paying taxes for 10 years. His wife, who had nearly no income, got the proceeds of a life insurance policy, their residence and some funds from his state retirement fund. These assets came directly to her, passing outside his estate. The unidentified widow asked the IRS if she was liable for his unpaid taxes or if the IRS could file liens on the assets she inherited.

If she hadn't filed a joint return with her husband and the estate doesn't file one for them, she wouldn't be personally liable for his tax debt, the IRS said. And IRS authority to seize the life insurance depended on whether her husband had been assessed for the delinquent taxes before he died. Because he hadn't, the IRS couldn't touch the insurance proceeds.

Property that passed directly to her outside his estate was protected from the husband's creditors so long as it passed in the absence of fraud, according to New York law, the IRS noted, indicating that she needn't fear Uncle Sam trying to collect from her.

IRS letter ruling 7825086
11/22/78

⌢

The IRS might owe you money. The 1978 laws have some refund possibilities.

Parts of the new tax law are retroactive. Taxpayers often can apply the new rules by filing amended returns and get refunds. Leon M. Nad, tax partner at Price Waterhouse & Co., says the new law could benefit heirs of decedents who died after 1976—or hurt them. Heirs retroactively aren't subject to the so-called "carry-over basis" rules effective in 1977. Under the new law, inherited property may be valued higher (or lower) than it was under carry-over basis.

That can mean bigger (or smaller) depreciation write-offs, or smaller (or larger) taxable gains if the property is sold, Nad says. There isn't any choice about dropping the carry-over basis; it's mandatory. Some taxpayers will benefit and get refunds, while others will have to pay more tax. There's relief, though, for many people who set up Individual Retirement Accounts. The new law helps those who put too much in their IRAs, or fouled up a "roll over" from a company pension fund into an IRA.

Taxpayers should check out the law because there are different deadlines for applying the new rules.

11/22/78

∽

A trust can shield insurance money, a divided Tax Court ruled.

People often want to keep life insurance proceeds out of their estates to shield them from estate tax. The late Robert B. Margrave was insured under a policy "owned" by his wife Glenda. She paid the premiums and had the power to change the beneficiary. The beneficiary was a trust controlled by Robert. When he died the insurance paid the trust $85,000.

The IRS said Margrave's control over the trust

gave him control over the insurance proceeds, making
the money part of his estate. But nine of the Tax
Court's 16 judges rejected the IRS argument. Margrave
didn't have enough control over the money to make it
part of his estate because his wife could have changed
the beneficiary. Thus, the proceeds escaped estate tax,
the majority ruled.

*The trust served much the same purpose as
the estate in carrying out Margrave's testamen-
tary wishes, noted Judge William H. Quealy, one
of the dissenters. If the insurance were payable to
the estate rather than the trust it would have been
taxed, the judge observed. Allowing the proceeds
to escape tax because they were paid to the trust—
as the majority decided—"produces an absurd
result."*

Estate of Robert B. Margrave v. Commissioner, 71 T.C. 2
10/18/78

Is a loophole open for a deceased who didn't own
all his firm's stock?

Life insurance death benefits usually are included
in an estate if the deceased had control over the insurance. Milton Levy owned 80.4% of Levy Brothers, a
New Jersey retailing corporation. The company owned
two life insurance policies on his life; his wife, Iris, was
the beneficiary. The policies paid her $206,000 when he
died; his estate didn't count the money as estate assets.
But the IRS did.

The tax agency argued that Levy could control the
policies through the corporation. But his estate said
Congress considered such situations and the legislation
it passed applied only to someone who owns 100% of a
firm; Levy owned only 80.4%, so the tax rule doesn't ap-

ply. However, the Tax Court said that the 100% stock-holder was cited merely as an example in a congression-al committee report and didn't restrict the tax code as narrowly as Levy's estate contended.

Congress clearly intended to cover those who "controlled" corporations with 100% or 80.4% stock ownership, the court said. Levy's estate must pay $42,000 of added estate taxes, the court con-cluded.

Estate of Milton Levy v. Commissioner, 70 T.C. 80
9/27/78

⌒

Weight Watchers is more than diets. It is the for-um for a tax fight.

Jean Nidetch, a founder of Weight Watchers Inter-national Inc., became dissatisfied with the running of the company. As a substantial shareholder and director, she decided to begin a proxy fight for control of the con-cern. In assaying potential votes for and against her po-sition, Nidetch had to consider 50,000 shares of Weight Watchers stock—about 5% of the total—held by two trusts that she had created for the benefit of her sons. The trustees were opposed to her view of company management, so she decided to replace them with allies who could be counted on to vote the stock her way.

Changing trustees proved to be a complex affair, costing Nidetch $102,500 in legal fees. Moreover, she settled her differences and never waged the proxy con-test. She deducted the legal fee on her tax return, how-ever, contending that it was incurred as an expense of producing income for herself. She reasoned that she would have waged the battle as a means of increasing her dividends and improving corporate policies. The

IRS barred the deduction because she didn't actually mount the proxy fight.

The Tax Court found Nidetch persuasive. The replacing of the trustees was crucial in inducing the company to come to terms with her complaints, the court said.

Nidetch v. Commissioner, T.C. Memo 1978-313
8/23/78

⌒

Did a wife help the family business succeed? The IRS didn't think so.

Over the 43 years of their marriage, Bessie and Clarence Craig built a sizable farm operation from scratch. When Clarence died, the IRS said all the farm equipment had belonged to Clarence and thus was included in his estate. But a federal district court in South Dakota declared:

"This court will not ignore this farm wife's contribution to the success of the business as the IRS seeks to do." Bessie was equally responsible for the farm's success: She cared for hired hands, marketed eggs, helped harvest grain, hauled cattle and kept the books (and raised five children, too). Half of the farm equipment belonged to her as an equal partner in the farm, said the court.

That meant the IRS had to refund some $40,000 of estate tax collected on the equipment, plus interest.

Craig v. U.S., U.S. Dist. Ct., So. Dakota, 1978
8/2/78

⌒

Uncle Sam comes first with a few exceptions, the IRS told an executor.

Administrators of estates have to be careful about

paying the decedent's bills. If the wrong creditors are paid first and there isn't enough left to satisfy the IRS, the executor can be personally liable for the federal taxes. A man died owing $74,000 in income taxes—he hadn't filed returns for 10 years. His executor sought IRS guidance about paying some of the deceased's expenses before paying his federal tax bill.

The executor could safely pay the funeral expenses and the estate's administrative costs, the IRS said. But the executor would be "personally liable for the income taxes of the decedent" if he paid the mortgage on the dead man's house or state income taxes or general creditors before paying Uncle Sam, the IRS warned.

IRS letter ruling 7824073
8/2/78

Can an estate deduct a fee paid an underwriter to sell a block of stock?

The estate of Helen Baker Jenner sold 300,000 shares of Baker, Fentress & Co. stock to raise cash. That was more than 10% of the shares in the closed-end investment firm, and the stock was sold through an underwriter who agreed to pay the estate $38.85 a share, or $11,665,000. But the stock was sold to the public at $42 a share, or $12.6 million. The difference, $945,000, was the underwriter's discount, or fee for the deal.

The estate deducted the discount, but the IRS barred the deduction. The stock simply had been sold to the underwriter for $38.85 a share, the IRS contended, so the discount wasn't a deductible expense. The Tax Court agreed with the IRS a few years ago, but the Seventh Circuit Court of Appeals recently sided with the estate. The underwriting was a "necessary conduit for the public sale of the stock," the court determined, and the discount was the charge to conduct the underwriting, and thus deductible.

With this decision, the Seventh Circuit joins the Ninth Circuit in ruling favorably for estates to deduct underwriting fees.

Estate of Helen Baker Jenner v. Commissioner,
U.S. Ct. of Appeals, 7th Circ., 1978
7/19/78

~

Granddad's trust. To keep it from the IRS cost $135,000 in legal fees.

William S. Bertram was getting $9,000 a year from a trust his mother's father set up years ago. But when mother died, there was a question about who owned the trust assets. Lawyers feared the $1.4 million trust fund might be counted in mother's estate and be subjected to about $875,000 in estate taxes. A suit in a state court to prevent the IRS from getting the trust assets succeeded. (Bertram was awarded the $1.4 million.)

He paid $135,000 in legal fees, which he deducted. But the IRS said the legal costs were incurred to gain title to assets and weren't deductible. Bertram argued that the outlay was "to maintain property held for the production of income," and thus deductible. However, Bertram hadn't title to the assets before the suit, the Tax Court noted.

Expenses for "asserting one's right to property . . . as heir or legatee, or as beneficiary under" a trust aren't deductible, the court said.

Bertram v. Commissioner, T.C. Memo 1978-247
7/12/78

~

A dying man's charity saved taxes during his life and after.

A Chicago man ill with cancer gave $203,000 to

charity in the last three years of his life. Deducting the donations saved him $123,000 of income taxes before he died. After his death, his estate used the gifts to save some $113,000 of estate tax: It counted the gifts in the gross estate because they were made "in contemplation of death." The estate didn't pay tax on the $203,000, though, as it, too, could deduct the sum as charity. But including the sum enlarged the gross estate and thus the size of the marital deduction.

The bigger the marital deduction, the lower the tax on the estate. The IRS argued the gifts weren't in contemplation of death, and, thus, didn't count in the estate. But the Tax Court said they should be included. (The IRS's argument that the gifts weren't in contemplation of death can apply only to gifts before 1976; after that, all gifts within three years of death normally count in the estate, whether in contemplation of death or not.)

"This situation may indeed reveal a loophole," the Tax Court asserted. But closing it is up to Congress.

Estate of Thomas C. Russel v. Commissioner, 70 T.C. 6
4/26/78

～

He raced, he drank, while she tended to business but for no pay.

Jack owned a golf driving range with a big piece of land when he married Marie. He sold chunks of the land over the years and acquired other enterprises: amusement parks, restaurants, a foreign-car dealership. Jack spent a lot of time racing cars; he wasn't a "detail man," and Marie looked after the businesses. In fact, she didn't want him around much because he had a drinking problem. Yet she didn't get any salary.

When Jack died, the IRS counted the entire value

of their businesses in his estate. She wanted to count only half and avoid estate tax of $66,000. She contended half was hers. But the tax code says a wife must prove she contributed equally with her husband to acquire their assets. Marie argued that her services to their businesses were responsible for earnings that permitted them to acquire the businesses. But the businesses weren't profitable, and the IRS showed that sales of the golf-range land financed their other acquisitions.

"Unfortunately" their finances were handled to give her little credit for her work, the Tax Court said, but excluded a minimal $18,300 out of some $815,000 from estate tax as her separate property.
Estate of Jack Robins Ensley v. Commissioner, T.C. Memo 1977-402
12/7/77

⌒

It's hard in Texas to shed a community-property interest.

Texas is a so-called community-property state, meaning husband and wife share ownership 50-50. And Texas law makes income from one spouse's separate property community property of both. But Charles J. Wyly Sr. figured he had shucked his interest in stock owned with his wife when both of them transferred it to a trust. The trust was to pay any income from the stock to his wife, nothing to Charles. Yet, when he died, the IRS counted half the stock in his estate.

The IRS argued that Texas law gave Charles a right to half the income from the stock, and that interest made the stock includable in his estate under federal law. Charles' estate argued that the income was separate property, that he hadn't retained any interest in the stock. But the Tax Court ruled that under Texas law Charles was entitled to half the income from his wife's separate property, and thus part of the stock was includable in his estate.

The result of both his and his wife's transferring their interests to the trust was to give him a lifetime interest in 50% of the transferred stock, so half its value was taxable in his estate, the court concluded. (Lawyers say this ruling probably doesn't apply outside Texas.)

Estate of Charles J. Wyly Sr. v. Commissioner, 69 T.C. 17
11/30/77

⌒

A new way to value a debt owed a dead person is aired in Tax Court.

G. R. Robinson had a note paying him $80,000 a year from a firm that bought his business. When Robinson died, 15 payments remained. His heirs will share the payments, but will owe income tax on most of the money. Robinson's executrix figured the note's value for estate taxes by reducing its value by the anticipated income tax on the payments. The IRS rejected that idea and said the estate owed $153,000 of added estate tax; the note must be taxed on its "fair market value."

Robinson's estate urged the Tax Court to adopt a novel approach: value the note at its worth in the heirs' hands to reflect the income tax liability inherent in the note. But that would result in a myriad of variables, for, among other things, the heirs' tax brackets and tax deductions would vary, the court noted.

Notes in an estate must be valued at what a "willing buyer and willing seller" would agree is the value. In this case, that's the worth of the future payments, the court asserted.

Estate of G.R. Robinson v Commissioner, 69 T.C. 16
11/23/77

While he lay dying: A tale of a late **IBM** heir's $8 million of "flower bonds."

Arthur K. Watson, of the IBM family, lay comatose nine days from head injuries before he died in 1974. Some years before, he gave his brother and his lawyer power of attorney to buy securities. They bought $8 million of "flower bonds" while Watson was in a coma. Flower bonds sell below their face value, for they pay a low interest rate, but the Treasury usually accepts them at full value in payment of estate taxes.

But the Treasury refused the $4.7 million out of the $8 million tendered by Watson's estate. The government argued that he didn't own the bonds as they were bought pursuant to a power of attorney invalidated by his unconscious state. But his comatose state didn't revoke the power of attorney, a U.S. district court determined. Had he recovered, he mightn't have ratified the purchase, but he didn't recover; and his heirs didn't object to the bond purchase, which benefited the estate and them, the court observed.

The government must accept the $4.7 million of bonds tendered, and any more of the $8 million that might be used to pay added taxes on Watson's estate, the court concluded.

> Estate of Arthur K. Watson v. Secretary of the Treasury,
> U.S. Dist. Ct., So. Dist. N.Y. 1977
> 11/23/77

 ⌒

Poky lawyers: Don't rely on them to file a return in time.

Herbert Richter knew that, as executor of his father's estate, he had to file an estate tax return within 15 months of his dad's death. He asked a law firm to do the return for him. The firm dawdled; the return was about a year late. The IRS penalized Richter $18,000.

He paid under protest and sued for a refund. If he could prove he hadn't "willfully neglected" the law and had "reasonable cause" for being late, he could get the late penalty rescinded.

He had nagged the firm to get the form in, so he hadn't "willfully neglected" the law, a U.S. District Court ruled. But it didn't agree with his reliance on the laggard law firm was "reasonable cause" for the tardy filing. U.S. appeals courts have ruled both ways on this point, the district court noted; it chose the harsher view and upheld the penalty.

An executor can't delegate the responsibility to file the form, the court asserted. It's up to him "to ensure" that filing is on time.

> *Richter v. U.S., U.S. Dist. Ct., Dist. of Minnesota, 1977*
> *10/26/77*

Family trust promoters claim they can help people avoid taxes. A family's income is assigned to a trust, which in turn pays the family's upkeep. Promoters, who charge as much as $10,000 to set up a trust, claim the income will be taxed to the trust, rather than the family. But the IRS and courts say income earners still are liable for tax. And the Supreme Court has let stand an appeals court ruling that two couples with trusts are liable for the taxes they hoped to avoid.

> *Horvat and Minesal v. U.S., U.S. Supreme Ct. Docket 78-1047*
> *3/21/79*

Trouble with the IRS

How secret is an unlisted phone number if the IRS wants to know who has it?

Special IRS agent Donna S. Love issued a summons to South Central Bell Telephone Co. for names and addresses of people whose phone numbers appeared on the telephone bill of a man she was investigating. Their identities might help determine the man's tax liability, she said. The phone company provided information for the customers listed in the phone book, but refused to supply it for two customers with unpublished numbers.

South Central Bell argued that the IRS must notify the owners of the unlisted numbers that the agency had subpoenaed information about them. Usually the IRS must notify taxpayers when the agency issues a summons to a third party for information about them; the notice gives the taxpayer a chance to fight the summons. But that rule applies to taxpayers under investigation, a U.S. district court noted. The unlisted phone owners weren't under investigation and weren't entitled to notice of the summons.

The phone company was obliged to disclose the unlisted names and addresses, the court concluded.

U.S. and Donna Love v. South Central Bell Telephone Co., U.S. Dist. Ct., Mid. Dist. of Tenn., 1979
5/2/79

∽

A "terrible" witness appeared for the IRS, so the judge said, anyway.

Joel A. Lutz's home in Farmington, Mich., was ruined by heavy rains. Water poured into his basement, collapsing part of a wall; the swimming pool was so badly damaged it later was bulldozed under, and a new pool was put in; parts of the first floor were covered with mud. Lutz deducted $62,700 as a casualty loss for the flood damage, which wasn't covered by insurance.

But the IRS said the loss amounted to only $20,000. The issue went to Tax Court. While an IRS witness was testifying about the amount of damage, Judge Cynthia Holcomb Hall recessed the hearing. In her chambers she told lawyers for both sides that the IRS witness was "terrible." Yet she later concluded that the IRS was closer to the right amount than Lutz and ruled he had only a $27,500 loss. However, the Fourth Circuit said Lutz should have a new Tax Court trial.

His lawyers said they figured from Judge Hall's remarks that they had the case won, so they didn't put on as strong a case as they would have.

Lutz v. Commissioner, U.S. Ct. of Appeals, 6th Circ., 1979
3/28/79

‿

He beat the IRS in the Supreme Court and wanted the U.S. to pay his lawyers.

When Dr. Ike Slodov bought a food business, it owed $250,000 in withholding taxes. The Cleveland orthodontist wasn't liable for that, but he would be personally liable if the firm didn't remit withholding after he took over. An IRS agent agreed to let the business stay open despite the $250,000 tax debt, if Slodov kept current with withholding payments. Payments were to be credited to withholding taxes, the agent agreed.

But the IRS agent didn't keep his word. He had payments credited against the business's share of Social Security taxes rather than as withholding payments.

Later, Slodov filed a bankruptcy petition, and the IRS said he was liable for $314,000 of unpaid withholding. He argued that the withholding would have been paid had the IRS honored its agreement with him. But he didn't succeed with this argument until he took his case clear up to the Supreme Court, which exonerated him.

And just recently another federal court said the government must pay $25,000 of his lawyer's fees because the IRS had acted in "bad faith."

In Re: Slodov, Debtor, U.S. Dist. Ct., No. Dist. Ohio, 1979
3/7/79

Can the IRS use its mistake to wreck a book company's lawsuit?

Publishers Guild Inc. considered its salespeople independent contractors and didn't withhold or pay payroll taxes on them. But the IRS said they were "employes," so the New York City publisher owed at least $2,700 of employment tax. The firm paid, but quickly filed to have the $2,700 refunded. While pursuing the issue at the IRS, in expectation of going to court, the firm got a $2,700 check from the IRS.

The company sent $2,700 to the IRS, explaining it was returning an erroneous refund. It heard nothing from the IRS for some 18 months and filed a refund suit in the Court of Claims. Then the IRS came out to argue that the case should be dismissed because a refund—though in error—was paid, and thus there wasn't any basis for the suit. But the court said the IRS error won't frustrate this lawsuit; it can proceed.

The IRS could have responded sooner and differently than to "belatedly" try to make this company begin its legal action all over again, the court remarked.

The Publishers Guild Inc. v. U.S., U.S. Ct. of Claims, 1979
3/7/79

Gloves off: The Tax Court hit a balky man with a long-dormant punch.

The court can sock a taxpayer with a $500 fine for a suit filed merely to delay paying taxes. The fine had last been imposed in 1933 when it was laid on a fellow named Coombs. In the past two years the court threatened tax protesters, whose cases are clogging the court, with the fine. Well, Judge Cynthia Holcomb Hall finally unleashed it; she zapped Roger D. Wilkinson with the full $500.

The Boise, Idaho, salesman had dragged the IRS into Tax Court to contest a $729 assessment. He refused to supply any evidence to prove his case. Instead he raised a string of constitutional objections, all of which the court told him were "groundless" and "frivolous." Still, he insisted on a full trial, during which he didn't provide any evidence and reasserted the constitutional arguments. Apparently that was more than enough for Judge Hall.

"We believe the time to act has arrived," she asserted when she slapped him with the fine. She added that the $500 doesn't "begin to indemnify the U.S. for the expenses which (his) frivolous position has occasioned."

Wilkinson v. Commissioner, 71 T.C. 59
2/7/79

〜

An about face on the IRS ordering people to give it handwriting samples.

Tax evaders often resist providing handwriting specimens to the IRS, knowing they can be incriminating. The IRS can compare a specimen with checks and other documents that reflect taxable income. A few years ago, the Eighth Circuit said the IRS can compel people to provide handwriting specimens. But recently the appeals court, sitting en banc (all judges on the case), reversed itself.

The lastest ruling adopts the position that compelling someone to make up handwriting examples "is a search and seizure" within the meaning of the Fourth Amendment. The powers of the IRS are "clearly subordinate" to the Fourth Amendment, and thus the agency isn't authorized to compel such samples unless Congress or the Supreme Court says it is. And so far neither one has provided such authority.

The Eighth Circuit has joined the Sixth and Second Circuits in denying this power to the IRS. But the Fourth Circuit has concluded that the agency can compel handwriting samples.

U.S. and Marvin v. Campbell a/k/a Holliday, U.S. Ct. of Appeals, 8th
Circ., 1978
12/6/78

⌒

A protester got loads of publicity that drew criminal charges for nonfiling.

The IRS selects tax protesters for criminal prosecution based on the amount of publicity they get. Usually, protesters who don't seek the spotlight are pursued by civil actions; criminal is reserved for the publicity hound. Richard Ralston Catlett is a notorious war and tax protester. The 68-year-old Columbia, Mo., health-food-store owner argued that criminal charges of failing to file returns should be dropped because the IRS was guilty of "selective prosecution."

The government is barred from selecting people to prosecute on grounds of race, religion or the exercise of free speech, or other "impermissible grounds." Catlett claimed that basing a criminal prosecution on publicity isn't permitted. But an appeals court disagreed. His exercise of free speech wasn't involved here, the court said. The IRS seeks criminal prosecution against publicized protesters to promote compliance with tax laws, the court observed.

"The government is entitled to select those cases for prosecution which it believes will" promote compliance, the court declared.

U.S. v. Catlett, U.S. Ct. of Appeals, 8th Circ., 1978
1/11/78

⌒

Bad paper: Are thousands of IRS power-of-attorney forms inadequate?

Before the IRS can deal with a taxpayer's representative, it is supposed to obtain a power of attorney signed by the taxpayer. The current form gives more limited authority than an earlier form—perhaps too limited. A dispute over an attorney's authority to give accounting papers to the IRS arose recently.

The taxpayers argued that the power-of-attorney form didn't empower the lawyer to hand over any data to the IRS. The taxpayers' arguments "are very persuasive," the Tax Court noted. But the court said that if it "cast a serious doubt" on the IRS form, "the effect on administration of the tax laws could be chaotic" as thousands of the forms are currently in use. Such a decision should be made "only if necessary" to the outcome of the case, the court said. It found other reasons to exonerate the taxpayers, and thus averted specifically ruling adversely on the forms.

However, William L. Raby, national tax director, Touche Ross & Co., a big CPA firm, says that if the issue clearly had to be decided in this case, the court "probably would have decided against the IRS."

Abatti and Gruis et al. v. Commissioner, T.C. Memo 1978-392
10/25/78

A jury trial. Can you get one when the U.S. sues you to collect income taxes?

A man quit making instalment payments on a $2,900 tax bill and the IRS sued to get a judgment against him and foreclose its tax lien on his assets. He urged the court to provide a trial by jury as called for in the Seventh Amendment to the Constitution. But a U.S. district court refused, ruling that this kind of case didn't entitle the taxpayer to a jury trial.

The crux of the case was whether a jury trial may be had as a matter of right in a case brought by the government for the collection of taxes. The IRS argued that it wasn't a matter of right. The Tenth Circuit Court of Appeals noted that the right to a jury trial in the Constitution is the right that existed under English common law when the Seventh Amendment was adopted.

Under English common law in 1791, a suit by the Crown to collect taxes was a suit in which the right to jury trial existed, the appeals court said. So the taxpayer could have a trial by jury.

U.S. v. Anderson, U.S. Ct. of Appeals, 10th Circ., 1978
10/18/78

⁓

IRS agents must go by the book so they don't deceive people, a court asserted.

Revenue agents investigate civil tax matters and are supposed to bring in special (criminal investigation) agents when they find "firm indications of fraud," the IRS Manual states. A revenue agent interviewed Andrew Toussaint, an IRS employe in Houston, about a $190,000 theft loss deduction. Toussaint said a $190,000 Picasso painting had been stolen from his home. He claimed he got the picture from his grandfather, though grandfather was so poor he left nothing when he died.

Toussaint couldn't explain how the poor man got the picture except that it might have been stolen. The IRS employe also said he didn't insure the painting for fear of tipping off thieves that he had it. That tale was a "firm indication of fraud" and the case should have quickly gone to the criminal division, a U.S. district court said. Because the case wasn't immediately referred to the criminal section, the evidence the revenue agent got was tainted; what he learned from Toussaint in five more interviews was barred as evidence, the court said.

The result of "continuing the investigation by himself was to deceive Toussaint into believing the investigation was routine and that criminal charges weren't contemplated," the court declared.

U.S. v. Toussaint, U.S. Dist Ct., South Texas, 1978
10/11/78

〜

A CPA goofed, but the IRS wouldn't accept a return correcting the error.

Mutual irrigation companies that provide their owners' water may be exempt from tax if 85% or more of their income comes from members. Sunny Slope Water Co., of California, was a tax-exempt water firm. It sold some land at a $64,000 profit. It was an installment sale: The buyer paid the sales price off over a number of years.

However, Sunny Slope's CPA inadvertently showed the full $64,000 on the water firm's tax return. The IRS suspended Sunny Slope's tax exemption because for that year it didn't get 85% of its income from its members. The company filed an amended return when it learned of the error, but the IRS rejected the return and collected $18,250 from the company.

However, the IRS was all wet: Sunny Slope's error was made in "good faith," and the IRS should have accepted the amended return correcting the mistake, a U.S. district court determined. Sunny Slope was due an $18,250 refund plus $6,500 interest, the court said.

Sunny Slope Water Co. v. U.S., U.S. Dist. Ct., Cent. Dist. Calif., 1978

9/27/78

⌒

He learned how much free advice from the IRS can cost.

Gene Gorrest lived apart from his wife pending their divorce. He asked the IRS how to file. Jointly with his wife, or as single head of household, the IRS advised. He used head of household, for it meant less tax. Later, the IRS said he didn't qualify as head of a household and owed $215 based on rates for single taxpayers. He agreed to pay. But then the IRS said he wasn't legally separated so he couldn't file as "single" and owed $812 based on rates for married filing a separate return.

However, he appealed to an IRS conferee who cut the amount to $142. Gorrest gave him a check. The IRS returned the check and demanded the $812. The IRS didn't tell Gorrest he could amend his return and file a joint one with his estranged wife to avoid the added tax. Nor did it tell him that if he appealed the matter to the Tax Court that would bar him from amending his return. He appealed to the court but didn't get any relief there.

"Misrepresentations of law were consistently made" by the IRS, but that didn't block the agency from collecting the $812, the court said.

Gorrest v. Commissioner, T.C. Memo 1978-239

7/19/78

I didn't file for 10 years for my Dad's sake, a lawyer insisted.

Alton G. Dunn's father underreported income from an insurance agency in which they were partners. His father refused to correct the misdeed when Alton confronted him. Alton was a practicing lawyer, yet he didn't want to turn his father in; nor did he want to file a return himself on which he knowingly misstated his income. But he feared that if he reported the correct partnership income on his own return it would directly implicate his dad.

So Alton didn't file at all, hoping the IRS would audit him and the partnership and force his father to end his tax cheating. But when the IRS finally came after Alton, he hadn't filed for eight years, and he missed two more during the IRS audit. Eventually, he paid back taxes for the 10 years. However, he contested $9,900 of fraud penalties, arguing he wasn't guilty of fraud, only negligence, as he was trying to force an audit to end his father's cheating.

That was his motive for the first five years. But for the other five he "wasn't so loath to incriminate his father as he was to blow the whistle on himself" and was guilty of fraud for those years, the Tax Court said.

Dunn v. Commissioner, T.C. Memo 1978-204
6/28/78

∽

The IRS was called a "cat's paw" doing the insurance industry's dirty work.

An informant gave the IRS reams of information about nearly all the lawyers in Philadelphia handling negligence cases. The IRS opened a probe of 14 of them and issued a summons to obtain fee agreements with their clients that the attorney had filed with a state court. But nine of the lawyers challenged the summons, contending the IRS was abusing its powers.

A U.S. district court agreed. The anonymous informant was "wedded body and soul to the insurance industry," which of course ends up paying most of the judgments that negligence attorneys win. "The IRS had to realize that the informant . . . was pursuing its own business purpose" when it gave the IRS the information, the federal court said. The IRS was guilty of abusing its power and letting itself be used "as a cat's paw to accomplish (an act) of retribution against . . . negligence attorneys," the court asserted.

"Cat's paw" comes from the tale of the monkey who used the cat's foot to rake chestnuts out of a fire. Among other things, it means "dupe or tool," says Webster's New World Dictionary.

U.S. v. Cortese, U.S. Dist. Ct., East. Dist Pa., 1978
6/7/78

∽

A wife obeyed her husband and didn't make a "knowing, intelligent decision."

Ruth Gillings and her husband were "tax protesters." They claimed, among other things, that filing in a federal tax return violated their rights against self-incrimination. The Justice Department prosecuted the California couple for willful failure to file a return, a misdemeanor with a maximum penalty of a year in jail and a $10,000 fine. The couple dismissed their court-appointed lawyers during the trial and acted as their own counsel.

The trial judge spoke at length to Ruth's husband about dismissing his lawyer to see if he knew what the consequences might be. The judge didn't speak to Ruth about it as extensively. She had told the court she followed the Bible's command for a wife to obey her husband before she dismissed her lawyer. The couple was convicted, but an appeals court overturned Ruth's conviction.

Ruth's husband made "a knowing and intelligent decision" to dismiss his lawyer, but the trial record didn't show that she was as well informed by the judge when she dismissed hers, the Ninth Circuit asserted. Ruth can be retried. Or the government can decide not to retry her and then she'll get off scot-free.

U.S. V. Gillings, U.S. Ct. of Appeals, 9th Circ., 1978
5/10/78

～

A sly way to mess up an IRS probe uses the Freedom of Information Act.

The act provides access to a lot of government records. But it normally won't give someone access to IRS investigation files, even if that someone is the object of the probe. Yet, asking for the file is a way to disrupt the agency's investigation for a while, at least. The effectiveness of this tactic is attested to by none other than IRS Deputy Commissioner William E. Williams.

"When a request is made for an open investigatory file, the steps necessary to process the request will tend to disrupt the investigation," Williams told a Senate panel. "The file itself becomes temporarily unavailable" to IRS investigators while other IRS personnel study it to see whether any of the contents should be released, he explained. Some taxpayers and attorneys have used the Freedom of Information Act as a way "to do what they couldn't do in court," an IRS spokesman remarks.

5/3/78

～

Life copies art: A case drags on and on as in Dickens's "Bleak House."

Back in 1971 the IRS office in Los Angeles sent Claude E. and Delores E. Brimm a notice that they owed $27,432.30. The tax issue has yet to go before the Tax Court, though the case has been there seven years. A side issue recently was laid to rest. It involved an underling's signing the district director's name to the notice. He wasn't authorized to sign it so the notice was invalid, the Brimms argued.

This obliged the court to plod through delegation orders handing authority down from the Treasury Secretary to the IRS Commissioner to the district directors to their subordinates. All was in order, said the court; the notice was valid. But the court clearly was fed up: "Procedural nitpicking" has consumed "more than half a decade," in which time Mr. Brimm has died.

This case evokes a passage about a lawsuit in Dickens's novel "Bleak House," the court asserted: "Jarndyce and Jarndyce drones on . . . innumerable children have been born into the cause . . . innumerable old people have died out of it . . . but Jarndyce and Jarndyce still drags its dreary length before the court."

Estate of Claude E. Brimm and Delores Brimm v. Commissioner, 70 T.C. 3
4/19/78

∽

A dawdling IRS mounted a misdirected attack to recoup a loss.

A group of cases involved the same facts and issues. So the taxpayers and the IRS agreed that the outcome of all the cases would be determined by the decision in one "test case." The IRS lost the test case. Yet it didn't free the taxpayers in the other cases from assessments it had made against them. So they asked the Tax Court to enter judgments in their favor. However, the IRS said the court shouldn't rely on the test case because a fraud had been committed on the court in the case.

The fraud involved the taxpayers' lawyer getting an IRS attorney to stipulate to "untrue facts," the IRS alleged. These cases aren't the place to raise that issue, the court said. The IRS must raise it by asking to re-open the test case. But the test case was decided four years ago; the IRS first alleged fraud 11 months ago, yet it hasn't moved to set the decision aside. Whether the "lengthy delay" killed the chances of overturning the test case can't be determined until the IRS moves to have it put aside, the court said.

In the meantime, the decision stands and the other cases will be decided in the taxpayers' favor. If the test case is set aside, the final outcome will apply to the other cases, the court concluded.

Sennett v. Commissioner, 69 T.C. 57
3/1/78

⌒

The only way to reap the benefits of a joint return is to file one.

Seems simple enough. But it isn't if you haven't filed returns for years. That was the case with Joseph and Evelyn Yetman. They didn't file for five years. When the IRS caught up with them, it computed their delinquent taxes at rates for married people filing separate returns. That resulted in more tax for the couple than if the IRS had used joint-return rates.

The couple complained to the Tax Court that the IRS should have to use joint rates. But the court disagreed. The tax code "clearly predicates the benefits of joint-return rates on the filing of a joint return," the court asserted. The Yetmans hadn't filed joint returns and thus they were barred from getting the benefits, the court concluded.

*A tip for nonfilers who get caught: Don't wait
for the IRS. If joint rates are better, file a joint return before the IRS sends a deficiency notice.
Some cases indicate delinquents can get joint-return benefits this way, Research Institute of America says.*

> *Yetman v. Commissioner, T.C. Memo 1978-52*
> *2/22/78*

Must the IRS follow the rules like everyone else, or
is it special?

The Tax Court sometimes rules on whether
amounts are taxable, then it will delay entering a final
decision until the IRS submits a claim for taxes based
on the ruling. But the agency overlooked claiming tax
for a sum that the court ruled was taxable. Finally, the
court entered a decision excluding tax on the sum. Later, the IRS tried to correct its mistake by asking the
court to change its decision to include the tax.

But the court said the IRS in effect was asserting
"an absolute right to present a claim," even after a final
decision has been entered. That assertion "overstates
the (IRS's) rights," the court asserted. The agency
failed to claim the tax in its deficiency notice to the taxpayer before the court got the case, and overlooked
claiming after the court ruled the amount was taxable.

The IRS "is required to conform" to the rules "like
any other party before this court" and the rules bar
such late claims, the court concluded.

> *Koufman v. Commissioner, 69 T.C. 35*
> *12/28/77*

Indian giver: The IRS hoped to be one after giving
away $19,600.

That tidy sum went to an estate Sara and Walker

Groezinger shared equally; so they ended up with the money. The IRS erred in refunding the estate tax and told the heirs to return the money. They refused. The IRS sent them a "deficiency notice" for $19,600 of unpaid tax on the estate. The Groezingers claimed there wasn't a "deficiency" as defined by the tax code.

They argued that the IRS couldn't use a deficiency notice to get back the money; the Tax Court hadn't jurisdiction over the matter, and the IRS must sue in a U.S. district court. The IRS contended the $19,600 was a "rebate," which if paid in error can be recouped through a deficiency notice, over which the Tax Court has jurisdiction. The court said it wasn't a rebate; however, that didn't let the heirs off the hook:

There was an "underpayment of tax," collectable by deficiency notice, which gave the Tax Court jurisdiction, and the heirs must return the $19,600, the court asserted.

Groezinger v. Commissioner, 69 T.C. 24
12/14/77

〜

"To punish and harass." Is that why the IRS went after an ACLU official?

"Discovery" usually allows a plaintiff to question a defendant and obtain pertinent documents prior to trial. Jay A. Miller, a career employe of the American Civil Liberties Union, which has defended many unpopular defendants, has sued the IRS to bar it from auditing his 1973 and 1974 returns. Miller says the since-disbanded IRS Special Service Staff kept a file on him, as it did on other political activists. He contends the SSS file was the basis for the audit which was intended "to punish and harass" him for his political activities.

The IRS denies that. But it refused to hand over documents or answer questions he posed. However, a

U.S. District Court granted Miller a measure of discovery: His probings are limited to matters specifically relating to the IRS's decision to audit him.

If Allen finds the audits "weren't properly initiated, then the court can expand the scope of discovery to include other related issues," the court said.

Miller v. Alexander et al., U.S. Dist. Ct., Dist. of Col., 1977
11/30/77

⌒

I want to see tax returns from Tax Court cases, a law professor told the IRS.

This Columbia University law prof could have seen the returns at the Tax Court, where they were publicly available as evidence in cases. However, after the cases were decided, the court sent the returns back to the IRS, as it does routinely with such documents. The professor, George Cooper, sued the IRS for the documents under the Freedom of Information Act.

The IRS argued that it is forbidden to disclose tax-return information to the public. The returns were publicly available at the Tax Court, but once back at the IRS regained their confidentiality, the government argued. However, a U.S. District Court recently rejected that argument. When the tax returns became part of the public record, they lost "all semblance of confidentiality" and didn't regain it when they returned to the IRS, the court asserted.

The court ordered the IRS to hand over the documents, and told the government to pay Cooper's legal costs.

Cooper v. I.R.S., U.S. Dist. Ct., Dist. of Col., 1977
11/9/77

⌒

Did an IRS agent blab to her husband about an acquaintance's tax return?

Michael Blickman, a Baltimore salesman, contends IRS auditor Ellen Demareck told her husband, Stanley, about Blickman's 1974-75 returns, which were being audited. Blickman only knew about it because he bumped into Stanley one day, and his old high-school classmate related what he had been told by his wife, Blickman alleges in court papers in a U.S. district court.

The IRS auditor's husband repeated details about Blickman's income, alimony and travel and entertainment deductions, Blickman alleges. It's a felony for an IRS employe to disclose such information. Blickman says he went to a U.S. attorney about the matter, but he declined to prosecute. Blickman's suit against Ellen, Stanley and the government seeks $250,000 damages.

Has the IRS taken action against Ellen? Leon Levine, an IRS spokesman, says privacy rules bar him from saying.

Blickman v. U.S., U.S. Dist. Ct., Baltimore, 1977
10/12/77

⌒

Pay up: The IRS lost a case and this time had to pay the winner's legal costs.

Do courts have authority to order the IRS to pay legal costs for taxpayers who beat the agency in lawsuits? The Tax Court has ruled it can't award attorney's fees; other federal courts say fees can be awarded only if the IRS acts in "bad faith," meaning with malice. Yet, a federal district court in Alabama recently awarded attorney's fees, asserting it needn't find the IRS acted in bad faith.

It was enough that the agency put "an unnecessary and vexatious burden" on the taxpayer, the court said. The IRS had asked the court to enforce a summons for a firm's books. But an IRS agent had pored over the books for a week and said he was done with them.

The IRS can take a second look only if the Treasury Secretary finds it is necessary and notifies the taxpayer in writing. But this agent didn't seek a letter from the Secretary; he issued a summons, which was wrong, the court concluded.
U.S. v. Garrison Construction Co., U.S. Dist. Ct., No. Dist. of Ala., 1977
10/5/77

Play hard . . . not foul. That's a shibboleth for U.S. prosecutors.

One of them successfully prosecuted a businessman for failing to report $263,000 of income. But the prosecutor phrased questions to witnesses to give the jury a damaging and false impression of the defendant, who appealed his conviction. He claimed the prosecutor's actions denied him a fair trial.

The taxpayer argued that the government's lawyer asked some improper questions, including this one: "His real method of accounting wasn't to report income, wasn't it?" A U.S. appeals court said the prosecutor "overstepped the bounds of fairness." The judge's instructing the jury to disregard the prosecutor's words wasn't sufficient to assure a fair trial, the court said.

A U.S. prosecutor "may prosecute with earnestness and vigor indeed, he should do so," the court asserted. "But while he may strike hard blows, he isn't at liberty to strike foul ones." The taxpayer must have a new trial, the court ordered.
U.S. v. Meeker, U.S. Ct. of Appeals, 7th Circ., 1977
9/7/77

He survived the Bay of Pigs and a Cuban jail. Then he faced the IRS.

Raul Ramon Gonzalez was a high roller in pre-Castro Havana. As head of the Havana Hilton Casino, he had his own hotel suite, several homes and a yacht. Gonzalez had been friendly with Castro since childhood but cooled toward him after he took power. Eventually, Gonzalez stashed $325,000 of his own cash aboard his yacht and sailed to Florida. He decided to participate in the Bay of Pigs invasion, and was captured and jailed in Cuba. After his release, he operated a private club in Miami, worked as a dealer in a Haitian casino, and began associating with suspected criminals.

The IRS investigated Gonzalez as part of its "narcotics project"—in which it tried to curb drug traffic by prosecuting narcotics suspects for tax crimes. The IRS failed to prove any drug connection, but Gonzalez was indicted for tax evasion. A judge acquitted him. The IRS then dropped its tax fraud charges and proceeded only to collect back taxes it said were due. Gonzalez argued that his acquittal proved that the entire investigation had been improper and that the IRS should be barred from collecting anything.

The Tax Court allowed the IRS to press its case. The court said the investigation was started in "good faith" and the government must have "certain latitude in pursuing leads."

Gonzalez v. Commissioner, T.C. Memo 1977-240
8/24/77

～

The IRS agent dropped by for a drink and found less than met his eye.

Agent John W. Burke had a hunch that Augusta, Ga.'s Partridge Inn Lounge, one of the city's most popular spots, wasn't declaring all its income. After a drink at the bar, he examined the books. Sure enough, Burke concluded, the proprietor of "The P.I.," as it was known, had filed incorrect tax returns. It turned out that the returns had been prepared by one Paul Huckaba, later described by the Tax Court as a "gypsy-type tax preparer" because he operated out of his car. The proprietor, Billy Sipes, lacking sophistication in the vagaries of tax law, had turned everything over to Huckaba.

Agent Burke wanted to impose a 50% fraud penalty against Sipes. The fraud charge was crucial. The statute of limitations had expired on infractions that weren't fraudulent, so if the IRS couldn't prove fraud, it couldn't collect anything. The Tax Court dismissed the case and assailed the IRS and Agent Burke. His testimony was "confusing and vague" and his investigation "careless," the court said. Moreover, the case lacked the usual signs of fraud: Sipes was cooperative and didn't try to hide anything.

If the IRS has a policy of "presenting for trial each and every fraud case its agents recommended, it should reexamine its policy," the court asserted. "If such a policy exists, it is intellectually dishonest and basically unfair to taxpayers."

Sipes v. Commissioner, T.C. Memo 1977-148
8/17/77

⌒

A victory in Tax Court won't win you anything extra to cover legal costs.

Some lawyers thought folks who beat the IRS in Tax Court could be reimbursed for attorney's fees under a law enacted in the fall of 1976. The legislation was designed to protect people from harassing government lawsuits, but Sen. James Allen got Congress to add a clause to include tax cases. But it hasn't been clear whether Allen's amendment covered the Tax Court. There, suits are always brought by taxpayers against the government, and the law pertains to a "proceeding by or on behalf of" the U.S.

But an auto dealer argued that before a taxpayer can sue the IRS in Tax Court, the IRS must issue a deficiency notice of tax due, and thus the case results from a "proceeding by" the U.S. The dealer also argued that Sen. Allen told Congress he intended to cover Tax Court cases. Still, the Tax Court concluded it wasn't authorized to award anyone attorney's fees. The court said that issuing a deficiency notice wasn't "a proceeding by or on behalf of" the U.S. "Proceeding" meant a court proceeding, not an administrative act.

The law that Congress changed deals only with district courts, indicating reimbursement applies only to district court cases, the Tax Court asserted.

Key Buick Co. v. Commissioner, 68 T.C. 17
5/25/77

⌒

Again: The IRS must give Taxpayer Compliance Measurement Program data to Philip and Susan Long, an appeals court said. They got statistical analyses, but the agency refused to give them the raw material that includes return and audit information. The court said the Bellevue, Wash., couple can have the raw data with taxpayer identities erased. The Longs won a case some years ago that first opened many IRS internal directives to public scrutiny.

Long v. U.S., U.S. Ct. of Appeals, 9th Circ., 1979
5/23/79

⌒

"I want the IRS to know that this judge thinks that this trial, this gentleman never should have been prosecuted." Thus spoke U.S. District Court Judge John W. Reynolds as he chastised the government for criminally prosecuting an emotionally disturbed man who hadn't reported $21,700 of income, three years' interest on some savings accounts. The judge fined the man $1, declaring that "a government has to be humane."

U.S. v. Worklan, U.S. Dist. Ct., East. Dist. Wisc., 1978
12/13/78

⌒

Can't do: A law firm manages clients' money, maintaining a bank account for each one to pay their bills and handle their earnings. The firm also prepares tax returns. Return preparers are prohibited from negotiating refund checks. So the law firm can't deposit its clients' refund checks in the bank even if it has a power of attorney signed by them, the IRS ruled.

IRS letter ruling 7824017
11/22/78

⌒

What happens when a taxpayer believes an IRS rule isn't valid, but the preparer of his tax return believes it's valid? If the preparer doesn't follow rules he believes valid because his client or the client's adviser believes they're invalid, the return preparer may be liable for penalties for negligent or willful disregard of tax rules, the IRS ruled.

IRS letter ruling 7813019
6/21/78

⌒

It's income: A taxpayer was penalized due to an error by the person who did his tax work. The tax preparer paid the penalty for the taxpayer. The payment is taxable income to the taxpayer, the IRS ruled.

IRS private letter ruling 7749029
12/21/77

⌒

Attorney's fees: The government was ordered to pay $3,350 of lawyer's fees for some Montana cattle raisers who won a tax case. A U.S. district court said the award was okay under the Civil Rights Attorney's Fees Awards Act.

Levno v. U.S., U.S. Dist. Ct., Montana, 1977
11/2/77

❧

Two money-order outfits are in bankruptcy proceedings; money orders they sold aren't being honored. If a check or money order is returned unpaid, the IRS usually penalizes the taxpayer $5. But the agency won't fine people who paid their taxes with the two companies' "rubber" money orders. Of course they must still pay their taxes.

IRS Manual, Supplement 52G-145
6/8/77

❧

Bad IRS advice. Taxpayers who have relied on erroneous information published by the IRS won't be liable for fraud or negligence penalties, but must pay any added tax later found owing. A Wichita Falls, Texas, taxpayer got that opinion from a Treasury lawyer in a letter disclosed by Tax Notes, a weekly publication. However, the taxpayer would owe interest on the additional tax, an IRS spokesman says; the agency can't waive interest in such circumstances.

Tax Notes Volume V, Issue 21
6/1/77

❧

Silver coins: A person died owning U.S. silver coins with a face value of $25,000. But they had a market value of $50,000; they were the old-style silver coins that aren't minted anymore. The IRS said the coins must be valued at market value rather than face value for estate tax purposes even though the money was still legal tender. It wouldn't matter if the owner were a coin dealer or not.

Rev. Rul. 78-360
10/11/78

Assessments, Liens and Seizures

He rescued a car from the tax enforcers and was towed into court.

Main Cob Co., a corn cob dealer, owed payroll taxes of $58,000. Main Cob's president, Robert Main, wasn't home when a gang of IRS collectors came to his house and without a warrant seized a company-owned car in his driveway. The next day Main went to the garage where the IRS towed the car and drove it off. The Gibson City, Ill., resident was convicted and sentenced to a year in jail for "forcible rescue" of seized property.

His timing proved to be awful: Just a few months after he rescued his car, the Supreme Court ruled in another case that the IRS can't seize property on private premises without a court order. Main appealed his conviction, arguing that the IRS seizure was illegal. But an appeals court said the Supreme Court decision didn't apply retroactively, so the IRS collectors acted lawfully at the time. Main's free on bail pending further appeals.

His lawyer notes that Main rescued his car before the Supreme Court decision, but he wasn't indicted until the day after the decision was announced. Today, IRS collectors must get court approval to seize autos on private premises.

U.S. v. Main, U.S. Ct. of Appeals, 7th Circ., 1979
6/20/79

Some cops told an IRS agent Johnny sold dope, and the IRS clobbered him.

If you fight an IRS assessment in Tax Court, the burden's on you to prove the IRS wrong. Based on what some policemen said, an IRS agent believed Johnny Weimerskirch, of Coulee City, Wash., was selling heroin and assessed him $10,000 tax and penalties for failing to report $25,000 of drug income. Weimerskirch went to Tax Court, but the court said he hadn't overcome the presumption of the IRS's being correct.

However, on appeal to the Ninth Circuit, Weimerskirch's lawyer, Richard P. Algeo, of Spokane, argued that the IRS must have "some substantive evidence showing that the taxpayer received income from the charged activity." Weimerskirch was never arrested for drug involvement, and the IRS hadn't any evidence of bank accounts, extravagant spending, or anything else to show he had unreported income. The Tax Court erred in upholding the IRS assessment, the appeals court said.

The court added that the IRS "is affixing a label, 'heroin pusher,'" without any proof, and that "runs afoul of every notion of fairness in our system of law."

Weimerskirch v. Commissioner, U.S. Ct. of Appeals, 9th Circ., 1979
5/23/79

◡

Like a clenched fist: The IRS wouldn't let go of $138,000 it seized.

Detroit cops found $280,000 when they searched Chester Campbell's home for guns. The cops told the IRS, which issued a "jeopardy assessment" to seize $138,000 of the cash the cops had. A week later, a Michigan court said the money was seized illegally and ordered it returned. The IRS ignored the order, but a U.S.

district court said the IRS had acted improperly and should return the money.

However, the court agreed to stay the return until the IRS appealed. An appeals court also ordered the money returned. Still the IRS didn't comply. Instead, it made a new jeopardy assessment and used it to convince the district court to change its ruling so the IRS could keep the money. These maneuvers didn't sway the appeals court, which recently ordered the IRS to return Campbell's $138,000.

Giving back the money didn't hurt the IRS so much, the court observed. The IRS "is simply returned to the position it would be in if it hadn't illegally seized the funds in the first place."
Campbell v. U.S. et al., U.S. Ct. of Appeals, 6th Circ., 1979
3/21/79

∽

What's in a name? Quite a bit if you can't spell it, the IRS learned.

When he got into "tax trouble" Manuel de J. Castillo owned several California properties, including his home. The IRS filed tax-lien notices with the Los Angeles County Recorder against Castillo. But his name was misspelled as "Manual Castello." Soon after the liens, he transferred one property—it wasn't his home—to Isidore Schuman, who sold it to Henry T. and Jane S. Haye.

In summer 1978, the IRS seized the Hayes' property and tried to sell it for Castillo's tax debt. But the Hayes cried "foul" and asked a federal court to void the lien against their real estate. The IRS argued that despite the misspelling of Castillo as "Castello," a diligent searcher would have turned up the lien. But the court didn't buy that. Such liens list only name and home address; searching the lien list wouldn't have uncovered the lien notice because "Castello" was listed some 1,000 names away from Castillo.

The lien was invalid against the Hayes' property, the court concluded, noting that the IRS had a duty to have its lien-notice forms correct, especially because "the name of the taxpayer is crucial" when the notices are filed by name, and not also by each property.

Haye et al. v. U.S., U.S. Dist. Ct., Cent. Dist. of Calif., 1979
3/14/79

～

He shipped lots of bread to Nassau, so the IRS seized his dough.

When it slaps jeopardy assessments on people, the IRS practically has carte blanche to seize their money and property. The IRS is supposed to use a jeopardy assessment only when there's reason to believe taxpayers may owe a bundle in taxes and might put their assets beyond Uncle Sam's reach. The IRS slapped a $1.8 million jeopardy assessment on Felix "The Cat" Vicknair after a boatload of marijuana was seized in front of his Florida residence.

Vicknair argued that the IRS acted unreasonably, as there wasn't any indication he wouldn't pay. But a district court noted that Vicknair had exported more than $800,000 in cash to the Bahamas. That was for a legitimate shipping business, his lawyer, Robert Breier, said. Even so, currency exports, "legitimate or not," indicate a "structure oft employed for the dissipation of assets beyond the bounds of the U.S.," the court asserted.

The IRS acted properly in making the jeopardy assessment and seizing Vicknair's assets, the court determined.

U.S. v. Vicknair, U.S. Dist. Ct., So. Dist. Fla., 1978
12/20/78

To get in: Here's how the IRS can enter private property to seize assets.

For years, the IRS entered private property to grab delinquent taxpayers' property without a search warrant. The IRS presumed the law authorized such action. But in 1977, the Supreme Court ruled that the agency must get a court order in most instances to enter private property to seize assets without the owner's consent. So the IRS began asking U.S. district courts for warrants.

One district court balked, contending it couldn't issue a warrant on an *ex parte* basis—that is, without the taxpayer being heard first by the court. However, the 10th Circuit Court of Appeals said district courts are empowered to issue search warrants for the IRS on an *ex parte* basis just as they do in criminal cases; the taxpayer needn't know a warrant is being sought.

The "probable cause" required for a warrant in a criminal case doesn't apply to the IRS. Requirements for civil enforcement warrants "are yet somewhat loosely defined," the appeals court said. But if the IRS follows authorized tax-collecting methods, that would justify granting its search warrant request, the court suggested.

In re Tax Indebtedness of Dell W. Carlson, U.S. Ct. of Appeals, 10th Circ., 1978
7/26/78

⌒

The "leaden feet" of the IRS trod without mercy on a poor man.

When his business failed in 1969, he owed about $5,000 of payroll taxes. But now he's 68 years old, lives on Social Security, and his only asset is the cash value in $10,000 of life insurance. He can't pay the premiums, but the cash value will pay them through 1986. The IRS wanted to seize the insurance. He pleaded to have it spared, arguing that if he died before the insurance ran out there'd be enough to pay the tax bill and bury him.

Since 1974 he has been in court trying to save his insurance. But "the government has simply been dragging its leaden feet," a U.S. district court exclaimed recently. "Why the government should seek to force a harder bargain on this admittedly indigent defendant, who asks only that he be allowed funeral expenses from policies that might expire before his death, totally escapes this court."

"There are and must be times when the strong arm of the law should be stayed out of pure mercy," the court said, and ordered the IRS to keep its hands off the man's policies.

U.S. v. Armbruster, Whitelaw and Metropolitan Life, U.S. Dist. Ct., So. Dist. N.Y., 1977
3/15/78

⌒

A late change can stop the IRS from selling our property, a couple argued.

Ray and Macine Knoefler filed a joint return that showed they owed $7,000. They didn't enclose any payment. The IRS tried to collect the money without success and finally seized real estate the couple owned. In the midst of the IRS collection efforts, the couple filed an amended return for the year. It showed they owed nothing instead of $7,000. Still, the IRS went ahead and advertised the seized property for sale.

Acting as their own lawyers, the Knoeflers went to court to stop the sale. The IRS must complete an audit of our returns before it can sell our property, they contended. However, a federal appeals court ruled against the couple. Filing an amended return doesn't stop the collection process, the court asserted.

The IRS could have delayed collection efforts until the audit was done, the court said. But that was in the IRS's discretion and there was nothing to show an "abuse of that discretion."
Knoefler v. IRS agent, U.S. Ct. of Appeals, 9th Circ., 1977
1/25/78

⌒

Its word is its . . . The IRS accepted a settlement in Tax Court and agreed that a couple owed $49,800 in added tax. But a few years later, the agency assessed the couple $44,000 more for the year involved in the Tax Court case. The assessment was "illegal and erroneous," a federal district court said, and ordered the government to pay the couple's legal costs to fight the assessment.
Fluor v. U.S., U.S. Dist. Ct., Cent. Dist. Calif., 1979
6/13/79

Matters of Timing

It got there despite the way this fellow mailed it to the Tax Court.

Orthel E. Cassell had 90 days—until Aug. 2—to petition the Tax Court to hear his case involving a $1,117 IRS assessment. But his petition arrived at the court on Aug. 8. When a petition arrives late, the postmark determines if it was mailed in time. But the postmark on Cassell's petition was illegible to the naked eye.

So the court had the postal crime lab examine it. The lab discerned that the postmark was "PM 2 AUG. 1978," and thus in time. But late petitions also must be "in an envelope or other appropriate wrapper, properly addressed," and Cassell had addressed the petition to the IRS instead of the court. So his petition had to be rejected and he'll have to pay the $1,117, the court said.

He can sue later for a refund in a district court, but the Tax Court reminded him that there also are "time limits involved in proceeding along the refund route."

Cassell v. Commissioner, 72 T.C. 26
6/13/79

⌇

How a "dead" firm can become a sitting duck for the IRS.

Padre Island Thunderbird Inc. was dissolved by Illinois for failing to pay state franchise taxes. Four years later, the IRS assessed the corporation $37,300. The assessment was too late, the firm argued, because Illinois law bars actions against dissolved corporations more than two years after they have been dissolved.

State laws don't set time limits for IRS assessments, federal laws do, the Tax Court said, and it related more bad news. Illinois law bars a corporation that hasn't paid state franchise taxes from bringing a lawsuit. So, the firm couldn't challenge the IRS assessment in Tax Court, the court concluded.

Padre Island Thunderbird Inc. v. Commissioner, 72 T.C. 37
6/13/79

⌣

What if the post office postmarks your letter to the court a day after you mail it?

To get a case into Tax Court, a petition must be mailed to the court within 90 days of the date the IRS mailed a deficiency notice demanding added tax. The IRS sent a deficiency notice to the estate of Stephen B. McGarity for $72,000. The last day to mail a petition to the Tax Court—and thus avoid payment until the court decided the disputed issues—was Aug. 8, 1978.

But Aug. 9, 1978, was the postmark on the envelope when it arrived at the court. That was a day too late. But executors for the estate of the late Atlanta cop said the petition was in time, as it had been delivered to the Lawrenceville, Ga., post office Aug. 8, the day before the post office postmarked it. Still, the petition was too late, the court determined, because a legible postmark determines the mailing date despite other evidence to the contrary.

Estate of Stephen B. McGarity v. Commissioner, 72 T.C. 19
5/9/79

⌣

Can a move become a $20,000 change-of-address tax shield?

Philip and Judith Reddock moved from Brooklyn to the Upper East Side of New York City. They filed a power of attorney with the IRS, saying that any communications about their 1974 tax return should go to their lawyer's office. With the three-year limit almost over, the IRS sent a deficiency notice for $20,000 of added tax for 1974 to the Reddock's old Brooklyn address. It came back undelivered.

By then the three-year limit had expired, yet the IRS remailed the notice to the couple's new address shown on more-recent tax returns. The couple urged the Tax Court to declare the notice invalid because it wasn't sent in time to their last known address. The IRS argued that the couple waived any defects in the notice when they petitioned the court. But the court said they "waived nothing."

Furthermore, the IRS notice was worthless as it hadn't been sent to the proper address before the three-year limit expired, the court concluded.

Reddock v. Commissioner, 72 T.C. 2
4/11/79

◃

Sure, we erred, but you must ignore our mistake, the IRS told the court.

Erle and Bonnie Heath paid $18,000 that the IRS said they owed. But they didn't believe they owed the money and requested a refund, the first step toward taking the matter into court. The IRS refused the refund in a letter of May 21, 1976. But the letter had the date of their refund claim wrong. So, in a letter in July the IRS corrected the date and said the couple had two years from this letter to go to court.

The Heaths filed a refund suit in the Court of Claims, within two years of the July letter. But the IRS said that was too late; the deadline expired in May, two years from its first letter. The court didn't see it that way. The IRS confused the couple about the filing deadline and then "urges us to ignore the confusion engendered by its actions," the court said.

The couple's refund suit could proceed, the court determined. In effect, the second IRS letter was a "formal notice" that extended the two-year deadline to July. However, if the IRS had merely phoned the couple instead of writing, the deadline wouldn't have been extended, the court said.

Heath v. U.S., U.S. Ct. of Claims, 1979
2/21/79

Two postmarks are worse than one, a last-minute lawyer found out.

A taxpayer's lawyer finished a petition to the Tax Court at 10 p.m. on the last day for mailing the petition, Oct. 25. He ran the envelope through the office postage meter and dropped it in a mailbox before midnight. When it arrived at the court, the envelope had two postmarks; the post office postmark read Oct. 26, a day past the deadline. The taxpayer was out of luck.

The Tax Court is the only court where you can contest an IRS deficiency notice of tax due without paying the deficiency first. But when a postage meter and a post office mark are on a petition, the post office mark establishes the mailing date. The attorney could have avoided this foul-up by taking the letter to the post office and making sure it was postmarked there on Oct. 25, the Tax Court said, adding:

"The possibility of untimely filing is a risk the sender takes if he fails to do so."

Pete James Enterprises Inc. v. Commissioner, T.C. Memo 1978-243
8/9/78

"Surprising carelessness" was shown by the IRS, a court said.

Garry and Louise Peters had a dispute with the IRS over a return filed in 1973. The law gives the IRS three years from the filing date of a return to issue a deficiency notice for additional tax—unless taxpayers agree to an extension. Some do agree to allow more time for negotiating a settlement. But this couple's dispute wasn't settled; the IRS sent them a deficiency notice for $3,500 in 1977.

The notice came too late, so we don't have to pay, the couple said. You agreed to an extension, the IRS insisted, though it couldn't find their consent form in its files. An IRS clerk did say she sent the form to the couple's lawyer and recalled receiving a signed form from him. But the attorney swore he didn't return the form. And the clerk's superior, who reviewed signed forms, couldn't recall seeing one for the Peterses.

"Disturbing irregularities in the handling of this case by the IRS . . . show surprising careless-ness," the Tax Court remarked. The couple needn't pay the $3,500 as the IRS couldn't show they had agreed to extend the three-year limita-tion.

Peters v. Commissioner, T.C. Memo 1978-219
7/5/78

⌒

She missed the mailman but collided with the tax collector.

Beatrice Davis wasn't home when the postman tried to deliver a certified letter on Dec. 31. When she got home it was too late to pick up the letter at the post office. So she got it Jan. 2—a year later. To her surprise it was her severance pay. She had been awarded $17,000 severance, but was told it would be sent several months later. Her employer, though, mailed it before year-end, and listed the sum on her W-2 that year. Davis didn't count it as income until the next year when she had it in her hands.

But the IRS said it counted in the earlier year. Which meant the $17,000 went on top of her regular earnings that year and put her in a much higher bracket, resulting in about $4,000 of tax on the $17,000. The IRS argued that her employer committed the money to her that year and she would have actually got it except "she chose" to be out when the mailman came. But she couldn't make such a choice for she expected the money much later, the Tax Court determined.

She had "no inkling that the certified mail was her severance pay," the court asserted, and it rejected the IRS claim.

Davis v. Commissioner, T.C. Memo 1978-12
2/1/78

Be "clear and concise" when you tell the tax man your address is changed.

The IRS must mail a deficiency notice of taxes due to a taxpayer's "last known address." The taxpayer normally has only 90 days from the mailing date of a valid notice to appeal to the Tax Court. The IRS is barred from collecting the disputed amount until the court concludes the case. A notice for $237,000 went certified mail to Lewis and Jeanne Johnson at the New Orleans, La., address on their tax return. But they were separated and weren't at that address.

Later, Mr. Johnson asked the Tax Court to hear the dispute even though the 90-day deadline was with the IRS listing his business address. But he hadn't specifically notified the agency, as he was obliged to, that that was his new address, nor that he and his wife had separated and left the address listed on their return.

Absent "clear and concise" notice "directing the (IRS) to use a different address," the agency can treat the tax return address as the last known address, the court asserted.

Johnson v. Commissioner, T.C. Memo 1977-382
11/16/77

⌒

Money back: The CPAs got the IRS to pay back a payroll-tax penalty.

The IRS usually imposes a 5% penalty on employers late with payroll-tax deposits. A New England firm paid the penalty when it was late because some anticipated financing was delayed, leaving the firm temporarily strapped for cash. It did make the deposits as soon as it could. When the firm's accountant, Peat, Marwick, Mitchell & Co., learned of the penalty, it sought a refund.

The CPA firm told the IRS the late deposits were due to "reasonable cause." The local IRS office refused to refund the penalty. But an appeal to the recently created post of Penalty Appeals Officer resulted in a refund. The Penalty Appeals Officer process is being tested by the IRS. Appeals can be made before or after a penalty is paid.

10/26/77

⌒

A French lawyer was in the U.S. the day the IRS

notice of tax due usually must be made within 90 days from the day the IRS mails the notice. An exception allows 150 days "if the notice is addressed to a person outside the U.S." A lawyer, a resident of Paris, practiced sometimes in the U.S., and happened to be in New York the day the IRS mailed him a deficiency notice. He left for Paris the next day.

His appeal to the Tax Court was made 91 days after the IRS notice. That's too late, the IRS argued: He was in the U.S. the day the notice was mailed, so he's barred from the 150-day privilege. If the IRS had its way, the court noted without approval, an IRS notice mailed at 12:01 a.m. could be appealed in 150 days by a taxpayer who left the U.S. at 11:59, but in only 90 days by one who left at 12:02.

Someone's "ephemeral presence at the moment the deficiency is mailed isn't controlling," the court asserted, and ruled that the Paris attorney had 150 days to appeal.

Lewy v. Commissioner, 68 T.C. 66
9/14/77

⌒

How swift is mail from Dallas to Washington? Well, three days. But. . . .

The Tax Court must receive a taxpayer's petition appealing an IRS notice of taxes due within 90 days of the IRS notice, or the court can't take the case. The day the taxpayer's petition is mailed counts as the day the court receives it. Eugene R. Mason had to appeal an IRS notice by July 7, but the court got his petition July 12. He mailed it July 6, he said, but the postmark was illegible.

end and mailed it at a Dallas post office the night of
July 6, he swore. But a postal inspector testified mail
shouldn't take six days from Dallas to Washington: A
postal study showed 100% of Dallas-Washington mail
was delivered in three days. He conceded, though, that
Mason's letter could have been slowed by the Bicenten-
nial celebration that week. And the Tax Court noted recently that postal data the inspector cited was for 1977,
not 1976, when Mason mailed his petition.

*His story "is entirely reconcilable with that
offered by the postal official," the court asserted,
and it granted Mason his day in Tax Court.*

Mason v. Commissioner, 68 T.C. 29
6/29/77

⌒

Confusion, he said, made him miss a critical deadline.

Alas: An IRS deficiency notice arrived in the mail
saying he owed over $1,500 in tax and penalties. When
he set about contesting it in Tax Court, he couldn't find
the court in Detroit, which was confusing. It's in Washington, though the judges "ride circuit" for hearings in
other cities. When William D. Perkins did locate the
court, the form he got to petition the court to take his
case was for a "small tax case" and his case exceeded
the small-case $1,500 limit. That was more confusing.

He had 90 days from the date of the IRS notice to
get his petition to the court. When he finally asked a
lawyer's help, he was told it was the last day and to get
the petition form mailed that day even if it was for a
"small tax case." Perkins said he put the form in a mailbox that day. But it was a weekend and the form wasn't
postmarked until two days later, too late to meet the

the matter was litigated. He was so confused he missed the deadline, he claimed. But the court said it must reject his case.

The court wondered why he was so confused as the IRS notice tells how to petition the court.

Perkins v. Commissioner, T.C. Memo 1977-58
6/8/77

⌒

Choose well: Ralph and Clarita Riedel filed a joint return. Later they discovered that they would have been better off filing separate returns. But they were out of luck because the filing deadline had passed. Once the deadline is passed, the decision to file jointly becomes irrevocable, a court told the Riedels.

Riedel v. Commissioner, T.C. Memo 1978-468
2/7/79

⌒

A secretary's word that she had mailed a Tax Court petition before the deadline for filing it was enough to convince the court that the petition had been filed on time. The postmark on the petition was illegible and the IRS had contended that the petition was late and therefore void.

Felt v. Commissioner, T.C. Memo 1978-286
8/16/78

Matters of Records

My books are wrong like they were the last time the IRS got me, he insisted.

The IRS ignored Ben L. Selig's books when it nailed him for $7,600 for the years 1961-63. His books were inadequate, so the IRS figured how much he should have reported by computing changes in Selig's net worth. But when the IRS went after Selig again—for 1972-74—it used his books to calculate that he owed $24,000 in tax. Selig complained that the IRS used his books this time.

He argued that his books were still inadequate and insisted the IRS figure his delinquent taxes by the net worth method. "Incredible," exclaimed the Tax Court. Here was Selig, after "poor bookkeeping" cost him dearly in the past, the court said, arguing that he hasn't changed his record keeping and was paying the same bookkeeper "to keep inaccurate and inflated books for over a decade even after he became aware that the books were inaccurate." The court refused to swallow that.

But Selig will have to cough up $24,000, the court ruled; he hadn't any right to have the IRS use the net worth method even though the agency used it before.

Selig v. Commissioner, T.C. Memo 1978-249
7/12/78

Confused or stubborn? A judge wondered of a pilot landing in court.

Grady Olen Klutz made $18,100 one year as a pilot. And the Lincolnton, N.C., resident deducted some $8,800 as business expenses. The IRS jettisoned $8,000 of the deductions, which included $3,100 for "auto & driver expense," apparently for Klutz's wife to drive him to and from work. The IRS said he hadn't substantiated the deductions.

Acting as his own attorney, Klutz took the matter to the Tax Court, where Judge Leo H. Irwin upheld most of the IRS assessments. The judge's opinion states: "It is unclear whether this case is a result of confusion or stubbornness on the part of petitioner. He has been audited nearly every year since 1962. Also, he has apparently been apprised of the necessity of maintaining adequate records. However . . . he failed to do so."

Klutz v. Commissioner, T.C. Memo 1979-169
5/23/79

⌒

Caesars Palace was told to divulge his records, but the IRS didn't tell him.

When the IRS subpoenas information about a taxpayer from "third-party record keepers," it must tell the taxpayer. Yet, an IRS agent, Shirley L. Moore, issued a summons to Caesars Palace for records of Arthur Weisberg without notifying him of the action. He found out anyway and asked a court to quash the summons because he hadn't been properly notified.

The IRS argued that he didn't have to be notified because a gambling casino such as Caesars Palace isn't a "third-party record keeper." Besides banks and savings and loans, the tax-code definition of third-party record keeper includes "any person extending credit through the use of credit cards or similar devices." Caesars Palace extends credit; Weisberg had one of its credit cards. But the IRS contended that the tax code meant such charge cards as American Express or Visa. Its argument crapped out in a U.S. district court.

Caesars Palace credit activity made it a record keeper included in the tax code, and Weisberg should have been notified; and because he wasn't, the court threw out the IRS's summons.

U.S. v. Desert Palace Inc., U.S. Dist. Ct., Nevada, 1979
4/18/79

⌒

He's easy: An "inadequate personality" meets a demanding IRS agent.

Agent Smith asked Joseph W. Richey for his business records. Richey handed them over. But later he sued to get the records back and to block the IRS from using them against him. Richey was "less capable than the average person" in handling the confrontation with the agent; he is a "passive person with an inadequate personality," a psychologist averred. Richey "panicked, became mentally confused and wanted very much to reduce the stress and tension" the agent's presence caused.

Richey is "authority-bound," and under stress "reacts pretty much to what a person tells him to do," a U.S. district court found. So the IRS must return the records because Richey couldn't have given them to Agent Smith "freely and voluntarily," the court concluded. Still, the IRS can try to get them again with a proper court order, the court added.

As for Richey, he and wife Blanche were indicted on criminal charges while the issue of their business records was in litigation.

Richey v. Smith, U.S. Dist. Ct., East Dist. Texas, 1977
2/22/78

She said, he said he was done with them. He said he didn't say that.

The IRS usually can make only one inspection of a taxpayer's records, unless special notice is given that a second inspection is necessary. IRS agent Mark Cohen was going over a taxpayer's records, but returned them to an accountant who had to supply them to a court under a subpoena issued in the taxpayer's divorce case. Agent Cohen got the records again, but again returned them because of a second subpoena in the divorce case.

When Cohen asked once more for the records, the accountant and her client balked. In court, fighting an IRS summons for the records, the accountant testified that Cohen had said, "he was through with them." If he said that, it meant the IRS had completed its inspection and couldn't see the records again without special notice to the taxpayer. But Cohen said he hadn't said that.

A federal appeals court approved a district court's accepting the agent's testimony over the accountant's, and affirmed that the records must be given to the IRS once more.

U.S. and Robert J. Pyle v. June Myslajek, Irwin L. Pollack and I. L. Pollack & Associates, U.S. Ct. of Appeals, 8th Circ., 1977
1/11/78

⌢

Maybe doctors' wives shouldn't be their husbands' bookkeepers.

When Carolyn left Richard Haley, she took expense and income records she kept for his medical practice. She refused to return them. He didn't know how much his income was and asked the local IRS office for advice. An IRS employe had Richard sign what he thought was an extension to file by July 15. By June 30 he still hadn't retrieved his books from his ex-wife; the

IRS told him to file based on his return the year before. Richard filed before July 15, paying $30,000 tax.

Later, the IRS found that he owed $4,000 more, and that the form he signed wasn't an extension to file late. The IRS told him to pay $10,000 in penalties for late filing and underpayment. However, his tardiness was due to reasons "beyond his control," his ex-wife's taking his records, the Tax Court said. And he filed by July 15, the deadline he believed he had after talking to the IRS. He didn't have to pay the late penalty, the court ruled.

He hadn't been negligent and hadn't intentionally disregarded the law, so he didn't owe the underpayment penalty either, the court concluded.

Haley v. Commissioner, T.C. Memo 1977-348
10/19/77

～

ZZYZX springs wells up in a tale of ministry, health food and a raid.

Helen and Curtis Howe Springer shipped health foods from a spot in the desert. Curtis named it Zzyzx (Zi-zex) Mineral Springs and hoped to perfect a claim to the federal land. He preached on gospel radio and promoted their products on the air. The couple quit selling the items and gave them to people donating to their Zzyzx Springs development effort.

One day California health agents raided the place and grabbed the Springers' books. Then the U.S. evicted them. Then, the IRS charged they had underreported a year's income. Only Helen filed returns. Curtis had deeded the business to her and believed its profits were hers alone. Helen reported $5,108 of income for the year; the IRS said the business provided the couple $212,000. Records for that year were lost after the raid.

So, the IRS figured their income from shipments and prices charged when the goods had been sold. But the prices didn't apply, the Tax Court noted; goods were sent for donations of varying amounts.

And the evidence showed Helen's returns for other years were correct, indicating she had also reported fully for the disputed year, the court asserted in rejecting the IRS allegations. Curtis, though, should have filed; state law made half the profits his, the court concluded.

Springer v. Commissioner, T.C. Memo 1977-191
8/10/77

Cases of Property

Bloomingdale's would build if the land was rezoned, otherwise no deal.

The chichi New York City-based store agreed to pay $330,000 a year rent for some 19 acres outside Washington, D.C., where it would build a store if the land were rezoned from single-family to commercial use. The landowner, Chevy Chase Land Co. of Montgomery County, Md., paid $105,000 for reports, studies and legal fees for the rezoning effort.

The land company agreed that only a Bloomingdale's store would go on the land if it were rezoned. That was supposed to ease nearby homeowners' concerns. But the rezoning was hotly opposed anyway and eventually was denied. The Bloomingdale's deal was lost. Any commercial development of the land was foreclosed, Chevy Chase Land figured, so it deducted the rezoning expenses as an "abandonment loss." Rezoning costs normally aren't deductible, but this was an unusual case, the Tax Court said.

The rezoning effort was "inextricably tied" to the lease that fell through when the zoning change was denied. The adverse zoning ruling "brought the entire matter to an abrupt end," so the costs could be deducted, the court concluded.

Chevy Chase Land Co. v. Commissioner, 72 T.C. 45
6/27/79

～

A banker, with Harvard behind him, left red ink in the snows of Vermont.

Truett E. Allen built a ski lodge in Vermont back in 1965. The Irving Trust Co. vice president figured skiing would blossom and he could reap a profit providing room and board. But Allen, who spent two years at Harvard Business School, never saw a profit in 12 years of owning the lodge. Poor snow, increased competition, the 1973-74 gasoline shortage from the Arab oil embargo and increased competition all hurt his lodge.

He wrote off the losses, which amounted to $52,000 for 12 years. But the IRS barred the deduction, claiming he didn't intend to profit from the place. However, the banker never made personal use of the lodge (he rented a room from a neighbor); he tried to make money by changing from overnight room and board to seasonal rentals, and when seasonal rentals slumped, he changed to shorter rentals. He kept adequate records. And some of the losses came out of his pocket; they weren't just tax losses.

All this tended to show he meant to make a profit but had been thwarted by unforeseen events, the Tax Court said and it concluded that he could deduct the losses.

Allen v. Commissioner, 72 T.C. 3
4/11/79

⌒

A "tainted" spouse could "poison" the $100,000 tax-free home-sale bonus.

Up to $100,000 of the proceeds from selling a house can be received tax-free if one of the sellers is at least 55 years old. This tidy tax exclusion applies to a married couple even if only one spouse is 55 and the other is a lot younger. But once the exclusion is used, it can't be used again—by either spouse. That's true even if they don't file a joint return to claim the exclusion. When one uses it, the other must consent to it in writing, the tax code says, and then it's unavailable again to either one.

So assume Hortense, aged 35, is married to Alan, aged 55; they sell their home, take the exclusion and sometime later either they divorce or Alan dies. Whoever marries Hortense will be giving up the $100,000 exclusion in the nuptial bargain, notes Israel Blumenfrucht, assistant professor of accounting and taxation at Iona College. The fact that Hortense and her first spouse used the exclusion bars its use in her second marriage. "The younger one's tainted for life," he says.

And there apparently isn't any way around this, short of ignoring the law.

2/14/79

◠

A change of mind by the Tax Court makes it hard for investors, the court says.

Expenses to conserve property held for investment usually are deductible. But often, outlays connected with investment property are considered capital outlays that aren't deductible, but rather must be added to the acquisition cost of property for figuring gain or loss when it was sold. A Modesto, Calif., landowner wanted to deduct legal and engineering expenses incurred to fight condemnation action against his vacant land and paid in trying to have it rezoned.

However, the expenses were incurred mainly to enhance the value of the land, the Tax Court said, and thus weren't deductible. Some years ago, the court ruled differently in a similar case, but was overruled by an appeals court. With its recent decision, the Tax Court said it was adopting the appeals court's position.

The court's new stance places a "difficult bur-

*den on the taxpayer to prove" an expense "is ordi-
nary and necessary rather than capital in nature
when incurred in connection with an investment,"
the court acknowledged.*

Soelling v. Commissioner, 70 T.C. 93
10/11/78

⌒

Condominium: Was it a vacation home, profit venture or tax shelter?

Richard H. Nelson, an Indianapolis civil engineer, deducted $4,275 for depreciation and $7,186 in interest and other expenses of maintaining an apartment he had purchased and rented out in Punta Gorda Isles, Fla. But the IRS balked. It contended that Nelson didn't own the place for the purpose of making a profit—a requirement for the deductions—but that he in fact had bought it as a personal residence and a tax shelter because his income had risen sharply that year.

The Tax Court said the IRS had "few facts" to support its case. The court concluded that Nelson had made a "good-faith" effort to make a profit on the apartment. He had advertised in newspapers and hired a real estate agency to solicit renters; he rarely made personal use of the place; and he showed a "pattern of investing" in Florida real estate for profit.

*Nelson had bought nine parcels of land in the
state over a six-year period.*

Nelson v. Commissioner, T.C. Memo 1978-287
8/16/78

⌒

A landed man put property in a partnership and was put upon by the IRS.

John H. Otey inherited some land valued at $18,-500. Eight years later, he and a builder formed a partnership to build apartments on the property. Otey deeded his land to the partnership. The partnership borrowed $870,000 and paid Otey $65,000, the current market value of the land. Otey figured the land was his capital contribution to the partnership, and the $65,000 a partial return on his interest in the partnership, and thus untaxable.

But the IRS said Otey had sold the land to the partnership. This is a murky area: It often is unclear if a partner who deals with the partnership is making a contribution to capital or selling it something. In this case, the Tax Court rejected the IRS contention. Otey hadn't sold the land to the partnership. The property was the partnership's only capital because the other partner put in only his good credit rating, which allowed the partnership to borrow the $870,000.

Without Otey's land to build on, the partnership hadn't any reason to exist, the court observed.

Otey v. Commissioner, 70 T.C. 28
6/14/78

∾

For want of tenants: A house for rent filled up with red ink.

Terrence D. Clancy paid $72,500 for a two-bedroom pad in a resort area near San Francisco. A real estate agent told him "considerable rentals" could be earned from the house, so Clancy spent $5,000 to make it rentable. But it was seldom rented: Two years' rents totaled only $1,500 while expenses including depreciation ran $21,000. He deducted the net loss, $19,500. But the IRS barred the deduction and said he owed $6,400 of tax.

Owners usually can deduct expenses on property held "for the production of income." But he hadn't held onto the house for that purpose, the IRS said. Clancy countered that he had spent $5,000 to attract tenants, used the place only 18 days one year, none the other, and had it ready to rent nearly all the time. Also, he noted, property an owner holds to sell at a profit later normally is considered held for the production of income.

And Clancy expected to sell at a gain; in fact he got $86,000 from a sale last year, the Tax Court noted, when it ruled that he could deduct the entire $19,500 of losses.

Clancy v. Commissioner, T.C. Memo 1978-85
3/29/78

Here's how a firm figured to deduct a loss on its owner's winter home.

The company owned the house in Palm Beach, Fla. But it wasn't used for business purposes; it was the firm's owner's winter vacation home. The business sold it at a loss and deducted the loss. But the IRS barred the deduction. The house didn't serve any business purpose, so the firm couldn't take the deduction, the IRS said.

However, the company said a loss is deductible even if the property that produced it isn't used for business purposes. A 1963 change in the tax laws ended such deductions, the IRS claimed. The prohibition doesn't apply to losses, only expenses, the company argued. It also contended that businesses don't take deductions for losses, they offset them against capital gains, and the law doesn't mention such offsets.

Even if the law doesn't mention offsets, Congress intended to cover them, the Court of Claims said. The firm couldn't use the loss to cut its taxes.

A loss must qualify as "a deductible item" or it can't be offset against capital gains, the court concluded.

W. L. Schautz Co. v. U.S., U.S. Ct. of Claims, 1977
1/11/78

～

My three homes: How to tally tax if you sell two homes.

A tax break usually results if another home is bought within 18 months of selling a principal residence: Profit on the first home is taxed only if it exceeds the new home's cost. A taxpayer who owned two residences sold one, moved into the other, making it his principal residence, then sold it and bought a third one —all within 18 months.

If he could lump the two sales together, he would avoid tax on his profit by offsetting his gains against the third home's cost, which exceeded his profit on both sales. But he couldn't do that, the IRS ruled. He must offset the profit from the first house against the cost of buying the third one. His profit on the second sale is fully subject to tax, as he hadn't any home purchase to offset it.

Rev. Rul. 77-371
10/19/77

～

Some earful: The racket from the road sounded like a tax tune to them.

David and Joan Adams built a home on land they knew was near a proposed highway. After their house was done, the highway was completed. It became a preferred truck route; traffic and noise rose markedly. The couple got their property-tax assessment lowered 30% by arguing the highway noise reduced their home's market value.

They also deducted $45,000 as a casualty loss, figuring the property was worth $130,000 before the noise increased, but due to the racket it was worth only $85,000. The IRS disallowed the deduction and billed them for $21,500 added tax. The couple, acting as their own lawyer, found they were spinning their wheels in appealing to the Tax Court: Road noise isn't a "casualty" for tax purposes, the court instructed; the racket wasn't of an "accidental character," it wasn't due to "some sudden, unexpected or unusual cause."

Also, the couple hadn't proven their home's value before and after the noise increased, the court noted.

Adams v. Commissioner, T.C. Memo 1977-308
9/21/77

⌒

A speculator trounces the IRS in a fight over a resort land sale.

Herman Siemers, a real estate salesman in Hilton Head, S.C., bought a parcel of land from his employer for $18,000. He executed a promissory note for the purchase price and agreed to pay principal and interest on the note, as well as taxes and maintenance fees on the land. He paid nothing on these obligations until two years later when he sold the land for $35,000. The day of the sale, he paid off the note, plus interest, taxes and fees that had accumulated from the date of purchase. Siemers treated his profit as a long-term capital gain.

Property must be held at least six months for the profit from a sale to qualify as a long-term gain. The IRS claimed that Siemers didn't really own the Hilton Head land until the day he sold it. For one thing, he didn't fulfill the tax and other obligations until then. Thus, the six-month requirement wasn't met, the agency said.

The Tax Court disagreed. It ruled that Siemers had borne the "burdens" of ownership, including liability for taxes and other expenses, from the time he bought the land, even though he didn't pay up until later.

Siemers v. Commissioner, T.C. Memo 1977-221
8/24/77

Manana was soon enough for some folks who lost property in Cuba.

Congress enacted a tax break in 1964 that granted a deduction for property seized by Cuba, but the loss had to be claimed by Jan. 1, 1965. The lawmakers had failed to permit a deduction for seized intangible property such as stocks and bonds. To correct that, Congress amended the tax code to allow a deduction for intangible property if the loss was claimed by July 1, 1971. Some taxpayers who had failed to claim Cuban losses by the 1965 deadline have been arguing for some time that the 1971 law gave them another chance.

The tardy taxpayers filed for tax refunds. After years of hassling at the IRS, their claims went before a federal district court. They argued that a phrase in the 1971 law could be read to mean a new deadline for taxpayers with tangible as well as intangible property. The IRS contended the amendment meant only intangible Cuban property losses could be claimed by the 1971 deadline.

The court agreed with the IRS. The tardy taxpayers "seek to twist the meaning" of the words "beyond (their) normal meaning," the court declared.

Ogden v. U.S., U.S. Dist. Ct., So. Dist. Miss., 1977
7/27/77

Savings and loan associations won't be pleased with this ruling.

Special tax rules apply to thrift concerns. But the rules aren't clear on treating costs of selling property acquired by foreclosure when a debt goes bad. It's an important issue, especially for savings and loans in such volatile real-estate markets as California and Florida. A test case involves Allstate Savings & Loan, of Los Angeles. Allstate took deductions of some $260,000, mostly for real-estate commissions, incurred in selling foreclosed property.

The IRS barred the deductions. The expenses must be reflected as adjustments to the bad-debt loss reserve, the IRS said. That would cause Allstate to owe $55,000 more tax. But Allstate argued that the sales costs should be deductible as "ordinary and necessary" business expenses. The Tax Court didn't buy that, though. Costs to sell foreclosed property reduced the amount from the sale that can be applied against the loan, the court reasoned, so the sales expenses should be reflected in the bad-debt loss reserve.

Allstate Savings & Loan Assoc., 68 T.C. 27
6/22/77

⌣

One shot is all: You can exclude from tax up to $100,000 of profit from selling your home if you are at least 55 years old. But if the profit is less than $100,000 —say $50,000—and you elect the exclusion, that's the end of all of it. The unused $50,000 is lost forever. So taxpayers should be careful about electing the one-time exclusion, cautions Robert M. Greenberger, a New York tax accountant with Morris Teichman & Co.

11/29/78

Free homes: The chancellor of education and a state school president have homes provided free by the state. After reviewing these arrangements, the IRS concluded that neither official could be taxed on the value of the free residences.

IRS letter rulings 7823006 and 7823007
8/9/78

◇

Artists Peter Hurd and Henriette Wyeth, his wife, can't deduct losses from their ranch in New Mexico. Their 2,400-acre spread includes a 17-acre polo field and a separate swimming-pool building and lost money every year from 1962 to 1975. Hurd, whose portrait of Lyndon Johnson the late President rejected as "ugly," didn't intend to make a profit from the ranch, the court concluded.

Hurd v. Commissioner, T.C. Memo 1978-113
4/5/78

◇

Wreck, then lease: Often buildings are demolished so the land they occupy can be leased. If the building is demolished before a lease is signed, the entire wrecking costs usually can be deducted at once. But if a lease is signed before demolition, the wrecking costs may have to be written off over the life of the lease, Touche Ross & Co., a CPA firm, relates. If a 50-year lease is involved, only 1/50th can be written off yearly.

2/22/78

Capital Gains and Losses

It was a deal until one of the CPAs who signed it had to pay his taxes.

Bernard D. Spector, a Dallas CPA, unloaded his accounting partnership to go to work for one of his clients. He agreed to merge his partnership into another accounting partnership. Three days after the merger, he was to withdraw from the new partnership and be paid four installments totaling $96,000, the value of his practice. The buyers set it up this way for their tax benefit.

They could deduct the $96,000 as "guaranteed payments" to a "retiring partner." But this also meant Spector was taxed on the money as ordinary income. He balked and reported most of the payments as capital gain from the sale of his accounting practice to outsiders. But the IRS wanted to hold him to the terms of the deal. He argued that he never really was a "partner" in the newly formed firm, so he couldn't have "retired" from it.

The Tax Court agreed with the CPA. The parties didn't intend to "join together" to conduct "an enterprise." Spector could count the payments as capital gains, the court concluded. This suggests that the IRS will tell the buyers they shouldn't have deducted the $96,000.

Spector v. Commissioner, 71 T.C. 91
4/4/79

A sting is hidden in the alternative minimum tax for folks with tax credits.

Congress appeared to have enacted the alternative minimum tax in 1978 to benefit people with capital gains. But the law was written with a trap for some tax-payers who haven't any capital gains, but who have siz-able tax credits. They would be better off if the provision didn't exist, Albert B. Ellentuck, national tax part-ner at Laventhol & Horwath, a CPA firm, says.

The sting comes from the alternative minimum tax limiting the use of investment, job, child care or energy tax credits, which otherwise could cut a person's tax bill. For example, someone with a taxable income of $100,000 and a $35,000 investment tax credit would pay only about $6,800 of tax. But the alternative minimum tax pushes the tax bill to $12,000, mainly by cutting the use of the $35,200 credit. "We doubt that Congress real-ized it was voting for this result," Ellentuck asserts.

2/14/79

⌒

Off the farm: A cut in tax rates encourages farmers to sell out.

Many farmers were discouraged from selling their farms in past years because so much of the profit goes to Uncle Sam in taxes. But the 1978 tax bill cut capital-gains taxes and "encourages the selling of farms," as-serts Robert C. Estes, partner in the San Francisco of-fice of Touche Ross & Co., a CPA firm. Estes, a farm-tax strategist, shows how the tax burden on a sale has been eased.

Assume a farmer makes $100,000 of taxable income a year from his farm and sells it for a $5 million profit. Under the old tax rates, the IRS would have snatched away about $2 million in taxes. But under new rates the tax-bite shrinks to about $1.4 million, so the farmer pockets $600,000 more.

1/24/79

⤳

She fought to get back her stock and to deduct the legal costs of the battle.

Mrs. Fay T. Cruttenden, of Corona del Mar, Calif., lent more than $100,000 and some stocks to a family-owned brokerage firm. Another company took over the family firm, but it didn't pay back her loan or return her stocks. She retained a lawyer who finally recovered her money and her securities. Mrs. Cruttenden deducted the legal costs to recover her stock. But the IRS barred the deduction.

The IRS claimed that costs to recover investment property are capital expenditures and aren't deductible; they must be added to the cost of the property. She argued that the IRS was too strictly interpreting the tax code, which, if properly read, permitted a deduction for costs of recovering investment property. A Tax Court majority reasoned that deductions are allowed for conserving income-producing property, and thus she could deduct the legal expenses.

But three dissenters said her loan to the family firm was capital in nature and the expenses to recover it must be considered capital, too.

Cruttenden v. Commissioner, 70 T.C. 18
5/24/78

⤳

Oh, it can hurt not to keep track of which stock certificates cost what.

If you own 3,000 shares of XYZ stock, and bought 100 shares at a time at different prices, it gets tricky keeping track of what you paid for the shares represented by each stock certificate; the certificates don't show the purchase price. You should keep a list of each certificate number and what you paid for the shares. You need to know what you paid for the shares to figure gain or loss when you sell.

And the tax code says the gain or loss must be figured on the cost of the actual certificate delivered for sale. A group of investors in New Jersey failed to keep adequate records of the thousands of stock certificates they bought and sold and couldn't prove which certificates were delivered for sale. When the IRS discovered the records were inadequate, it recomputed the sales as if the first shares the group bought were the first sold. That resulted in a $600,000 tax bill. The Tax Court said the law empowered the IRS to recompute the sales, and the investors, a family group, owed the added taxes.

Kluger Associates Inc. et al. v. Commissioner, 69 T.C. 80
4/12/78

⌒

Mattel's settlement: Does it mean capital gains or ordinary income?

The toymaker settled some class-action lawsuits for $30 million, but litigation delayed payment two years. The settlement fund, which has grown to $34 million, can be paid now. Roughly 30,000 stockholders who lost money on Mattel stock have been cleared to share in the settlement. They'll get only between 10% and 15% of their claimed losses, someone at the Mattel Claims Processing Center says.

The money is capital gains, says Warren S. Shine, of S. D. Leidesdorf & Co., a CPA firm. That's true even if part of the loss was written off against ordinary income as the tax code permits. "The recovery keeps the original nature of the loss, which was capital in nature," he explains. The lawsuits charged that Mattel issued false financial information.

3/1/78

〜

I won't compete is a costly promise to make, a seller learned.

Marcel Malgoire sold the Brown Jug liquor store to George. George paid $90,000. The sales contract allocated $20,000 of the price to Marcel's pledge he wouldn't compete with George. Marcel figured his tax on the sale entirely as capital gains. But the IRS said the $20,000 was ordinary income because it was for a noncompetition covenant.

Alas, Marcel. He didn't know the tax consequences of allocating $20,000 to the covenant. But George knew: It meant he could deduct the $20,000 while Marcel had to count it as ordinary income. Marcel argued that the noncompetition clause hadn't any substance and should be ignored. But there must be "strong proof" for a court to set aside such agreements, the Tax Court said, and Marcel hadn't presented any.

He understood the legal effect of the agreement, so it is valid, and he owed some $4,000 tax because the $20,000 was ordinary income, the court said.

Malgoire v. Commissioner, T.C. Memo 1978-29
2/8/78

〜

Like craps, cheap bonds are a gamble, luckless taxpayer insisted.

Walter Jasinski paid only $6,300 for bonds with a face value of $10,000. He expected to collect $10,000 when they matured in three years, and interest until then. He got some interest, but the company that issued the bonds sought protection under the bankruptcy laws, and Jasinski didn't get the $10,000 when the bonds matured. He wrote off his $6,300 loss, but the IRS challenged the deduction.

Among the arguments Jasinski made in Tax Court was that low-priced, high-yield bonds are a gamble, and thus he should be able to treat his loss like a gambling loss. An unusual argument, but like "snake eyes" in a crap game gained him nothing. Investing in "capital assets (such as bonds) isn't a wagering transaction in the sense" that term is used in the tax code, the court remarked.

Jasinski v. Commissioner, T.C. Memo 1978-1
2/1/78

A frugal Irishman had an unusual notion about his brokerage account.

Patrick McWeeney grew up in Ireland, immigrating to the U.S. at age 23. He didn't marry, own a car or a house. He lived frugally and eventually became the owner of Paddy's Tavern. He opened a brokerage account in 1937, but never withdrew any funds from it. The IRS found $62,000 of stock market capital gains and $21,000 of dividends McWeeney failed to report.

The IRS said he owed $44,000 of back taxes and $22,000 as a fraud penalty. To make fraud stick, the IRS must show "intentional wrongdoing." Among other things, the agency argued that McWeeney lied to an IRS agent about his stock dealings when he said: "I took no money out, and therefore I had no transactions." However, the Tax Court absolved him of fraud.

McWeeney hadn't lied. He had only a fourth-grade education and didn't know he must report stock-sales gains even if proceeds stayed in his brokerage account, the court said.

McWeeney v. Commissioner, T.C. Memo 1977-428
1/4/78

A split tax court sets a tough line on selling partnership interests.

Selling capital assets results in capital gains or losses; selling "ordinary" assets produces ordinary income or losses. A consultant bought into a partnership because it promised him consulting work. But the partnership changed its plans and he saw he wouldn't get any consulting jobs. So, he sold his interest, losing $27,000 that he deducted as an ordinary loss.

But the IRS said it was a capital loss. Sales of partnership interests are capital transactions and don't produce ordinary income or losses, the IRS argued. The consultant said his partnership interest wasn't a capital asset: He invested in the venture to gain consulting-business income, and therefore he acquired an ordinary asset. His motives didn't matter, a Tax Court majority said. In a precedent-setting ruling, the judges said the law specifically bars ordinary income or loss treatment to investments in partnerships.

Two dissenters, though, said the court has considered whether corporate investments are ordinary or capital and shouldn't deny the same consideration to partnerships.

Clinton and Pollack v. Commissioner, 69 T.C. 11
11/9/77

⌒

If you buy a pregnant horse, how much have you paid for its unborn foal?

Launce E. Gamble, a San Francisco investor, paid $60,000 for a mare, Champagne Woman. He figured it was a bargain, as she was carrying a foal sired by Raise A Native, who had sired Majestic Prince, winner of the Kentucky Derby and the Preakness Stakes. Gamble insured the unborn foal for $20,000.

When the colt was about a year old, Gamble sold it for $125,000. He computed his gain by deducting from the sales price $12,500 of selling costs and $30,000 as his cost of the colt. The IRS said his cost was zero: The $60,000 paid for the mare applied entirely to her, none of it to the foal, though she was pregnant when Gamble bought her. The Tax Court said "nay" to that idea. Part of the $60,000 for the dam applied to its unborn foal, but the correct amount was $20,000, what the foal has been insured for, the court concluded.

Gamble v. Commissioner, 68 T.C. 69
9/14/77

A $1.2 million case produces an historic decision.

Percy and Harold D. Uris, of the New York real estate family, ended up as the only owners of a corporation's stock after it paid some unhappy shareholders $2.9 million to buy back their shares. The $2.9 million redemption exceeded the company's accumulated earnings at the time, and left its capital accounts in the red.

Seven years later, the corporation paid Percy and Harold $1.3 million each. They treated most of the money as capital gains. Payments to owners that exceed a company's earnings usually aren't dividends, the tax code says. The Urises said the payment to them exceeded the firm's earnings. But that was because the Urises applied the deficit created by the earlier stock redemption against later earnings. The IRS said they couldn't do that and owed $1.2 million of tax.

In the first decision on this arcane matter, the Tax Court agreed with the IRS. Deficits created by stock redemptions can't be carried forward to "reduce earnings . . . in subsequent years," the court asserted.

Uris v. Commissioner, 68 T.C. 38
8/10/77

Water was its business, but some water was special, this firm argued.

Assets such as shoes, ships or water held for sale in the usual course of business normally aren't capital assets; selling them produces ordinary income. Buena Vista Farms Inc. sold water from wells and its river rights to farmers and treated the revenue as ordinary income. But the San Francisco firm provided the state with water and as compensation was to get state water later.

Buena Vista sold its right to the state's water and treated the $105,000 from the deal as capital gains. The IRS said it was ordinary income. The firm argued it hadn't held the right to state water in the "ordinary course" of its business, and thus the water right was a capital asset. But the company hadn't made an investment in the state water, it acquired a right to it by selling water to the state which produced ordinary income, the Tax Court said.

Buena Vista's "right to receive exchange water from the state represents, in substance, a right to receive income" and selling that right produced ordinary income, the court determined, meaning a $19,000 tax bill for the firm.

Buena Vista Farms Inc. v. Commissioner, 68 T.C. 34
8/3/77

〜

A Christmas tree grower sought a sugar plum from the IRS.

Selling standing timber can produce earnings that are treated as capital gains, and thus taxed less than ordinary income. "Does a fell-it-yourself Christmas-tree business get the capital gains goody?" a grower asked the IRS. A tax break hung on whether "standing timber" was being sold, the agency responded.

Yuletide customers came to the farm, picked a tree, cut it down themselves and paid for it. The IRS decided the buyers hadn't any interest in the trees until after they were cut down, so sales of cut—rather than standing—timber were involved. That meant the grower couldn't treat himself to capital gains. But the ruling didn't leave him entirely out on a limb:

He might qualify for another tax break that lets tree owners, in effect, treat a part of profits as capital gains, the IRS said.

Rev. Rul. 77-229
7/13/77

Tax Shelters

A cattle-feeding tax dodge stampeded the court into a split decision.

Kenneth and Fred Van Raden, Hillsboro, Ore., sold a business in 1972 and faced tax on $4.6 million of capital gains. But in mid-December they invested in a cattle-feeding partnership, Western Trio VR. Western spent $360,000 on a year's supply of feed Dec. 26, and deducted the expense, thus providing a $360,000 loss for the Van Radens. But the IRS barred the deduction and told the Van Radens to pay $206,500.

The IRS argued that deducting a year's grain supply before it was used up distorted Western Trio's income. But the partners convinced a Tax Court majority that there was a business purpose in addition to the obvious tax purpose for the purchase: Feed would cost more later. However, four of the court's 16 judges dissented. A dissenter noted, "Quite simply the provisions (of the law) have been exploited and abused by a clever gimmick. . . "

This victory probably applies only to cattle-tax-shelter expenses before 1976. Congress has restricted farm-syndicate deductions after 1976 to feed actually consumed each year.

Van Raden v. Commissioner, 71 T.C. 97
4/18/79

∽

Call a doctor: A tax gimmick with government cars crashed into the IRS.

Teofilo Evangelista, an Appleton, Wis., doctor, got into a deal in which he bought 33 cars rented to a government agency. He financed the tax shelter with a $100,000 loan from the Park Bank, Madison, Wis. He deducted $68,000 depreciation on the autos before giving his interest in the cars to a trust for his kids; his wife was the trustee.

The trust paid off $62,000 remaining on the loan. Then came the IRS. The agency said the doctor realized taxable income when the trust assumed his indebtedness. He said he had merely made a "net gift": the cars' value less the balance due the bank. But after his fat, tax-cutting depreciation deductions, the cars were worth only $34,000 on his books, less than the $62,000 paid the bank. The Tax Court ruled that the doctor had realized taxable income when his debt was paid and he owed $13,000 in tax.

Another Wisconsin doctor in this same shelter lost on the same issue in Tax Court. Frank A. Ross Jr., the lawyer in both cases, says there will be an appeal. About six other doctors got into this deal, Ross adds.

Evangelista v. Commissioner, 71 T.C. 95
4/11/79

⌢

A tale of the joy the tax code can bring:

How shall we finance the $23 million of truck trailers we've ordered? wondered Flexi-Van Corp. Assign the order to Bank of America, let it pay for them, then lease the trailers from the bank, came an answer inspired by the tax code. And Flexi-Van did. And it made itself a deal with "negative interest," for the bank forgave interest on the lease. The bank got depreciation and investment tax credits for owning the trailers.

The bank needs the tax benefits to shelter its considerable profits from Uncle Sam's grasp. But Flexi-Van doesn't need any more deductions. So this deal allowed Flexi-Van to trade tax benefits for a lease that calls for payments totaling less than the trailers cost the bank. "It's what Congress intended: companies trading tax deductions for lower costs (on leases)," says a bank executive.

Though the deal was made near year-end, the bank can deduct six months of depreciation and investment tax credits this year.

12/21/77

⌒

Leaky shelter. A "family trust" proves to be one.

Some promoters are making money by showing people how to set up so-called family trusts which they claim will cut taxes. The IRS says the trusts are shams; the government is pushing prosecution of some promoters. Douglas H. and Teddi Damm set up a family trust. Douglas' employer refused to make Damm's paychecks payable to the trust, so the Medford, Wisc., resident endorsed them to the trust, hoping to have the money taxed to the trust at lower rates than if the couple paid tax on it.

The trust paid and took deductions for the Damms' rent and utilities, payments on a car they used but assigned to the trust and for other expenses. The IRS said the income was taxable to the couple and they owed $286 tax on his $4,000 of earnings (she had none). Assigning his income to another entity, the trust, didn't relieve the couple of their tax burden, the IRS said. The Tax Court agreed. The trust hadn't any control over the income: It couldn't direct Douglas' money-making efforts. He hadn't any legal duty to earn money for the trust and he controlled his earnings.

The couple owed tax on the income, the court said, but they could deduct some expenses the trust paid for them.

Damm v. Commissioner, T.C. Memo 1977-194
8/3/77

⌒

Three into 30 is 10 but not the right answer for the IRS.

A special break allows some small corporations' profits to be taxed directly to stockholders. The corporation doesn't pay income taxes, avoiding the so-called double tax: Once on its profits, again on its dividends taxed as income to its stockholders. However, to qualify for this tax break, the corporation, among other things, can't have more than 10 stockholders.

Some sharp mind figured that 30 owners could get around that rule if they split into three groups, each owning a separate corporation. Essentially, though, the three corporations would operate one business. Their three companies each had only 10 stockholders, so did they qualify, the 30 asked the IRS. No. In form they met the requirements, but the whole thing was done "for the principal purpose" of beating taxes, the IRS noted. And the Supreme Court has ruled that "elaborate and devious" schemes to avoid taxes, though meeting the letter of the law, can still be rejected, the IRS observed in rejecting this scheme.

Rev. Rul. 77-220
7/6/77

⌒

A way around tax-shelter restrictions uses U.S. securities bought on credit.

Congress barred the use of nonrecourse loans for most investments to stop tax shelters in which someone typically put up $10,000, signed a $90,000 note without personal liability and gained a $100,000 interest in the deal. Tax deductions were based on the whole $100,000; often first year write-offs ran three or four times cash invested. But now only the $10,000 of cash would count unless the investor was personally liable for the $90,000 loan.

That's meant most tax-shelter gimmicks have no appeal, for most people don't want personal liability on loans that may well have to be paid if the shelter runs into trouble. But shelter constructors aren't without imagination: William G. Brennan, a specialist who tracks shelters in his "Brennan Reports" newsletter, tells of a CATV deal using U.S. securities bought on margin, or credit. An investor puts up cash and becomes liable for the borrowing on the margin account. So, his investment will include the cash and the "recourse" loans.

Nonrecourse loans will bankroll the cable TV operation, but investors are supposed to be able to deduct the fruits of these loans: Interest expense, depreciation and investment credits from assets acquired.

5/25/77

Tax-Exempt Organizations

20/20 foresight could have kept a foundation from colliding with the IRS.

The H. Fort Flowers Foundation gave Vanderbilt University $200,000 in 1965. Income that year was only $35,000, and the trustees didn't want to consume assets, so they decided to "borrow" the $165,000 balance from foundation principal and repay it with future earnings. The foundation was still repaying itself in 1970 when a new law imposed penalties on foundations that didn't make minimum charitable contributions each year.

The IRS figured the foundation owed about $91,000 for failing to give enough of its income to charity. The trustees argued that the penalties didn't apply since the income was being used to repay a loan. But the foundation couldn't "borrow from itself," the Tax Court said. Thus, there wasn't a loan to repay, so the penalties applied.

If the trustees could have foreseen enactment of the penalties, they could have avoided them by having the foundation borrow from and repay a bank, the court observed.

H. Fort Flowers Foundation Inc. v. Commissioner, 72 T.C. 38
7/18/79

∽

Antifreeze? Drinking plagued Bethel, Alaska, so it opened a liquor store.

Alcohol got to be such a problem that at one point prohibition was voted into Bethel. But boozers could still get liquor elsewhere, so drinking problems continued. Prohibition was voted out, and the town decided to own and operate a liquor store, the only legal one in town, to control sales. The store was set up on a nonprofit basis. Profits were kept to buy more inventory.

Drinking still was a plague for the town, so five years later prohibition was voted in again. The liquor store's earnings were turned over to the city. Even so, the IRS said the profits were taxable as they hadn't been "accruing" to the city. The town argued that it had a right to the profits, and it could have made the store turn them over each year. But "could have" isn't good enough: Neither store nor city books reflected the town's right to the income, an appeals court noted.

The city-owned liquor store's earnings didn't "accrue" to the city as required by the tax code, so the profits were taxable, the court concluded.

City of Bethel, Alaska, and Community Liquor Sales Inc. v. U.S., U.S. Ct. of
Appeals, 9th Circ., 1979
6/6/79

⌒

The Big Mama Rag printed only articles that advanced the cause of women.

The monthly feminist newspaper refused to print anything it considered damaging to its cause. Still, The Big Mama Rag wanted to be considered a tax-exempt educational outfit. But the IRS said it didn't qualify, as it didn't publish "full and fair exposition" of the facts, and, in fact, refused to print the other side.

The Colorado-based paper claimed it was being discriminated against: An IRS official had said Big Mama was denied exemption because it was "pro-

moting lesbianism." Big Mama also argued that it used
volunteers almost exclusively to print 2,700 copies each
month, gave all but 600 of them away without charge
and was run on a nonprofit basis. Even so it didn't qualify, Watergate Judge John Sirica, of the district court in
Washington, D.C., ruled. The paper "has adopted a
stance so doctrinaire that it can't satisfy" the requirements for exemption as an educational publication, Sirica asserted.

The judge said the "unfortunate comments"
about lesbianism didn't represent an official IRS
position.

The Big Mama Rag Inc. v. U.S., U.S. Dist. Ct., Dist. of Columbia, 1979
5/30/79

⌒

Georgia beauties get their money if they do as
they're told. But is it tax-free?

Contestants in the Miss Georgia pageant, which
can lead to being Miss America, are given scholarships.
But they must agree to make public appearances when
pageant officials require, or else no scholarship. The
scholarship is paid directly to the contestant's school by
Miss Georgia Scholarship Fund Inc., a nonprofit outfit
that solicits, manages and disburses scholarship money
for the contest.

The scholarship fund sought federal tax exemption, which would let contributors deduct donations to
the funds. But the IRS said the scholarships amount to
"compensation," which bars the fund from tax exempt
status—and makes the scholarships taxable income for
the contestants. The fund sued in Tax Court for the exemption. But the court said the scholarships are compensation, paid "to attract a high quality of contestants," and "awarded in consideration of certain con-
tractual obligations assumed by" the contestants.

*All of which meant the fund wasn't entitled to
tax exemption, the court concluded.*

Miss Georgia Scholarship Fund Inc. v. Commissioner, 72 T.C. 22
5/9/79

⌒

A nonprofit translation service made the IRS see
red—and "pinkos," too.

The watchful souls at the IRS who dispense tax-
exempt status to applicants deemed worthy, turned
down the Peoples Translation Service, an Oakland,
Calif., nonprofit outfit that publishes Newsfront International, a bulletin of foreign-language articles translat-
ed into English. The IRS dismissed it as providing
"mere translations." But the service, which gets some
funds from the University of California at Berkeley,
went to court.

In court, the IRS came up with more justifications
for its action. Among them: The translations "have a
leftist bias and don't present a balanced view of the issues with which they deal." It was too late in the proceedings to raise the specter of a "leftist bias," the Tax
Court said. Peoples Translation Service sells its bulletin
below cost, makes available information about world
opinion and events and provides free translations to
scholars, the court noted.

*An opinion by Chief Judge C. Moxley Feath-
erston said the translation service qualified for
exemption.*

Peoples Translation Service/Newsfront International v.
Commissioner, 72 T.C. 5
4/25/79

⌒

Sorry, Werner, but est self-realization sensation
doesn't thrill a judge.

"est" stands for "Erhard Seminars Training," an

eclectic self-awareness method developed by Werner Erhard, who has turned on thousands of people. To boost est, some nonprofit corporations were set up in different states. The nonprofit est of Hawaii signed a licensing pact with several EST Inc.-related profit-making outfits, which split est Hawaii's proceeds, directed its activities and could cut it off if it wasn't granted tax exemption.

In two years, est Hawaii paid EST units $481,000 in royalties and was billed by them for $152,000 more in expenses. The IRS denied est Hawaii tax-exempt status, and the Tax Court endorsed the IRS denial. The court said that est Hawaii's "only function is to present to the public for a fee ideas that are owned" by the profit-making EST affiliates. The "ultimate beneficiaries are" the profit-making est concerns, the court noted.

The est Hawaii operation "was simply the instrument to subsidize the for-profit corporations and vice versa and had no life independent of those corporations," the court asserted.

est of Hawaii v. Commissioner, 71 T.C. 96
4/11/79

⌣

Taxing me violates a promise not to molest Indians, a Chippewa told the U.S.

A treaty signed in 1795 provides that the Red Lake Band of Chippewa Indians and some other tribes were to live and hunt on their reservations "without any molestation from the United States." Roger A. Jourdain, Red Lake Band's council chairman since 1959, was paid $16,000 one year and $18,000 another, none of which he reported.

But the IRS said the Red Lake, Minn., tribal official had to pay $6,700 in taxes on that money to Uncle Sam. Among other things, Jourdain argued an income

tax would be "an unwarranted intrusion by the U.S. into Indian affairs" in violation of the treaty's promise not to molest the Chippewas. However, the treaty didn't expressly exempt the Indians from being taxed, the Tax Court noted, and tax exemptions must be "expressly granted" Indians; they aren't "granted by implication."

"The molestation the (treaty) had in mind was interference in the Indians' rights to hunt, etc., not the right to be free from taxation," the court said.

Jourdain v. Commissioner, 71 T.C. 87
3/21/79

⌒

This church "has no sincere belief in the Bible," the IRS divined.

The Free Church of America, "a religious corporation" created in 1976 in Illinois, applied to the IRS for tax exemption. The IRS asked the church to provide details of its operations, but the church refused, citing the Bible as the basis for refusing. So the IRS denied the tax exemption, contending it didn't know enough about the church to make it tax-exempt.

The church appealed to the Tax Court. In court papers, the IRS asserted that the church was trying to avoid disclosing its "true operations" by citing the Bible but "has no sincere belief in the Bible." Perhaps the church was being "evasive," the court said, but the IRS was "unduly harsh" in questioning its beliefs. However, the court said it wouldn't be the "arbiter" of what the church believed or didn't believe.

The court did find a reason to deny the tax exemption: The church failed to assure that its assets wouldn't revert to its members if the church should be dissolved. The court added that the

church can amend its bylaws to correct this flaw
and apply again to the IRS for tax exemption.

General Conference of the Free Church of America v.
Commissioner, 71 T.C. 82
3/7/79

Some Callaways formed a family association and wanted the IRS to bless it.

The Callaway Family Association Inc. was created as a nonprofit corporation to focus on the history and genealogy of the Callaway family and thus "study immigration to and migration within the U.S." Among the Callaways is Howard "Bo," a former Army Secretary and ex-member of Congress. The association has about 600 members, puts out "The Callaway Journal" and holds a yearly gathering. It sought tax-exempt status from the IRS but was rebuffed.

The IRS said the outfit served some public purposes but also served substantial private interests of the Callaways—too substantial to qualify for tax exemption. The association asked the Tax Court to overturn the IRS. But the court found the association unqualified for tax exemption. "Any educational benefit to the public created by (its) activities is incidental to" the private purpose the association serves.

Without tax exemption, dues and donations
paid the association aren't deductible by those
who make them. And the association probably will
be denied special low postal rates for nonprofit
outfits.

The Callaway Family Association Inc. v. Commissioner, 71 T.C. 30
12/27/78

The IRS rebuked an outfit that aided parents opposed to public schools.

Some people don't want their kids in public school, so they send them to alternative schools or teach them at home. The National Association for the Legal Support of Alternative Schools disseminates legal information about alternative education. NALSAS is a nonprofit organization. But the IRS refused to grant it tax exemption, contending it didn't operate for a public purpose.

The IRS also said NALSAS "advocates disobedience of compulsory education laws," an illegal purpose that bars tax exemption. But the IRS arguments flunked out of Tax Court. Information is provided to everyone, member or not, at the same cost, so NALSAS serves the public, the court said. It does suggest alternatives to public school, but there isn't any evidence it advocates disobedience to school attendance laws, the court asserted.

NALSAS is entitled to be tax-exempt, the court said. Edward D. Nagel, NALSAS's founder, says the exemption will open doors to foundation funding that otherwise were closed. The association has about 100 members; it responds to about 2,000 inquiries a year, he says.

National Assoc. for the Legal Support of Alternative Schools v. Commissioner, 71 T.C. 11
11/15/78

⌒

Charity began with the IRS in mind; the IRS didn't think that was charitable.

Christian Stewardship Assistance Inc., a nonprofit Texas concern, showed rich folks how to give to charity to minimize income and estate taxes. Claiming it furthered a charitable purpose, the concern sought to be exempt from federal income taxes. However, the IRS refused to grant tax exemption, contending the outfit "served private rather than public purposes" as it helped the rich cut their taxes, something that didn't qualify as an exempt activity.

But Christian Stewardship argued that many charities give similar advice without jeopardizing their tax exemptions, and that its counseling spurred "Christian fund raising." However, its activity provided more private than public benefits, the Tax Court determined, so the organization didn't qualify for a tax exemption.

"We don't find within the scope of the word charity that the financial planning for wealthy individuals described in this case is a charitable purpose," the court asserted.

Christian Stewardship Assistance Inc. v. Commissioner, 70 T.C. 91
10/4/78

Spell it out, or your trust fund can be taxed, the IRS maintained.

There's an excise tax on foundations. But certain funds can escape the tax if they are "organized and operated exclusively" for the benefit of charities, hospitals or schools or other such publicly supported organizations. Joan R. Goodspeed's will established a $1 million trust fund, the Warren M. Goodspeed Scholarship Fund, to aid Yale students from Duxbury, Mass.

However, Mrs. Goodspeed's will didn't specifically say the fund was exclusively for Yale's benefit. And the IRS seized on that lack of specificity to deny the fund exemption from the excise tax on foundation assets. However, the Tax Court said the will "reveals quite clearly" the purpose for which the fund was set up. "We see no use in requiring language more specific than that which Mrs. Goodspeed actually used," the court asserted. The fund was exempt from the tax, the court ruled.

Warren M. Goodspeed Scholarship Fund v. Commissioner, 70 T.C. 43
7/5/78

Bingo brings in lots of money for a nonprofit group, but is it tax-free money?

A Veterans of Foreign Wars post in Minnesota had to pay tax on bingo income, the IRS said. The games provided "unrelated business income" taxable to the otherwise tax-exempt veterans group, the agency said. The VFW argued that Congress meant to tax unrelated business income only when exempt organizations made money competing with taxpaying concerns. The bingo games didn't compete with taxpaying outfits because only nonprofit groups can legally run bingo games in the state, the VFW argued.

But competition wasn't necessary, the IRS contended; earnings from "a trade or business" unrelated to an exempt organization's exempt purpose are taxable. The Eighth Circuit Court of Appeals, split two-to-one, agreed with the IRS. Bingo was an unrelated activity, so the VFW must pay some $12,000 of tax on four years' bingo income, the majority ruled.

Clarence LaBelle Post, VFW, No. 217 v. U.S., U.S. Ct. of Appeals, 8th Circ.,
1978
6/28/78

～

Too much control. The IRS frowns on it for funds set up to aid charity.

A 4% tax is levied on private foundations' investment income. However, foundations that support public charities may escape the tax if they comply with some laws involved. A Chicago family set up a fund to benefit three charities. The IRS said the fund must pay the 4% tax even though it was established to support public charities.

The fund's trustee was empowered to stop aiding any of the named charities if the trustee determined it "no longer adapted to the needs of the public"; the foundation could then pick another charity to help. The tax code bars such judgments, the IRS said. Substitutions are allowed, the IRS argued, only due to events beyond the trustee's control—for example, if a charity fails or ends its operations. The IRS was correct; the fund must pay the 4% tax, the Tax Court determined.

"It is essential that such authority (to substitute charities) be strictly limited" for a foundation to escape the 4% tax, the court asserted.

Quarrie Charitable Fund v. Commissioner, 70 T.C. 17
5/31/78

∽

A school for babies can't provide much education, the IRS figured.

The San Francisco Infant School was formed by a couple, both lawyers, who wanted an all-day school for their young daughter. The school catered to children six months to three years old. The IRS refused to grant the school tax-exempt status as an educational organization. The agency said the school's primary service wasn't education, it was custodial day care, and that didn't qualify for tax exemption.

The school did provide a lot of purely custodial care because the children were so young. But it also provided them an extensive curriculum and facilities designed to develop language and motor skills, and to engender social development. It "has become a model infant school," the Tax Court observed when it ruled the facility qualified for tax-exempt status.

"We see no reason why the tender age of (the school's) students should preclude qualification," the court declared.

San Francisco Infant School Inc. v. Commissioner, 69 T.C. 83
4/12/78

Money may flow faster from foundations after this IRS ruling on lobbying.

Private foundations are more restricted from lobbying than "public charities." Many foundations have feared funding public charity projects that include lobbying costs because the IRS can levy a tax on foundation expenditures for prohibited activities. Much of the fear should be dispelled by a recent IRS ruling for the McIntosh Foundation, experts say, though strictly speaking it applies only to McIntosh.

"It's a very important ruling because the degree of timidity among foundations is enormous," says Manhattan lawyer Stanley S. Weithorn. The Council on Foundations says it should allay fears about some grants. A safe grant, for example, would be $50,000 to partly fund a charity's $100,000 project that includes $80,000 for research and $20,000 for lobbying, says Thomas Troyer, a Washington, D.C., lawyer. He says a $90,000 grant for such a project probably would mean a penalty on the foundation because part of the money obviously must go directly for lobbying by the charity.

The McIntosh Foundation ruling involves proposed funding for the National Resources Defense Council.

12/21/77

⌒

A hair piece, or how the IRS scalped the master barbers.

For years, the Associated Master Barbers & Beauticians of America Inc. was exempt from tax. But the IRS revoked the group's exempt status. Tax-exempt outfits generally are forbidden to engage in a regular business of a kind usually run for profit. If they do, they can lose their exemption.

The IRS said the barbers' outfit was in a regular business, selling insurance to members. But the haircutters' group argued that insurance was only an incidental activity and providing insurance was related to "exempt activities" of promoting the well-being of its members. That didn't wash with the Tax Court. The court determined that a substantial amount of the association's financial activities involved insurance, and the barbers' group was in a regular business that barred tax exemption.

"Relatively few" of the association's efforts "were intended to promote and elevate the standards" of the profession, the court asserted.
Association of Master Barbers & Beauticians of America Inc. v. Commissioner, 69 T.C. 5
11/2/77

⌒

Bottled booze sales proved a sobering activity for this club.

Social clubs often are exempt from federal income tax. They usually can engage in such nonexempt activities as renting their premises to nonmembers without losing their tax exemption. But the IRS revoked the Santa Barbara Club's exemption for selling bottled liquor to its members for consumption outside the club. The sales flowed nearly $30,000 a year into the 83-year-old club's till, about 25% of its total receipts.

The IRS argued that this recurring, substantial, profitable activity voided the club's exemption. The California club argued that sales were confined to members, so its exemption shouldn't be affected. A Tax Court majority blackballed the club's contentions. However, loss of the tax exemption cost the club only about $800 a year for the three years involved in this lawsuit. Its receipts exceeded $100,000 each of those years.

Santa Barbara Club v. Commissioner 68 T.C. 19
6/1/77

⌒

Bob Jones University won a historic decision when a U.S. district court ruled that the IRS overstepped its power in denying tax exemption to the fundamentalist Christian school because it barred interracial couples. The court said the school's policy on interracial dating and marriage was an integral part of its religious practice.

Bob Jones Univ. v. U.S., U.S. Dist. Ct., S. Carolina, 1978
2/14/79

⌒

College sports are especially lucrative for schools that share in millions paid for broadcasting their games on television. However, the IRS suggested in 1977 during an audit of some Cotton Bowl conference teams and the bowl association itself that TV revenues might be taxable. Later, though, the IRS relented. Broadcasts are "substantially related" to schools' educational activities, and thus tax-exempt, the IRS decided.

10/4/78

⌒

Spared: The American Physical Society is a tax-exempt scientific and educational organization after all. The IRS Manhattan District office said the society wasn't entitled to that status, but was overruled by the IRS North Atlantic Regional office. Retaining its tax exemption lets the society continue to use postal rates for nonprofit groups, saving it several hundred thousand dollars a year in postage.

9/20/78

Gay ruling: An outfit organized to "foster an understanding and tolerance of homosexuals and their problems" qualifies for exemption as an educational organization, the IRS ruled. That its materials "concern possibly controversial topics" doesn't bar it from tax exemption, the IRS noted, "so long as the organization adheres to the educational methodology guidelines" in the Tax Code.

Rev. Rul. 78-305
8/30/78

Golf game: A school proposes to buy a country club's golf course and lease it back to the club for a nominal amount. School faculty, students and some others associated with the school would be able to use the course on the same basis as club members. The IRS said this arrangement wouldn't threaten the school's tax-exempt status.

IRS letter ruling 7823062
8/2/78

To aid Tibetan refugees, a tax-exempt private foundation wants to buy carpets from a factory operated to employ the refugees and resell the rugs. That won't jeopardize the foundation's tax exemption, the IRS said. And if the carpets are sold entirely by volunteers, the proceeds won't be taxed to the foundation as unrelated business income, the IRS ruled.

IRS private ruling 7818021
5/10/78

Benefits, Bonuses and Perks

His grapes went into first-rate wine, but the IRS gagged on his salary.

Gewurztraminer, merlot, pinot noir, cabernet sauvignon are among the grapes grown at R & G Young Vineyards, 100% owned by Robert A. Young. The vineyard, in Geyserville, Calif., commanded top dollar from wine makers. When some growers got only $415 a ton for their merlots or cabernets, Young got $815. Some called him the best grower in the Alexander Valley.

And the vineyard paid him a vintage $181,000 in salary and bonuses one year, $120,000 the next. But the IRS said everything over $40,000 a year was "excessive" and nondeductible. Young argued that he was worth his pay: he worked nearly every day of the week from 7 a.m. to 6:30 p.m., and nights when there was frost danger. He did alone what other vineyards paid two or three supervisors to do. Still, the Tax Court corked his salary at $75,000 a year for the years in question.

Chateau St. Jean esteems Young grapes so much, it bottles wine only from them and says on the label produced at Robert Young Vineyards.

Young v. Commissioner, T.C. Memo 1979-242
7/11/79

⁓

Could a doctor, old, sick and semi-retired, earn $100,000 in 11 weeks?

Gunmen robbed Dr. Nathaniel Sandler and his wife in their home in Brooklyn's Williamsburg section, a once lovely but currently declining area. After the robbery, the 74-year-old physician put $133,000 in several banks. The IRS alleged the money was unreported income on which Dr. Sandler owed tax of $83,000. The physician died in the midst of this hassle.

But his wife argued that he couldn't earn so much: he saw few patients, he was old, diabetic and arthritic, walked with a cane and had a severe bronchial condition. Anyway, he reported $6,000 earned from his limited practice. He hadn't hidden any income, and he had put the money, which was a hoard built up over the years, into the banks due to fear from the robbery in his home, she said. And the Tax Court added that for the IRS to be correct in this case, the elderly doctor would have had to earn the improbable sum of $100,000 in an 11-week period.

The conclusion: The money wasn't unreported income; the IRS couldn't tax it.
Estate of Nathaniel Sandler, T.C. Memo 1979-229
7/11/79

⌣

Free meals for hotel workers aren't fare for the tax collector, a court said.

The Tropicana Hotel, in Las Vegas, gave employes free meals in a windowless, basement cafeteria. This kept workers out of hotel restaurants and from leaving the hotel to eat. It also made it easier to keep meal breaks down to 30 or 45 minutes. The IRS said the meals were "wages" subject to payroll taxes; the hotel paid Social Security and unemployment tax on the food, which the IRS said was worth $1.25 a meal.

But the Court of Claims ordered the IRS to refund the payroll taxes. Citing a Supreme Court decision, the court said the IRS was imposing "an expansive and sweeping definition of wages" that isn't consistent with the withholding tax system that Congress enacted. The court also noted that the meals were of "relatively small value" and criticized a Treasury regulation on payroll taxes as "brilliantly conceived," a "hunting license" for IRS agents "to flush up" tax dollars, but "as a guide to employers . . . it is nearly worthless."

This decision "will spawn more refund claims than any (decision) I've seen in 15 or 20 years," remarks William L. Raby, national tax director at Touche Ross & Co. Employers and employes normally have three years to claim payroll tax refunds.

Hotel Conquistador Inc. v. U.S., U.S. Ct. of Claims, 1979
5/9/79

⌣

Brace yourself and see what an orthodontist did to numb his tax bite.

Bruce M. Heflin incorporated his practice, which gave him some tax advantages. For one, the corporation could deduct its payments to a pension plan for the Columbus, Ohio, orthodontist. But the occlusion specialist also had it pay and deduct $250 for his home phone and $360 for his wife to wash office towels once a week. He considered the money business-expense reimbursements and didn't report it.

That set the IRS's teeth on edge, of course. The money was taxable income to Heflin, the agency said, and the corporation couldn't deduct the phone payment because it was really a dividend to the dentist. He argued that his phone was used for business: patients called his home, and he called his dad for investment advice for the pension plan. However, "medical emergencies aren't a way of life to an orthodontist," the Tax

Court said, and his need for advice as the pension plan trustee wasn't a need of the corporation.

As for the towel money, which amounted to $7.20 a load, it was his income. And he couldn't deduct anything as the cost of doing the wash, for he hadn't shown what it cost.

B. *Morgan Heflin Inc. and Heflin v. Commissioner, T.C. Memo 1979-62*
3/14/79

⌒

Did it matter that he forfeited his profit if he sold too soon?

A Mattel Inc. bonus plan gave Theodore M. Horwith, a vice president, 2,660 shares of Mattel common some years ago. Any profit from the shares was forfeited to the toy concern if he sold before six months elapsed; that was the penalty under federal securities law. The stock was taxable income, which Horwith figured to be $43,000 based on the market price six months from when he got the stock.

But the IRS said the stock must be valued as of the day he got it; it was worth $76,000 then, so Horwith owed $14,000 tax, the IRS said. He said the later date should be used because the stock was "nontransferable" and "subject to a substantial risk of forfeiture" until six months went by. But the law didn't forbid a sale, and it only penalized Horwith if he sold early, the Tax Court noted.

The stock could have been sold or transferred to another owner the day he got it, so for tax purposes it had to be valued then, the court concluded.

Horwith v. Commissioner, 71 T.C. 83
3/14/79

⌒

The collector's there even if you trade one thing for another thing.

Let's say a lawyer's home needs painting and a housepainter needs legal help, so they swap. The painter paints the lawyer's house and the lawyer tends to the painter's legal problem. Cash doesn't change hands. Nor does it when a professional artist gives an apartment owner a work of art for six months' free rent.

Yet, in both events all parties are subject to tax on their barter, the IRS says. The fair market value of the services or property count as income, the IRS said in a new ruling. So the lawyer is supposed to count in income the value of the paint job, the painter, the value of the legal services, and the apartment owner, the value of the work of art and the artist, the value of the six months' rent.

"The IRS ruling is absolutely correct technically," says James E. Power, a tax partner at Deloitte Haskins & Sells, a CPA firm, "but it will be difficult to enforce from a practical standpoint."

Rev. Rul. 79-24
1/31/79

⌒

A steel man was a one-man show of industry, but the IRS wasn't impressed.

What's an executive worth? That can be a taxing question when the executive is a major stockholder. The IRS often decides that owner-employes of closely held corporations are overpaid and denies the business a deduction for the "unreasonable" portion of their pay. The IRS considers the excessive pay a dividend, nondeductible by the corporation.

When Robert Hawes went to work for Steel Constructors Inc., a closely held firm in Grandview, Mo., he didn't own any of it. He did a bang-up job for the small steel-erecting concern, and the owners agreed to pay him $350 a week plus a bonus of 50% of the profits. Later, he bought into the firm and became its president and majority stockholder. One year his bonus amounted to $88,600, another $94,300. The IRS said only $29,000 was "reasonable compensation"; the balance wasn't deductible.

But Hawes worked from 5 a.m. to 9 p.m. making the business hum. He was the sine qua non of its success, the Tax Court asserted, and his remuneration was fully deductible.
Steel Constructors Inc. v. Commissioner, T.C. Memo 1978-489
1/3/79

Director, beware. It doesn't pay to serve on a board without pay.

Some directors of a firm that gave investment advice to a mutual fund learned that lesson first hand. The firm was sued by some stockholders, and the suit was settled for about $1 million. The directors weren't covered by insurance against such suits and had to dig into their own pockets. A question arose about their deducting the cost of settling the lawsuit.

Directors who were paid to serve on the board could take the deduction as an "ordinary and necessary" business expense, the IRS said in a private ruling. But the ruling indicates that directors who served without pay couldn't take the deduction, says C. Dixon Matthews, tax partner at Wolf & Co. of Massachusetts, a Boston-based CPA firm. Serving on a board for pay constitutes a "trade or business" and payment of such a settlement is a deductible business expense.

But unpaid board members wouldn't be considered in a trade or business for which they could

take the deduction, Matthews notes. "It doesn't
pay to be a good guy. Get paid," he asserts.

12/13/78

⌒

Free lunch: Three utility bigwigs got them and free
rides for their wives, too.

The men are a former chairman, the current chairman and a senior vice president of Columbus & Southern Ohio Electric Co. The utility reimbursed them for
lunches, up to 144 in one year. They ate usually at a
hotel near their offices in Columbus. Two of them usually ate together, the other often ate alone. When they
took their wives to some conventions, the company
picked up the tab.

The IRS said the company had paid the men's personal expenses, so the amounts were taxable to them.
The executives argued it was company policy to reim-
burse some officers for meals and to pay for their wives
to attend conventions. The women eased the way so-
cially and helped the men make valued business con-
tacts. The Tax Court rejected these contentions; the
men must count the sums for the lunches and their
wives as income.

The three also must count as income some
$1,000 a year the utility paid for country clubs for
each of them, the court said.

Fenstermaker et al. v. Commissioner, T.C. Memo 1978-210
6/21/78

⌒

The IRS bites a dentist whose corporation had insurance on his life.

A New York dentist set up a corporation to own
his office building and equipment. When he borrowed
$75,000, the bank made his corporation guarantee the

loan and provide life insurance on the dentist payable
to the bank. The corporation deducted the premiums.
But the IRS barred the deduction. A firm can't deduct
premiums if the firm benefits directly or indirectly from
life insurance on employes or officers, the IRS said.

The Tax Court has denied deductions for life insurance on loans but only when the corporation itself
borrows the money. Here an officer, rather than the
corporation, borrowed the funds; the firm merely guaranteed the loan, the dentist argued. But the court said
that didn't matter: The insurance relieved the corporation of further liability on the loan if the dentist died.
That benefited the corporation, so the premiums aren't
deductible, the court ruled.

D'Angelo Associates Inc. v. Commissioner, 70 T.C. 12
5/17/78

⌐⌐

A $200,000 keelhauling was the IRS's plan for the
user of a firm's yacht.

The company, which negotiated many of its construction contracts aboard a yacht, quit such cruises
when its boss sold the yacht. However, business
slumped, and the closely held concern decided to buy
itself a yacht designed for customer cruises. The 85-foot
craft had a large salon for meetings; its cabins were all
the same size, so that no guest would be slighted. The
corporate motto, "Krapfcandoit," was boldly lettered
across the yacht, so boldly that one yacht club barred
the vessel from its moorings.

The firm paid about $365,000 for the craft. The
boss sometimes used it for pleasure, paying the firm the
boat's charter fee of $500 a day. But the IRS said that
the boat was built for the boss's personal benefit rather
than a valid business purpose and that he had to count
the purchase price as his income. That meant a

$200,000 tax bill for him. The yacht did provide him personal benefits, the Tax Court observed.

But "the record demonstrates a need for a yacht to adequately conduct corporate business," the court said. The IRS was fishing in the wrong waters. The executive owed nothing.

Krapf v. Commissioner, T.C. Memo 1978-138
5/3/78

◇

A dentist drilled, filled and capped as D.D.S. Inc. to eschew a big tax bite.

He put his name on the corporation he set up to operate his dental practice, Sigel G. Roush D.D.S. Inc. He had the corporation pay him rent for two cars he owned, which he and his wife drove. The corporation deducted the lease payments, while he and his wife deducted depreciation on the cars on their joint return. He also had the corporation pay some $2,500 of their entertainment expenses, which the corporation deducted.

Most of the money paid for parties the Newark, Ohio, couple gave, he said, to promote "good will" for his dental practice. However, one party was for his daughter's college chums and he admitted that he didn't talk about dentistry at any of the parties. The IRS, of course, barred all these deductions and counted some of the corporation's outlays as income to the dentist and his wife. The corporation owed about $5,000 of added tax, the couple nearly $2,000, the IRS figured.

The Tax Court confirmed most of the IRS calculations, though the court did let the corporation deduct less than $50 for the dentist's using one car to get lunch for his office staff.

Roush v. Commissioner, T.C. Memo 1978-115
4/5/78

A tutor is touched by the defeat of a New Jersey State trooper.

He tutored students and got a free room in a dormitory. He also was to get free meals in the dorm's dining hall. But he was getting paid to work in the college laboratory and couldn't eat in the dining hall often. So the school gave him $730 as a meal allowance. He didn't count it as income. But the IRS insisted it was taxable income and billed him $114 in added tax.

Usually, meals provided by an employer for the employer's convenience don't produce taxable income for the employe. The tutor argued that cash paid in lieu of actual meals should be considered nontaxable, too. However, a similar contention by a New Jersey trooper was made a few months earlier before the Supreme Court, and the court rejected it—which was too bad for the tutor:

His case "must be decided" in favor of the IRS, the Tax Court said, in an opinion that appears to be its first to rely on the Supreme Court decision.

Austin v. Commissioner, T.C. Memo 1977-434
1/18/78

∽

Keep the change: How the IRS figured the tips for a recordless waitress.

Helen Thiefl waited tables in a bustling cafe, but she didn't keep track of her tips. She reported $290, or an average 16 cents of tips an hour, for the year. The IRS didn't swallow that. The cafe's credit card sales showed the average tip per sale was 13.9%, which the IRS pared to 12.5% because the waitresses gave the busboys a cut.

Then the IRS computed average sales per waitress per hour, multiplied that by 12.5% to get tips per waitress per hour, which came to $2.04. Mrs. Thiefl worked 1,833 hours, indicating she pocketed $3,739 for the year. The Tax Court recently modified the IRS's concoction. For one thing Mrs. Thiefl's schedule, 6 p.m. to 2 a.m., served a clientele that was "appreciably . . . the nontipping variety."

The court figured she averaged tips of only 8% of her sales checks, and owed tax on the unreported portion of $2,400 of tips she hadn't reported, plus a 5% penalty.

Thiefl v. Commissioner, T.C. Memo 1977-387
11/23/77

⌒

Worth it: A construction executive rebuffs an IRS attack on his pay.

Stanley Ledford got his start in construction when he helped build an air base on Guadalcanal during World War II. He started his own company in Washington, D.C., in the late 1950s and built it from 10 employes to 250 by 1970. Ledford ran all parts of the business. He often worked 12 hours a day, sometimes six or seven days a week. Ledford didn't pay dividends to himself or the company's other two stockholders, his son and daughter. He put all excess earnings back into the business.

But Ledford paid himself more than $80,000 in annual salary, and the IRS objected. The law prohibits paying executives or any other employes an "unreasonably" high salary. Salaries are tax-deductible expenses of corporations, and owners of small companies have been known to try to save corporate taxes by paying themselves most of the profits in salary. The IRS said Ledford's job was worth only $50,000 a year.

The Tax Court upheld his original salary. It

said he was "largely responsible" for the success of his business. And the court noted that a big corporation had tried to buy Ledford's company and had offered him $100,000 a year to stay and run it.
      Ledford Construction Co. v. Commissioner, T.C. Memo 1977-204
                                                              8/24/77

⌒

A valuable lady is worth only $40,000 a year, the IRS figured.

Loulu helped her husband run an auto seat cover business for many years without pay. After he died, she, her son and another man owned and ran the company, and she began to draw a salary. She tended the payables, oversaw the receivables and met cash needs by arranging loans. She also ran the whole show when the other owners were away on frequent, long trips. When Loulu was close to 75 years old, she was paid $62,800 a year. The IRS said more than $40,000 was "excessive."

The company had to show Loulu's pay was "reasonable." She earned the money, the company argued: She not only arranged loans, but personally guaranteed them, and coordinated colors for products. She had convinced the others the firm should sell auto accessories, a move that pushed sales over $4 million a year.

After reviewing her sizable contributions to the business, the Tax Court determined Loulu's entire pay was "reasonable," and, of course, deductible.
              Allison Corp. v. Commissioner, T.C. Memo 1977-166
                                                            6/15/77

⌒

Texas agreed to pay its employes' share of Social Security taxes beginning in 1978. The state wanted the amount it paid for the workers to be excluded from their taxable incomes. But the IRS said that an amount an employe normally would have paid, but was paid by the state, counts as the employe's taxable earnings.

IRS private letter ruling 7850029
12/27/78

⌒

A cop in the U.S. Canal Zone was obliged to live in a government-furnished house. Yet, he couldn't exclude the value of the house from his income, the Tax Court said. The house wasn't on his employer's "business premises," because he didn't perform a significant part of his work there, nor did the government conduct a significant portion of its business there, the court reasoned. But one dissenter said the entire Canal Zone was the government's "business premises" and the cop should get the exclusion.

Benninghoff v. Commissioner, 71 T.C. 19
12/6/78

⌒

Save 'N' Pay: A home building firm let workers buy its homes at a discount. One employe saved $3,200 on a house he bought. Neither he nor the firm reported the discount as the worker's income. But the IRS said it was a taxable fringe benefit. The Tax Court agreed with the IRS. In a summary opinion reported by the Research Institute of America, tax publisher, the court said the worker owes tax on the $3,200 discount.

Beckert, T.C. Summary Opinion 1978-211
9/13/78

Payroll Taxes

Family relations were its forte, but the IRS objected to its employe relations.

The American Institute of Family Relations, in California, offers marriage and child counseling. Most of its counselors are psychologists. They get a part of whatever a client pays the institute; if a client pays nothing, the counselor gets nothing. Still, the IRS insisted the counselors were "employes" and told the institute it owed $117,000 of payroll and withholding taxes.

Workers can be treated as "independent contractors" instead of employes if there's a "reasonable" basis to do so. The institute didn't control the way the counselors worked; they used the counseling methods they preferred. It didn't give them any equipment or secretarial help to aid them in preparing reports on clients. And it considered them "professionals" like doctors or lawyers, who are normally exempt from payroll taxes.

Indeed, the institute had a reasonable basis for not treating the counselors as employes, a federal district court said, and it ordered the IRS to refund $38,250 of payroll taxes the institute paid.

The American Institute of Family Relations v. U.S., U.S. Dist. Ct., Cent. Dist. Calif., 1979
6/6/79

~

Can the go-go girls at the Hello Doll bar gyrate around the IRS?

The dancing girls were the main attraction at a North Hollywood, Calif., bar where they performed on a mirrored stage. The bar didn't pay Social Security taxes for them or withhold income taxes from their paychecks because it considered them independent contractors. But the IRS considered them employes and told the bar to pay $32,000 in back payroll taxes.

Whether workers are independent contractors or employes often is determined by how much control the person employing them has over their work. In the case of the dancing girls, a federal court jury was told to consider, among other things, "whether the hirer can control the details of the dancer's performance." The jury was instructed that "if the services rendered are artistic in nature and not subject to control as to how they are to be performed, that is indicative of an independent contractor."

The jurors, all females, apparently didn't find the performances at the Hello Doll bar "artistic in nature," for they found the dancers were employes subject to payroll tax.

Theresa Enterprises Inc. dba The Hello Doll v. U.S., U.S. Dist. Ct., Cent.
Dist. Calif.
8/30/78

⌒

His iron hand made life rough, but it kept the IRS away from his wife.

He ran his moving company "with an iron hand" and badly: Checks bounced, payroll withholding taxes weren't paid on time. At one point employes demanded to be paid in cash. When creditors refused checks signed by him, he changed the bank authorizations so his wife, a director of the company, could sign checks.

If she resisted signing checks she knew weren't covered, he would compel her to sign by "berating her

publicly, threatening her and at times beating her." The
concern owed $19,800 of delinquent payroll withholding
taxes when he died. The IRS told her to pay. She was a
"responsible party" liable for the delinquent withholding payments because she was authorized to sign company checks, the IRS argued.

*To be liable, though, a person must have had
authority to make payments. She hadn't any authority and "was dominated by her husband," the
Court of Claims said. Thus the IRS couldn't compel her to pay.*

Barrett v. U.S., U.S. Ct. of Claims, 1978
7/26/78

〜

Make Uncle Sam wait so your company can earn
more interest on its money.

Doing that may involve changing payroll dates and
holding onto payroll taxes as long as possible. Some big
employers can save a lot of money, says Roy Johnson,
president of PCS Reports Ltd., payroll tax consultants,
in New York City. It gets complicated, but a simple example shows what's possible: A firm that pays workers
twice a month, on the 15th and the last day of the
month, must remit payroll and withholding taxes on the
payroll of the 15th within three days, meaning by the
18th.

But if payday were moved to the 16th, the law says
the payroll taxes aren't due until three days from the
22nd, which is the 25th. That means the employer could
earn interest for seven more days on these funds, Johnson says. The law also says only 90% of payroll taxes are
due on the 25th; often the remaining 10% isn't due for as
much as 70 days, Johnson asserts.

This strategy works best for employers who pay

either once or twice a month and have sizable payroll tax payments.

6/7/78

⌒

How to give workers a raise and save their employer some money, too.

Suppose employes making $15,000 get a raise to $16,500. It will cost their employer $17,498.25 a worker: $16,500 of wages plus Social Security tax of 6.05%, or $998.25. Social Security also takes $998.25 from each worker's $16,500, leaving $15,501.75. In this example, the employer can save about $100 an employe and the workers wouldn't be any worse off if they got only a $500 rise to $15,500 and their employer paid their Social Security tax for them, suggests payroll-tax strategist Roy Johnson.

Then the employer pays $15,500 plus 12.1% for Social Security, or $1,875.50, for a total $17,375.50. That's a $122.75 saving. And each worker has $15,500, only $1.75 less than if they got the full $16,500 and paid their own Social Security. Johnson, president of PCS/Reports Ltd., New York, says negotiating municipal pay raises this way could "save New York City a bundle."

4/5/78

⌒

Howdy, partner. It's a new IRS greeting for some accounting people.

Most states allow only certified public accountants to be partners in CPA firms. Most big CPA firms, though, have employes who aren't CPAs, but have nearly the same privileges as partners. To satisfy state laws, they aren't called partners, but "principals."

The IRS has told a CPA firm its principals were "partners" for federal tax purposes. That means, among other things, they aren't employes; the firm needn't pay federal payroll taxes for them. But the principals must pay self-employment taxes, suggests William Raby, national tax director, Touche Ross & Co., a CPA firm. (It isn't the firm in the IRS ruling.) If states accept the IRS's view, principals would pay state income taxes as partners and in some instances save money, Raby says.

Rev. Rul. 77-332
9/21/77

A local PTA stepped in to provide part-time teachers for a school "enrichment program" when other funding dried up. The teachers are employes of the Parent-Teachers Association for federal payroll tax purposes, the IRS ruled.

IRS letter ruling 7829031
8/2/78

Not so cuke: A crew leader is responsible for payroll taxes for workers tending cucumbers under this direction because he failed to have himself designated in writing as an employe of farmers using the crews, the IRS ruled.

IRS private ruling 7826062
7/19/78

Camp counselors' "free" meals and lodging are subject to Social Security tax. The Hartford, Conn., YMCA failed to pay and withhold on freebies for its counselors and ended up owing $7,000. From now on it will figure the tax based on $3 a week for lodging and 85 cents a meal, or $187.65 for nine weeks, Stephen J. Taylor, associate director, says. The American Camping Association says it advised its 4,000 members to count the value of meals and lodging as income subject to the payroll tax.

3/22/78

⌣

News carriers, who deliver papers to homes on a part-time basis, are subject to federal payroll taxes, Social Security, unemployment and withholding, the IRS said in a private letter ruling. The carriers are employes, it found; they didn't qualify as news vendors, who aren't considered employes for payroll-tax purposes.

IRS private ruling 7739011
10/5/77

⌣

Helping hands: As therapy, some mental patients prepare aluminum cans for recycling and get paid for the work. Their pay, though, is exempt from withholding and payroll taxes, the IRS determined.

IRS private ruling, 7737044
9/21/77

Other Taxes on Business Dealings

Buying a pet publisher unleashed a dogged tax problem.

Miracle Pet Products sold its pet-publishing operations to TFH Publications, of Neptune, N.J., for $1.1 million. As part of the purchase price, TFH gave Miracle $360,000 of free advertising in Tropical Fish Hobbyist or any similar magazines TFH might decide to publish. TFH treated the $360,000 as "future" income to be taxed when Miracle used the advertising space.

But the IRS said the $360,000 was taxable immediately, so TFH owed $165,000 tax. In effect, Miracle gave $360,000 of assets to TFH for advertising space that TFH normally would sell for cash, the Tax Court observed. The assets TFH got must be treated the same as cash, as "taxable income," the court said. TFH owes the tax, the court concluded. But the firm could have deferred the $360,000 if a fixed amount of advertising on a fixed schedule of use had been called for and there was a degree of certainty the advertising would have to be provided, the court said.

However, that wasn't the case here: "Because of Miracle's bankruptcy" (two years after the deal with TFH) TFH "may never" have to provide Miracle any more free advertising, the court said.

TFH Publications Inc. v. Commissioner, 72 T.C. 54
7/18/79

After 20 years his "special" policy paid off and the IRS wanted a cut.

Insurance dividends usually are considered a return of premium and aren't taxed. But the IRS tried to ignore that rule in the recent case of Ned W. Moseley, of Stuttgart, Ark. Moseley had paid $190 annually for a special 20-year life policy, "special" because $385 was credited to a fund. If he was alive 20 years later, he got a piece of the fund. He survived; his piece was $3,500.

Moseley figured he paid $3,800 in premiums over the 20 years and got back $3,500, so he didn't owe any tax. But the IRS said he put only $385 in the special fund and got out $3,500 for a profit of $3,115, on which he owed $1,400 tax. The IRS said he bought two things; life insurance and the right to be in the fund. But the Tax Court noted that the insurance company didn't treat them separately in its contract.

The special fund benefit couldn't be purchased without the life insurance benefit; they were inseparable, which meant Moseley didn't have to pay, the court ruled.

Moseley v. Commissioner, 72 T.C. 15
5/2/79

‿

A "bargain sale" greased the way for this deal, but the IRS wanted to be paid.

Three sisters inherited a road-building outfit from their father, but Charles D. Missimer, of Roanoke, Va., ran it. He wanted to buy them out for $144,000; they wanted much more. A deal finally was made. Missimer bought their stock for $144,000, and the corporation sold its land and building to the women for a bargain $12,000—it was worth $76,000. The firm stayed on the property, paying the sisters $900 a month rent.

The IRS said either the sisters owed tax on the $64,000 "bargain" element in the deal, or Missimer did. Because it couldn't decide which one, the IRS assessed them all, and they ended up in Tax Court. The deal could be seen either as the sisters getting $64,000 from the firm, or Missimer getting it, the court said.

Missimer benefited from the bargain sale; he couldn't have made the deal without it. So he owed some $30,000 tax, the court said.

Missimer v. Commissioner, T.C. Memo 1979-48
2/28/79

⌒

Is Dracula watching? She was paid to bleed and then was chased by the IRS.

Dorothy R. Garber's blood has a rare antibody known in only two or three other people in the world. It is useful in typing blood serums. Biomedical Industries Inc. paid the former Oshkosh, Wis., resident $25,000 to become a donor. She also got $1,600 a bleeding, a $200 weekly salary and a costly car. The IRS charged her with tax evasion for failing to report $273,000 she earned over a three-year period.

But Garber argued that the blood money was tax-free, as it was "damages" for the suffering of being a donor. She got headaches, dizzy spells and muscle pains from injections of a substance that stimulated her output of the rare antibody; her arms were scarred from needles. But that isn't the kind of suffering the tax exemption is for, an appeals court said. The exemption is for damages received for a tort, an injury from someone's wrongful act. The blood money was taxable, the court said.

She knew the "side effects involved . . . negotiated her contracts with this in mind and was sig-

*nificantly remunerated for her troubles," the court
declared.*

U.S. v. Garber, U.S. Ct. of Appeals, 5th Circ., 1979
2/28/79

～

Tongsun Park: The South Korean money man tried to shake the IRS.

Park, of course, is the fellow whose generous ways got some Congressmen in trouble for accepting his money gifts. At the peak of several probes into his affairs, the IRS slapped him with a $4.5 million bill for unpaid taxes and put liens on assets of Pacific Development Inc., a Park-owned U.S. corporation.

The IRS liens tied up two checking accounts, 50,000 shares of International Oil & Gas Corp., a Mercedes sedan, Cadillac convertible, Lincoln limousine and a $1 million policy on Park's life. The corporation tried to get the liens removed. But a federal court determined that the concern was Park's "alter ego," and thus its assets could be seized for his tax debt. The court noted that Park completely controlled the concern, which "neglected to have a genuine board of directors."

*Also, the concern's employes and facilities
were used for Park's personal benefit without
charge, noted the court, which suggested he created it to avoid U.S. income taxes. (He's contesting
the $4.5 million tax assessment in the Tax Court.)*

Pacific Development Inc. v. U.S., U.S. Dist. Ct., Dist. of Columbia, 1979
1/31/79

～

She bailed out people, but could she bail out of the 70% bracket?

The highest tax bracket is 70%, but personal service income qualifies for a maximum 50% rate. But the "maxi-tax" doesn't apply to 70% of business profit if capital is a material factor in the business. Dorothy Bruno owned a bail bond firm in Kansas City, Mo. She made more than $100,000 from her business and paid the 50% maximum rate on it. But the IRS said 70% of it didn't qualify for the maxi-tax.

The IRS argued that Bruno had to own property and deposit $15,000 with the city to be a bondsman, so capital was a material factor in her business. But the Tax Court said those were start-up requirements similar to an investment a doctor or lawyer makes to open a practice. Her business "was built by services rendered," the court asserted.

Her fees were like those earned by real estate salesmen and her earnings qualified totally for the 50% maximum rate, the court concluded.

Bruno v. Commissioner, 71 T.C. 17
11/29/78

~

An M.D. won $105,000 in a libel action against his alma mater. Is it taxable?

Dr. William Q. Wolfson sued Wayne State University for denying he was on its medical school faculty 25 years ago. The drawn-out litigation resulted from his going to the school to get a Class A medical school degree when he already had one from a Class B school and was practicing medicine. He attended Wayne State at the urging of its chairman of medicine, whose eye condition Wolfson cleared up.

Wolfson was both a student and a faculty member, but when the Detroit Free Press years ago reported he was merely a student unlicensed to practice in Michigan, the school didn't set the record straight. Later, it told those who asked about him that Wolfson wasn't ever on its faculty. But finally he won. The school settled with him, paying him $105,000 and correcting its records to reflect his faculty status. The IRS said the money was taxable income. Wolfson argued that it was compensation for damage to his personal reputation and thus was tax free.

But the Tax Court said his suit was brought to clear his professional reputation rather than his personal reputation, so he must pay tax on the $105,000.

Wolfson v. Commissioner, T.C. Memo 1978-445
11/15/78

⌒

The IRS moved in on trailer park owners for being too good to their tenants.

Self-employed persons usually must pay Social Security self-employment tax. Income from renting real estate, however, is exempt from the tax unless services such as food or maid service are provided tenants. Then part of the rent income counts as "personal service income" subject to the tax. The IRS figured Fabian and Florence Bobo's income from a 48-space mobile home park fell under the tax.

Their Novato, Calif., trailer park hadn't any recreational facilities, or even a public phone. But the Bobos supplied utility hookups, trash-hauling and grounds maintenance. The IRS contended that these were services for tenants that made the Bobos subject to the tax (which in 1978 amounted to $1,433). However, the Tax Court said the Bobos needn't pay; these services were for maintaining the trailer park and making it fit for occupancy rather than for the tenants themselves.

Services to tenants "must be of such substantial nature that (payment) for them can be said to

*constitute a material part of the payment made by
the tenant," the court observed.*

Bobo v. Commissioner, 70 T.C. 68
9/6/78

∽

Something smelled about a sewer builder's corporation, the IRS sniffed.

Preston W. Carroll built sewers, but he didn't have enough bonding capacity to bid on big jobs. To increase his bonding capability, he formed a corporation and had it take over some $2 million of equipment he owned. He rented the equipment back from the corporation, paying it $2 million rent in three years. The firm paid income taxes on its earnings, but having the corporate set-up saved Carroll $70,000 a year in income tax.

The IRS said the set-up was a tax-avoidance gimmick and should be ignored. All the rent the corporation got should be counted as Carroll's income, the agency said. That would mean he owed $1.1 million in taxes.

But the Tax Court bailed out the sewer contractor. There was a substantial business purpose for forming the corporation besides tax avoidance: to increase the business's bonding capacity, the court determined.

*Such transactions "may not be constructed
entirely from tax advantage. But if the foundation
and bricks have economic substance, the . . . inducement of the tax advantage can provide the
mortar," the court asserted.*

Carroll v. Commissioner, T.C. Memo 1978-173
8/9/78

∽

Did a firm sell a right to collect $130,000 sometime down the road?

Selling the right to collect income in the future usually means the sales proceeds are taxed to the seller as ordinary income. But an investment firm controlled by Robert H. Storz, owner of Storz Broadcasting Co., sold its assets and went out of business, and he treated none of the proceeds as ordinary income. The IRS said some of the proceeds were ordinary income as they bought the firm's right to collect fees on partially completed underwritings.

The buyer completed the underwritings and collected $130,000, the IRS noted. Mr. Storz argued that underwriters aren't entitled to a penny until they complete an underwriting. These weren't completed before the sale, so his firm hadn't the right to any income to sell. The Tax Court agreed with him, but an appeals court rejected his contention.

Efforts by the Storz firm before the sale gave rise to the underwriting income that the buyer eventually collected, so the firm had and sold the right to collect the money. Mr. Storz himself must count and pay tax on part of the sales proceeds as ordinary income, the appeals court said. How much? The appeals court directed the Tax Court to determine that.

Storz v. Commissioner, U.S. Ct. of Appeals, 8th Circ., 1978
8/2/78

⌢

A constructor of roads met the IRS and learned about constructive receipt.

Even if you don't have money in your hot hand, you may owe tax on it—you can have enough control over it to have "constructive receipt." The IRS thought that was the case with a contractor paid as work progressed on a highway job. Part of each progress pay ment was retained by the state until the job was completed.

The "retainage," $86,000 one year, was put in a bank escrow account. The bank needed the state's approval to release the account, and for the year in question the account wasn't given to the contractor. But the bank bought securities with the money after consulting with the company. However, that didn't amount to sufficient control for constructive receipt, the Tax Court ruled.

The contractor hadn't "unfettered or even substantial control" over the money, and didn't owe tax until it got the escrow account, the court determined.

Iler and Rankin v. Commissioner, T.C. Memo 1978-182
6/14/78

⌒

A blowup developed about the mobility of a film processor's huts.

Film N' Photos placed 2,000-pound, prefab huts on shopping-center parking lots. One employe occupied a hut, serving customers, who had to stay outside, through a sliding window. If a location didn't pay, the Houston film processor hauled the hut to a different spot. The company considered the huts movable personal property and took an investment tax credit for them. IRS barred the credit.

The IRS argued that the units were "inherently permanent" and thus were real property, which didn't qualify for the credit. The huts were welded to a concrete slab, which often was poured atop a parking lot surface, but in a way that kept the slab from adhering. So the hut and the slab could be moved together. The Tax Court noted that the units could be trucked around Texas without any special house-moving permit because they were so small.

The units rested on the ground but "were in no way attached," so they were personal property eligible and the firm was entitled to the credit, the court ruled.

Film N' Photos Inc. v. Commissioner, T.C. Memo 1978-162
5/10/78

⌒

A tax trap is found in the way the jobs credit works for some folks.

The credit was meant to spur employment by cutting taxes for businesses that added employes. But it can be a burr for partnerships that lost money in 1977, says Al Ellentuck, national tax partner, Laventhol & Horwath, a CPA firm. Partnerships that lost money don't owe any tax so the jobs credit doesn't help them. Yet, it hurts partners who use their share of a loss to offset other income to save taxes.

The tax code requires the partnership to reduce its deduction for wages paid by the amount of the jobs credit it's eligible for, even if it can't use the credit, the IRS has said. Cutting the deduction for wages cuts the partnership's loss, and thus reduces the amount of losses a partner has to offset against other income. "It's a trap that probably wasn't intended," Ellentuck says. "We're hearing the screams as people prepare partners' tax returns."

The same result applies to small corporations whose owners elect to have profits and losses taxed to them as individuals, says Steven Holub, of Laventhol & Horwath's Washington, D.C., office.

3/15/78

Peddling papers to a reluctant buyer cost two brokers $100,000.

The brokers persuaded Freedom Newspapers Inc. to buy three newspapers even though Freedom wanted only two of them. The brokers said they would sell the third paper for $700,000, what it cost Freedom, or they would pay Freedom $100,000. They couldn't sell it and paid the $100,000. Freedom treated the sum as a reduction in the cost of the third paper, which it sold later at a loss.

However, the IRS said the $100,000 was income because it was damages the brokers had to pay for failing to sell the third paper. That meant Freedom owed $48,000 tax on the $100,000. The newspaper concern argued that the money was an inducement to get Freedom to buy the third paper. Such inducements merely cut a buyer's cost; they don't produce income.

The Tax Court sided with Freedom. In effect, the brokers made a warranty that was tied to the purchase. So the $100,000 "must be characterized as a reduction in the purchase price," the court asserted.

Freedom Newspapers Inc. v. Commissioner, T.C. Memo 1977-429
1/18/78

⌒

A cotton-pickin' notion: It would have cost a Texan $22,000.

He grew cotton and normally harvested a crop late in the year. But bad weather delayed a harvest until early the next year, when he had another crop to harvest by year-end. The double harvests meant double income that year and a whopping tax bill. To avoid that, he delivered his cotton to the gin, but made an agreement to be paid the next year, when he got $45,000 for the crop.

The IRS said he had "constructively received" the money in the year of harvest and thus owed $22,000 of tax on the $45,000. Among other things, the IRS argued that the delayed payment agreement wasn't bona fide, as it was made to avoid taxes. The Tax Court didn't cotton to that notion. The agreement was valid; the farmer didn't have to pay, the court determined. A taxpayer "has a legal right to conduct his business . . . to minimize taxes," the court reminded the IRS.

Another cotton farmer beat the IRS in a similar case tried in 1977 before a federal jury in Texas.

Schniers v. Commissioner, 69 T.C. 40
1/18/78

∽

The people who made the IRS open its files win the fight that began it all.

A lawsuit by Philip and Sue Long forced the IRS a few years ago to make public its agents' manual and thousands of pages of other previously secret information about audit and collection practices. The Bellevue, Wash., couple filed the Freedom of Information suit in the course of disputing a $41,000 tax bill, much of it for "personal holding company" tax on two family corporations. The companies owned duplexes Long and his brothers and sister inherited from their father.

The IRS contended proceeds from selling off the duplexes were subject to the tax, which is a penalty on certain corporate income. The case hinged on whether the companies held the real estate "primarily for sale," rather than for investment purposes, and thus were real estate "dealers" exempt from the personal holding company levy. The Tax Court ruled in 1975 in favor of the IRS.

*But the Ninth Circuit, in a two-to-one deci-
sion, reversed the Tax Court. "This means we
have won on all the issues," says Long, whose historic tussle with the IRS began in 1969.*
Parkside Inc. and Beaconcrest Inc. v. Commissioner, U.S. Ct. of Appeals,
9th Circ., 1977
12/14/77

⌒

A sex-bias suit against Uniroyal got her $7,000; she figured it was tax-free.

Sophia M. Coats sued the big rubber company for "invidious and unlawful sex discrimination" in violation of the Civil Rights Act of 1964. Her lawyer persuaded her to settle out of court, advising any settlement wouldn't be taxed. Uniroyal paid her $7,000. But the settlement papers didn't say if the sum was back pay or punitive damages, which usually are tax-free.

However, the IRS said she owed some $1,700 of tax on the $7,000. Acting as her own lawyer, she argued in Tax Court that the money was paid as damages and shouldn't be taxed. But the court disagreed: It was back pay collected under the Civil Rights Act, which "is taxable in the same manner as back pay otherwise received," the court asserted.

*Her lawyer's bad advice about the money's
taxability didn't save her from the tax either, the
court said; but she could deduct the $1,500 she
paid him.*
Coats v. Commissioner, T.C. Memo 1977-407
12/7/77

⌒

Not my money. That's a broker's story about a $24,000 commission.

Who pays tax on income can be a tricky question sometimes. Consider the case of Jerry W. McIver, a Florida real-estate broker. Besides being a licensed broker, he was sole owner and chief executive of a firm that developed mobile-home parks. His company and another unrelated firm bought 80 acres for $486,000. The broker who represented the sellers got a $48,000 commission on the transaction and split it, giving McIver a $24,000 check, which McIver endorsed over to his firm. McIver's company recorded the sum as a reduction in its investment in the 80 acres.

However, the IRS wanted McIver to pay tax on the $24,000, arguing that it was his income. McIver said he only got the money as an employe of his firm; he claimed he had agreed to give the company any commission he got on the transaction. But McIver's firm wasn't licensed as a broker and couldn't legally accept commissions, the Tax Court noted. And the other broker considered McIver to be acting as a co-broker in the transaction from the outset; otherwise he probably wouldn't have split the fee.

It was McIver's income. He controlled the situation and "performed the acts which produced the income," the court asserted.

McIver v. Commissioner, T.C. Memo 1977-174
6/22/77

∽

Only if it fits: Some truckers use covers to keep cargo from blowing away. The IRS decided that the excise tax on truck parts applies to "fitted cargo covers." But "nonfitted" covers won't be taxed.

IRS private ruling 7914010
4/11/79

Such things occupy the IRS: Must an importer of special tires and inner tubes for amusement park bumper cars pay the excise tax imposed on vehicular tires? Yes, the IRS said, reasoning that, as the tire fits a "vehicle wheel" and is capable of "transporting a person," it's a tire for excise-tax purposes.

IRS letter ruling 7823-65
7/26/78

⌒

Among thy fungi: A structure built for mushroom growing didn't qualify for the investment tax credit because employes worked in it regularly as "an integral part" of the growing process. That made the facility a building ineligible for the credit, the IRS reasoned.

IRS private ruling 7752005
1/18/78

Business Losses and Bankruptcies

Reins of red ink made the IRS look for hobby horses on a dentist's ranch.

Losses from business ventures are deductible, but hobby losses aren't. Dr. Theodore N. Engdahl and his wife Adeline started an American saddle horse breeding venture on a Morgan Hill, Calif., ranch. It would supplement their income when he retired from orthodontics, they hoped. But for 11 straight years their horses ran in the red.

Clearly this is a hobby pursued without hope for profit, the IRS said and kicked out $53,000 of losses the Engdahls deducted. The couple argued that they weren't hobbyists: neither rode horses. They went into this for profit, they had sought expert advice, kept good books, worked hard—up at 5:30 a.m. feeding nine horses and mucking stalls—tried various ways to make the operation pay, but had been hit by bad luck. Some good breedstock died, and demand for their type of horses shrank.

It was "unlikely" they would have gone into "a hobby costing thousands of dollars and entailing much personal physical labor without a profit motive," the Tax Court said, and it concluded the losses were deductible.

Engdahl v. Commissioner, 72 T.C. 56
7/25/79

A fowl venture laid an egg, but saved a lot of scratch at tax time.

Chicken and turkey-raising units of Rocco Inc. lost money their first year. Rocco turned the losses to its tax advantage by filing a consolidated return reporting a $2.4 million loss. Eagle-eyed IRS auditors saw that the losses resulted from the units' use of *cash* accounting; if they used *accrual* accounting, the red ink disappeared.

The IRS swooped in, clucking that Rocco violated a law against acquiring a business for the "principal purpose of evading or avoiding tax." The agency crowed that it could force accrual accounting on the subsidiaries and make Rocco pay $455,000 as a result. This made Rocco cry, "fowl," of course. The subsidiaries weren't formed for tax avoidance, the company argued, and the tax code lets poultry raisers use cash accounting.

Even though its plans hatched a tax loss, that wasn't the main reason the company laid them, the Tax Court determined. So, the IRS couldn't pluck this taxpayer, the court said.

Rocco Inc. et al. v. Commissioner, 72 T.C. 13
5/2/79

⌒

Up in smoke? A whole lot of "the noxious weed" was missing from a warehouse.

A chewing-tobacco company, National Home Products Inc., stored bales of tobacco at its warehouses in Viroqua, Wis. But an inventory disclosed that some 44,000 bales of Wisconsin leaf, valued at about $934,000, had vanished. An investigation indicated that some supervisory employes were linked to the disappearance.

But the evidence wasn't strong enough to warrant criminal prosecution. The concern did file suit against the employes and its insurance company, which balked at paying the loss. The concern reduced its inventory to reflect the loss, which cut its taxable income. But the IRS said the concern had "a reasonable prospect of recovering" the loss, and thus couldn't take the inventory writedown. It's true that a loss can't be *deducted* if there's reasonable chance of recovery, the Tax Court noted.

But the concern wasn't taking a deduction for the loss, it was adjusting its inventory, and inventory reductions for such losses can be made whatever the prospects for recovery, the court said. Any later recovery would be taxable income, the court added.

National Home Products Inc. v. Commissioner, 71 T.C. 47
1/24/79

◇

He couldn't use one year's loss, so he tried to use another's.

Losses in one year often can be carried back to offset an earlier year's income to get a refund of the earlier year's tax. By carrying back a 1970 loss to 1968, Thomas H. Jones & Co. got a tax refund. Such refunds usually are tentative. After an audit, the IRS found that the carryback was improper and assessed the firm—owned by Thomas H. Jones, of Shaker Heights, Ohio—some $9,000 in tax for 1968.

Jones agreed that the 1970 loss had been carried back erroneously. But now he wanted to use a 1971 loss to offset the $9,000 the IRS wanted for 1968. The IRS said the time limit for carrying back the 1971 loss had run out. However, the 1970 loss had used up all of the 1968 income and the 1971 loss couldn't have been used until the 1970 carryback was disallowed, Jones argued.

The Tax Court agreed with him. When the

IRS threw out the 1970 carryback, it opened the
way to carry back the 1971 loss, the court conclud-
ed. Thus, Jones escaped paying the $9,000 the IRS
said was due for 1968.

Jones v. Commissioner, 71 T.C. 38
1/10/79

⌒

A dog story, or why the IRS howled about a divorced woman's kennel.

Eve M. Ballich's dogmanship was superb: She
raised and showed 66 fox terrier champions. Her business acumen wasn't so good: The kennel she ran at her
Stevenson, Md., home never turned a profit. It took in
as much as $18,000 one year, but then expenses ran
nearly $29,000. Losses for a four-year period totaled
$44,000. Ballich deducted the losses.

But the IRS growled that the kennel was a hobby,
so the losses weren't deductible. She argued that she
spent long hours on breeding, care and showing of her
dogs. She also said she maintained accurate records of
the operation for tax purposes. But the Tax Court noted
that her records weren't detailed enough to tell which
parts of the operation made money and which lost.

And Ballich, now in her 70s, conceded that
she wouldn't have kept the kennel going if she
hadn't got more than $27,000 a year in alimony
from an ex-husband. The kennel "was her hobby"
and its losses weren't deductible, the court said.

Ballich v. Commissioner, T.C. Memo 1978-497
1/10/79

⌒

You can ditch creditors and begin a new business
with a tax break.

A. L. Davis did it. His grocery chain lost $2.5 million before it was liquidated in bankruptcy, where $3.8 million of his debts were canceled. He started another grocery business, which turned a nice profit. But he avoided more than $500,000 of tax by carrying over losses from his bankrupt business. The IRS said he couldn't use those losses.

Davis didn't "own" the losses anymore, he lost them in the bankruptcy, the IRS argued. But the Tax Court rejected that argument. The law normally lets bankrupts carry-over losses incurred prior to bankruptcy, the court said. But that may change: A proposed law would reduce loss carry-overs by the amount of debts canceled in bankruptcy and would have denied Davis any tax benefits from his bankruptcy.

"This reform is long overdue," says David A. Berenson, national tax partner, S. D. Leidesdorf & Co. But the proposed law must be simplified, he told a congressional unit on behalf of the American Institute of Certified Public Accountants.

Davis v. Commissioner, 69 T.C. 69
3/22/78

∽

A new stance: The Tax Court assumes one on accepting bankruptcy cases.

The Tax Court doesn't accept tax disputes under the bankruptcy court's jurisdiction. But it isn't always clear when the bankruptcy court has jurisdiction. The Tax Court, for example, was hearing cases involving penalties when the tax on which the penalties were based was before the bankruptcy court, but the penalties themselves weren't. In two recent decisions, however, the court changed its position on this practice.

The IRS had assessed penalties against people in bankruptcy proceedings, but the IRS didn't file claims for the penalties with the bankruptcy court. The taxpayers argued the penalties weren't before the bankruptcy court for action, so the Tax Court could consider them. But a Tax Court majority found that the bankruptcy court can rule on taxes or penalties even if it hasn't been asked to, so the Tax Court can't hear such disputes.

But a dissenting judge said the court should retain jurisdiction unless the bankruptcy court is petitioned to act.

Sharepe v. Commissioner, 69 T.C. 3
11/2/77

~

A golden silence: Is there a tax break in a failed recording studio?

Irvine P. Dungan was a lawyer with an entrepreneur's urges: He controlled a radio station and a background-music firm and started a recording studio. The studio made some tapes for hopeful rock-and-roll groups and advertising jingles, but soon went bust. Dungan dropped about $22,000, and deducted all his loss as a worthless business loan.

But the IRS argued he hadn't lent the studio money, he had contributed to its capital, and thus could take only the less-useful capital-loss deduction. The issue came down to whether Dungan intended to lend the studio money, or invest it and assume the risks of an owner; that intent was to be perceived from the evidence, the Tax Court noted. There wasn't a definite timetable for the studio to repay Dungan, there was scant record of its debt to him and interest wasn't paid, nor, it seemed, was any called for.

The facts "typify equity rather than debt," the court concluded, so Dungan had a capital loss.

Dungan v. Commissioner, T.C. Memo 1977-324
9/28/77

She paints, sculpts, draws, designs, writes, films and deducts.

Not once during 20 years did Gloria Churchman's income from her artistic endeavors exceed her expenses. And the Mill Valley, Calif., woman didn't depend on art for her livelihood; her husband was a writer, lecturer and Berkeley professor. Generally, one must be in business for profit to deduct business expenses. Consistent losses over a long period typically are used by the IRS to show lack of profit motive, and the agency barred Churchman's home office and expense write-offs.

She contended, however, that she had tried hard to make her art pay. She participated in art shows, sold a number of paintings locally, traveled to New York and San Francisco in an effort to have her work displayed in galleries and received a monetary grant to make a film. The Tax Court sided with Churchman.

"She intends to make a profit from her art-work, and she sincerely believes that if she continues to paint she will do so," the court decided.

Churchman v. Commissioner, 68 T.C. 59
8/17/77

～

"Dementia Investmentitis." A man afflicted with it pleaded for relief.

Its victims possess a "pitiful lack of investment acumen," according to John W. Herrick, a Fort Worth, Texas, attorney, who hasn't a medical degree, but labeled and brought the "disease" to the world's attention recently. Herrick said he knew he had the sickness after every investment he made became worthless. He asked the Tax Court to be considerate of his condition and rule against the IRS, which he accused of a "total lack of understanding." The granite hearted agency coldly barred the suffering attorney's $50,000 deduction for a bad investment.

Flushed with the disease, Herrick sank $50,000 into stock of a coin-dispenser maker, which proceeded to sink to new lows thereafter: The firm lost a customer that bought 99% of its output, and its finances shriveled to where nothing would be left for such shareholders as Herrick if the corporate corpus were liquidated. That was a clear symptom his shares were worthless and entitled him to the $50,000 deduction, he said. But the IRS said the business wasn't a terminal case: The president put in more money and still hoped to salvage it.

Poor Herrick. Because he couldn't prove the company hadn't any future, he couldn't take the deduction, the court concluded.

Herrick v. Commissioner, T.C. Memo 1977-171
6/22/77

Corporate Expenses and Deductions

Hard times: A $285,000 fine paid by The New York Times isn't deductible.

The newspaper paid $100,000 criminal contempt and $185,000 civil contempt of court fines for defying an order of a New Jersey state judge presiding over the mid-1978 murder trial of Dr. Mario E. Jascalevich. Sometime before the trial, Times reporter M. A. Farber wrote about the hospital murders for which the doctor was on trial. The judge wanted to see Farber's notes, but the reporter and his paper balked.

Farber went to jail for 40 days, the paper got fined, and eventually Dr. Jascalevich was found innocent by a jury. The Times's tax advisers said the $100,000 criminal contempt fine isn't deductible, but they said the $185,000 civil fine might be. However, an IRS spokesman notes that the Tax Court has ruled that civil contempt of court fines aren't deductible. And a Washington tax attorney asserts: "Civil contempt fines aren't deductible since they changed the tax code in 1969."

1/10/79

⌢

A payoff to an ex-X-ray associate was an X-rated tax deal, the tax enforcers said.

Three radiologists practiced together in a professional corporation they owned equally. But the two younger ones told the older one, who was in his 60s, that they wanted to end their association with him. He said he would leave the practice for the book value of his stock in the corporation plus $100,000. The corporation agreed to pay him "consulting fees" and "deferred compensation" totaling $100,000, payable over five years, plus buying his stock at book value.

The corporation deducted its payments under the "compensation" agreement. But the IRS said the payments actually were to buy his share of the practice; none of the money was for compensation and thus wasn't deductible. The IRS stressed that he hadn't been consulted once since leaving. However, the Tax Court had a different diagnosis.

The parties had entered into a bona fide contract "knowingly, voluntarily and willingly," and there wasn't any reason to set it aside. The payments were deductible.
Muskogee Radiological Group Inc. v. Commissioner, T.C. Memo 1978-490
12/27/78

⌒

Full-court press: A basketball team and the IRS fight over players.

The owners of the Supersonics paid the National Basketball Association $1,750,000 for the Seattle franchise in 1967. They allotted $1.6 million of that sum to player-acquisition costs and depreciated it over five years. Such hefty tax write-offs make owning a pro ball club attractive. However, the IRS said $1.6 million was too much for the privilege to pick some second-string players from other NBA teams and to join in a college-player draft.

Initially, the IRS said only $450,000 could be written off for the players; it okayed the five-year depreciation period. But later the IRS argued that the owners acquired a "mass of assets" that were so entwined they couldn't be valued separately, and thus couldn't be depreciated at all. The Tax Court rejected the IRS massasset argument. But the court deflated the owners' write-off, too. Only $500,000 was depreciable for the players, the court determined.

First Northwest Industries of America Inc., successor to Seattle Supersonics Corp. v. Commissioner, 70 T.C. 79
9/20/78

⁓

The annual report: Don't let it take away a tax break on inventories.

Year-end statements usually are computed soon after the year ends, but businesses can put off filing federal tax returns until September. However, the way inventories are valued in the annual report controls the way they must be valued for federal tax returns and most state returns. If a firm uses FIFO (first in, first out) on its year-end statement, it normally can't use LIFO (last in, first out) on its tax return, though LIFO can cut the firm's tax bill in inflationary times like the present.

For example, using LIFO cuts taxable income by $60,000 when an inventory that cost $1 million at the start of the year costs 6% more at year-end, says Marvin A. Kaufman, a tax partner at Alexander Grant & Co. Federal and state tax rates combined might run 50%, Kaufman notes, so LIFO would save $30,000 of taxes in this example.

The IRS has ruled that once a financial statement utilizing FIFO has been issued, it can't be amended to gain the tax benefits of LIFO for that year.

1/18/78

A booze dealer broke state laws on prices. Were kickbacks involved?

The firm sold liquor at legal wholesale prices, but delivered extra bottles in violation of state law. A customer paying for 12 bottles got 13. The extra bottles didn't add to gross receipts, of course, but the firm counted their cost in cost of goods sold, which was subtracted from gross receipts to arrive at gross income. The cost of the booze given away can't be deducted as part of cost of goods sold, the IRS said, and asserted the firm's gross income should be raised $135,000 and its taxable income increased accordingly.

The tax code bars deduction for illegal kickbacks. But the Tax Court and the Supreme Court have ruled that price rebates are adjustments to gross income and aren't deductions the code bars. The prohibition only covers expenses deducted *after* gross income is computed, the courts indicated. The IRS agreed with the courts for about 10 years, but changed its stance recently. A Tax Court majority, though, wouldn't change the court's position and rejected the IRS's argument to do so.

But four dissenters said the bottles given away didn't produce any receipts, so their cost didn't belong in cost of goods sold.

Max Sobel Wholesale Liquors v. Commissioner, 69 T.C. 36
12/28/77

⌒

Oyster babies do better in cradles of shells, the IRS learned.

When about 14 days old, oyster larvae form rudiments of a shell, and the weight makes them sink. They must find a clean hard surface to attach to, or they usually smother in muck on the bottom. The surface on the bottom to which they can cling is known as "cultch." A Baltimore concern dredged up dead oyster shells and sold them for use as cultch. It deducted the maximum yearly depletion allowance for oyster shells, 14%. But the IRS said it could take only 5%.

The law allows 14% depletion for shells sold for some uses, but permits only 5% if the shells are sold for use as "rip rap, ballast, road material, rubble, concrete aggregates or for similar purposes." The IRS argued that use as cultch fell under the 5% depletion uses. To permit 14% would give oyster shells an unfair edge over other materials competing for use as cultch, the agency contended. But the Tax Court didn't find any pearls of wisdom in those arguments.

Other materials can't compete with shells as cultch, for shells are better suited for that purpose, the court said. The 5% depletion uses don't include cultch, so the dredging concern could take 14% depletion, the court concluded.

C.J. *Langenfelder & Son Inc. v. Commissioner, 69 T.C. 28*
12/21/77

⌒

Pitch on San Diego isn't deductible for a publisher, the IRS says.

Copley Press Inc., publisher of a San Diego paper and ones in other cities, deducted $450,000 for a presentation on the San Diego market to 323 advertising people apparently brought to the city to view it. The IRS disallowed the deduction, challenging Copley's contention the outlay was an "ordinary and necessary" business expense.

The IRS also barred $302,000 of deductions Copley claimed for payments to such outfits as the California News Boy Foundation and the San Diego Junior Chamber of Commerce. They were charitable contributions, which the tax code limits to 5% of a corporation's taxable income, the IRS claims. Copley won't discuss the case. Altogether, the IRS wants the publisher to pay $922,000 in added tax for 1969-73.

Tax Court, Wash., D.C.
11/16/77

∽

A card case: Wherein Master Charge costs gave two banks deduction headaches.

Each bank paid a one-time, nonrefundable $10,000 fee to join Master Charge's credit card system. They also spent heavily for credit-screening, promotion, postage and other expenses to start up their Master Charge programs. They deducted these outlays, but the IRS barred them, and figured one bank owed some $380,000, the other $124,000 in added taxes.

.The money went for "preoperating expenses" to enter a new business, the IRS said, and wasn't deductible. And the outlays were "capital" in nature as they paid for benefits or assets with a life beyond the year in which they were paid. Wrong on both counts, the Tax Court told the IRS: Credit cards aren't a new business for banks. And the startup outlays weren't capital expenses, they went for "common and frequent" banking activities. They were deductible "ordinary" business expenses, the court concluded.

    The $10,000, however, was a membership fee that was a capital outlay and wasn't deductible, the court determined.

Iowa-Des Moines Nat'l Bank, U.S. Nat'l Bank of Omaha v. Commissioner,

68 T.C. 76
9/21/77

To raise the take from audits of big companies, the IRS has started using statistical sampling. If a sample of, say, travel vouchers finds 10% aren't detailed enough to qualify for a deduction, the IRS would bar a deduction for 10% of *all* travel vouchers, though all of them weren't actually audited. Price Waterhouse & Co. is reviewing the IRS's use of sampling in auditing the CPA firm's clients, Leon M. Nad, national tax partner, says. Statistical sampling has been used for years by CPA firms to audit clients' books.

IRS Manual Supplement MS 82G04
2/14/79

No tax break: Federal savings and loan associations can be fined by the Federal Home Loan Bank Board if they don't maintain liquid assets at a required level. And the fine won't be deductible, the IRS ruled, because the tax code bars a deduction for fines or penalties imposed by federal, state or local law.

Rev. Rul. 78-196
5/31/78

Mine mouth: A coal-mining outfit couldn't take a depletion deduction for coal mined in Kentucky under a verbal agreement with a landowner. The IRS ruled the oral contract wasn't enforceable under state law, so the mining firm hadn't an "economic interest" in the coal.

Rev. Rul. 77-341
10/5/77

Interest and Debt

I got $24,000 from my brother who owed it to me, an accused tax evader averred.

A jury convicted Leland M. Carriger of tax evasion. The IRS calculated his unreported income by the "net worth method." First his net worth, assets minus debts, for the beginning of the year in question was computed, then his spending was analyzed and his year-end net worth determined. The IRS calculations showed a substantial chunk of money unreported and that Carriger owed $13,000 in tax.

But he contended that his net worth was unduly big that year because of nontaxable revenue, $24,000 his brother Vernon repaid on a loan. Leland had notes Vernon signed to show the debt, and some witnesses who said they saw Vernon give Leland "a pile of money." But the trial judge barred the notes as evidence, weakening Leland's defense, and he was found guilty.

The trial judge erred, the Sixth Circuit Court of Appeals said; he should have admitted the notes as evidence. The court overturned Leland's conviction and said he was entitled to a new trial.
U.S. v. Carriger, U.S. Ct. of Appeals, 6th Circ., 1979
3/14/79

〜

He prospered in the stock market and helped a pal who didn't fare so well.

For many years, Samuel B. Levin worked full time investing in the stock market. The New York City resident built a portfolio worth several million dollars. Along the way he befriended Irving Like, also an investor but on a smaller scale than Levin. Both men bought Central Railroad of New Jersey shares before the company went bust. Levin owned some $1.5 million of Jersey Central stock and got Like voted to its board.

Later, Like needed money and Levin lent it to him. The loan helped cover Like's wife's surgery and his margin debt on Jersey Central stock. Like never repaid $36,000 he got from Levin; after six years, Levin was barred by state law from pressing for payment. Some years later, when the stock market soured and Levin's fortune shrank, he deducted the $36,000 as a business bad debt. But the IRS said he couldn't because he wasn't in the "business of trading stocks," and even if he were, the loan wasn't business-connected.

The Court of Claims said Levin was one of those rare persons who, for tax purposes, was a "securities trader." Even so, the loan to his friend wasn't business-connected.

Levin v. U.S., U.S. Ct. of Claims, 1979
2/28/79

⌣

It wasn't so dandy when Tandy swapped some bonds for common stock.

Tandy Corp. exchanged a $40 million bond issue for Tandy common. For each $1,000 of bonds, a bondholder got a premium: $1,144.61 of Tandy common based on its market price at that time. Tandy deducted some $2.8 million for accrued interest and "premium" expense based on the value of the stock. But the IRS said the bond indenture agreement said there wouldn't be any "payment or adjustment" on conversion of the bonds "on account of any interest accrued."

That meant Tandy hadn't paid interest or a premium to convert its bonds; it had made a nondeductible payment to "eliminate" its bond debt, the IRS argued. Tandy said another clause in the indenture document suggested that bondholders could get accrued interest and a premium. Indeed, the indenture could be read either way, a U.S. district court said. Tandy created this ambiguity and must bear the consequences, the court asserted, concluding that the company couldn't take the deduction.

Tandy could have written the indenture agreement "so as to clarify the present ambiguity and to avoid the very confusion that has given rise to this litigation," the court said.

Tandy Corp. v. U.S., U.S. Dist. Ct., No. Dist. of Texas, 1979
2/21/79

⌒

The patient got back in the driver's seat; the doctor suffered in the "crash."

Truck driver Don W. Jeffery had a ruptured disk removed and a spinal fusion performed by orthopedic surgeon William N. Harsha of Oklahoma City. But Jeffery's back was still too unstable for him to resume the lifting drivers normally must do. He became depressed and considered himself a "parasite," reliant on a veteran's pension and welfare.

Getting Jeffery back to work could help, Dr. Harsha decided, and sank $10,000 into a one-truck business for his patient. The driver's spirits and physical condition improved, but the trucking operation didn't. To "save it," the doctor arranged to buy 23 trucks for some $600,000 and extended $75,000 more to keep the firm going. At one point, he had guaranteed $900,000 of debt for the firm; when it folded he was able to settle these obligations for $209,000, which he deducted as a business bad debt.

But the doctor was out of luck, a federal appeals court ruled. He hadn't advanced the money for profit-making reasons, and thus he had a non-business loss, which is deductible like a short-term capital loss: only $3,000 a year.

Harsha v. U.S., U.S. Ct. of Appeals, 10th Circ., 1979
2/14/79

⌒

A dutiful son might have learned this tax dodge when he was an IRS agent.

Harold W. Wales, a tax lawyer and ex-IRS agent, got $4,000 from his mother; he promised to repay $8,000. He paid her about $300 a month and deducted nearly $200 of it as "interest." But the IRS said there wasn't a bona fide loan between mother and son and barred his interest deduction.

The Phoenix, Ariz., lawyer argued that he signed a note and owed a legally enforceable debt to his mother. Yet, she hadn't said when it must be repaid, hadn't asked for nor seen the note he signed, hadn't required the 10% interest rate he said he was paying her, and wasn't sure why he needed the $4,000—he made nearly $100,000 a year. However, she had asked him to supplement her income by $200 a month, the Tax Court noted in denying his deduction.

The "loan" plan was "an elaborate scheme" he devised to convert to deductible interest a big part of his nondeductible support payments to his mother, the court concluded.

Wales v. Commissioner, T.C. Memo 1978-125
4/12/78

How to treat an appendectomy or a gift to a hospital put on Master Charge.

The operation and the contribution are deductible, of course, but when are they deductible if they're put on a bank credit card such as Master Charge? The IRS recently provided the answer: Using a bank credit card is like using borrowed funds, and expenses paid with borrowed money are deductible when they are paid regardless of when the loan is repaid.

So medical care or contributions charged to a credit card normally will be deductible when the charge is made, the IRS says in two recent rulings. Its latest stance on contributions reverses a 1971 ruling that said credit-card contributions weren't deductible until the charge was paid.

Rev. Rul. 78-39 and 78-38
2/8/78

⌣

The tycoon vs. the IRS: A protracted contest over a $100 million deal.

When he borrowed $100 million in 1963 to buy Union Oil stock from Phillips Petroleum, shipping billionaire Daniel K. Ludwig used as collateral stock of a foreign tanker corporation he owned *in toto*. His tanker company had retained earnings of $5 million. The IRS claimed Ludwig's use of the stock caused the $5 million to be taxable to him under rules for taxing earnings of controlled foreign corporations.

Use of the stock as collateral made the company a "guarantor" of Ludwig's loan, and that made its retained earnings taxable income for him, the IRS argued. But that was an "expansive interpretation" of the law, the Tax Court asserted. The corporation wasn't a party to the loan agreement, hadn't said it would pay if Ludwig defaulted, and if he did, the banks couldn't make the firm pay; they could merely take over his stock, the court noted. So the company wasn't a guarantor and its retained earnings weren't taxable, the court concluded.

While this case took about 14 years, Ludwig took only two from when he bought the stock to sell it at a $45 million profit. He paid Uncle Sam $11.5 million tax on the gain.

Ludwig v. Commissioner, 68 T.C. 85
10/12/77

~

My seal means I am bound to pay my debt, a giving brother argued.

Joseph Linder lived with his sister, Rose, in his house in Bayonne, N.J. He wanted to bestow a sizable gift on Rose, but lacked the money. So, he signed "under seal" a mortgage on his house payable to Rose, and recorded the document as a lien on the property. Joseph paid Rose $7,000 over two years and deducted it as interest on his "debt."

But the IRS barred the deduction. Joseph merely had made a "gratuitous promise" to pay Rose; she hadn't given him anything in return for the alleged mortgage and she couldn't get a court to enforce his promise, the IRS noted. So, he hadn't incurred a legitimate debt and couldn't claim an interest deduction, the IRS asserted. Joseph argued that such a promise is legally enforceable in New Jersey when it is signed "under seal," an old practice that bound the signer to his word. But that wasn't true any longer, the Tax Court said after reviewing New Jersey law.

The "magic of the seal has long since been . . . exorcised in most American jurisdictions," the court observed.

Linder v. Commissioner, 68 T.C. 68
9/7/77

A dry cleaner got in a spot because he knew so little tax law.

Small-business owners often don't realize the tax consequences of their actions. John and Irene Russos bought a dry cleaning firm for $45,000, with $8,000 down. Regrettably, they had the company pay about $11,000 on what they owed. The corporation deducted the interest paid on their behalf. But the IRS said the debt was the couple's, so the company couldn't deduct the interest.

In that case, the $11,000 is added salary for us, the couple said, and it's deductible by our business. But the IRS said the money was a nondeductible dividend, as the Russos' hadn't intended for their company to pay them more money. The couple deserved more, the Tax Court noted sympathetically: John labored 80 hours, seven days a week and was paid only $13,000 a year; Irene worked 20 hours weekly and got nothing. Yet, the corporate records showed there wasn't any intent to count the $11,000 debt payments as compensation, the court said.

The case must be decided on "what was done" rather than on "what might have been done," so, the business couldn't deduct the payments, the court asserted.

Russos v. Commissioner, T.C. Memo 1977-309
9/21/77

⌒

Good parents who help pay the kids' college loans get no help from Uncle Sam.

Mary, LeAnne and John got government-guaranteed loans to help cover college costs. Their parents didn't cosign or otherwise guarantee payment, but they did make some payments on their kids' loans and deducted $800 of interest. The IRS disallowed the deduction. Interest usually is deductible, but it isn't when paid on other people's debts—even your own kids', the IRS contended.

The helpful parents argued that they had promised to meet some loan payments for their children. Their promise was a contract that made them responsible for payment, and thus entitled them to deduct the interest. That's good parenting, perhaps, but it isn't recognized in the tax code. Even if the parents had contracted with their children to make payment, the Tax Court declared, they still were "only secondarily liable" as guarantors for the loan, and get no interest deduction.

We have "consistently held that (interest) payments made by a guarantor aren't deductible," the court instructed.

Secunda v. Commissioner, T.C. Memo 1977-185
7/6/77

⌒

The sole proprietor gets a break from the Tax Court's change of heart.

The court eliminated a tax burden for sole proprietors who form corporations to take over their business. For a long time, the court backed the IRS position, which, loosely stated, is that if a cash-basis proprietorship has more liabilities than assets assumed by a corporation, the proprietor was taxed on the excess of the liabilities.

The IRS reasoned that the owner gained by having the corporation assume payment for liabilities he had owed. But the proprietorship's accounts receivable didn't count as assets that could be balanced against the liabilities, and that produced a "harsh result" for the owner, the Tax Court noted in rejecting its earlier position on this issue. The court observed that two appeals courts had reversed the Tax Court on this matter. Two judges dissented.

But in a concurring opinion, Judge Charles R. Simpson praised the Tax Court's change-of-heart and quoted the late Surpeme Court Justice, Felix Frankfurter: "Wisdom too often never comes, and so one ought not to reject it merely because it comes late."

Focth v. Commissioner 68 T.C. 21
6/1/77

⌒

What is it then? Usually four quarterly insurance premiums add up to more than the single annual premium because most insurance companies charge more for paying other than an annual premium. However, this added charge isn't interest, the IRS ruled. That means it isn't deductible. The IRS didn't say what the extra charge is . . . just what it isn't.

Rev. Rul. 79-187
6/27/79

⌒

A good boy borrowed $1,000 from his mother and took it on himself to pay her $50-a-month interest until he paid back the $1,000. The IRS said he could deduct only $7.50 a month as interest; the rest acutally was a nondeductible gift to mom. But the Tax Court said he could deduct $600 he paid her one year; it was deductible interest, even though paid to a relative.

Barton v. Commissioner, T.C. Memo 1979-234
6/20/79

Giving to Charities and Others

Will an Indian giver get hog tied by strings attached to her gift?

Indians occupied Alcatraz Island some years ago demanding that the penal colony be made a "cultural, educational and medical center" for Native American Indians and Alaskan Natives. Mitzi S. Briggs, a rich woman from Atherton, Calif., decided to help them by giving her 184-acre ranch for such a center. But she wanted to assure that the Indians would avoid militancy.

So she put conditions on the gift. The foundation the Indians set up for the center must be headed by a woman Briggs picked; they must raise the construction money; and if they abandoned the effort, the ranch reverted to Briggs. She deducted $507,000 for the gift. But the IRS barred the deduction. She might get the ranch back, the agency argued: The Indians had no fund raising know-how, resented the woman picked by Briggs, and thus, the whole thing might be abandoned. She argued that the chance of that was "so remote as to be negligible."

However, there was more than a "negligible" chance it would happen, the Tax Court said, so the gift wasn't deductible.

Briggs v. Commissioner, 72 T.C. 55
7/25/79

The "gas-guzzler" tax dodge begins by giving your gas-hog to charity.

Some savvy folks are donating gasoholic cars to Goodwill Industries and taking a charitable deduction. "This has been a real boon for us," says Joseph E. Pouliot, a Goodwill Industries vice president, "One car makes up for a lot of clothes." The Goodwill in Washington, D.C., received about 70 cars in the first half of 1979. "We usually get about three or four a year," spokeswoman Betsy Forte says. The agency made $25,000 from selling the cars.

The Bridgeport, Conn., Goodwill got 38 cars within 45 days and has sold 13 of them for a total $2,800. Owners normally deduct the car's "blue book" value, which is usually more than a dealer would pay for it, and many times it's more than Goodwill ends up selling it for in a gasoline-anxious atmosphere.

But the deduction someone takes "is between them and the IRS," a Goodwill official says. "We don't set values for tax deductions on these cars."

7/25/79

⁓

They avoided the World Council of Churches and fell prey to the IRS.

E. H. and Betty Lee Jones Winn gave $10,000 to Sara Barry, a Presbyterian missionary working in South Korea. The Greenville, Miss., couple's church was raising money for Barry's work, but the Winns didn't support the World Council of Churches and believed part of any donation to their church might go to the council; so they made a direct donation to Barry, who was Mr. Winn's cousin.

Donations to individuals—rather than to charitable organizations—for charity overseas normally aren't deductible. The IRS said the $10,000 went to an individual doing overseas charitable work and thus was nondeductible. The Winns argued that the money went for the church's overseas work and was deductible. The Fifth Circuit Court of Appeals decided that the money went "to or for the use of" the church to support its South Korean missionary effort and was deductible.

The appeals court decision overturns a Tax Court decision of a few years ago that went against the Winns.

> Winn v. Commissioner, U.S. Ct. of Appeals, 5th Circ., 1979
> 6/13/79

⌒

He took a deduction for being a good scout, but the IRS didn't salute.

David L. Hamilton was a good scout to a bunch of Girl Scouts. His wife Maggy was a scout leader, and he drove their four daughters and some other girls to Girl Scout functions. Transporting the kids cost $74 out of pocket, he figured, and deducted that amount as a charitable contribution.

Auto expenses incurred to render services to a charity normally are deductible. But the IRS said the Blue Springs, Mo., resident couldn't deduct the $74 because the Girl Scouts didn't benefit from his driving— his daughters and the other children did. The Tax Court agreed. Hamilton's kids were the beneficiaries; the deduction was barred.

"The presence of a substantial, direct, personal benefit to the taxpayer or to someone else other than the charity is fatal to the claim for a charitable contribution," the court asserted.

> Hamilton v. Commissioner, T.C. Memo 1979-196
> 6/13/79

Give them nothing: Scrooge would have loved this IRS ruling.

A family owned 25% of a company and decided to give some employes each 10 shares of the firm's stock to commemorate its 50th anniversary. But first they asked the IRS if it considered such gifts tax-free, so that: The employes wouldn't be taxed on the stock, there wouldn't be payroll taxes on the shares' value and there wouldn't be gift-tax liability to the family for giving the shares.

In a ruling that's sure to stifle such generous urges, the IRS ruled: The employes would owe income tax on the value of the stock they got, there would be withholding, Social Security and federal unemployment tax on the stock's value and the family would be liable for gift taxes because the gifts wouldn't qualify for the annual $3,000-per-recipient gift-tax exemption.

"It's a tough ruling," says Donald C. Alexander, a tax lawyer and former IRS commissioner. "If it is upheld, it will put a crimp in big stockholders giving employes stock."

IRS letter ruling 7916097
5/23/79

⌒

He played Santa to some politicians. The IRS, of course, played Scrooge.

A savvy Kansas City, Kans., lawyer, David W. Carson, gave local candidates more than $200,000 in campaign contributions over a four-year period. The IRS claimed the contributions were taxable gifts and told Carson he owed $12,500 of gift tax. Gifts usually are taxed; the giver normally pays the tax.

But Carson argued that campaign contributions are exempt from gift tax. The IRS, though, contended that nothing in the tax code exempts them. A Tax Court majority determined that campaign contributions are gift-tax free. The court noted that donations don't benefit a candidate personally, but rather aid his campaign. Also, the giver makes the donation to further his own views and aims, the court said, and thus the candidate can "be viewed . . . as the means to the ends of the contributor."

Three dissenting judges insisted that the majority's ruling changes the tax laws—something only Congress is supposed to do. There isn't any clear legislative intent to exempt campaign gifts from the tax, so they should be taxed, the dissenters argued.

Carson v. Commissioner, 71 T.C. 22
12/20/78

⌒

Ever wonder how much those who itemize deduct on their returns?

Commerce Clearing House, a tax information service, has computed the averages for 1976, the most recent year for which figures are available. CCH stresses that the numbers are averages only, that falling within them doesn't preclude an IRS audit, and that substantiation is required in an audit.

Adjusted Gross Income	Contributions	Interest
$10-15,000	$414	$1,378
15-20,000	472	1,690
20-25,000	542	1,836
25-30,000	646	1,977
30-50,000	939	2,366
50-100,000	2,015	3,954
Over 100,000	9,901	9,249

8/16/78

Wrong numbers: A court connected its own value to a phone stock.

Margaret K. Burgi was 78 years old when she gave a nephew and his family stock in a little phone firm she controlled to induce him to take over the business. She paid gift taxes based on the 5,712 shares valued at $14.25 each. But the IRS said each share was worth $83.20, which meant she owed $88,000 more tax. The IRS said a bigger phone company would value the shares at the higher figure by calculating what it could earn if it owned Miss Burgi's business.

Experts on her behalf (she died in the midst of the dispute) argued that the stock wasn't worth even its $39-a-share book value as it wasn't traded. In valuing small firms' shares, book value, earnings history and dividend-paying ability usually are considered. But there isn't any "general formula," a federal district court said. "There is no way of obtaining an average of several factors and basing the valuation on the result."

So courts use their own judgment. This time the court came up with $55-a-share, indicating the gift was worth $314,160. That's more than the $81,396 Miss Burgi's experts said. But less than the IRS's $475,238.

Estate of Margaret K. Burgi v. U.S., U.S. Dist. Ct., West Dist. Wis., 1976
5/17/78

⌒

Is a law firm generous? Well, see what the Tax Court said in this case.

Edward A. Ruestow was a lawyer employed by Kenyon & Kenyon Reilly Carr & Chapin, a New York City law firm. The firm dismissed him when he was about 61 years old. Ruestow's contract with the firm stated he would be paid $2,000 severance pay. But the firm gave him $30,000 when he left. Ruestow counted $2,000 as taxable severance pay and $28,000 as a nontaxable gift.

There wasn't any gift; the entire $30,000 was taxable income, the IRS said, noting that the law firm accounted for the whole amount as severance pay on its books. But Ruestow, who acted as his own attorney, argued that as the firm was obligated to pay only $2,000, the $28,000 excess was a nontaxable gift to him. However, "The mere absence of a legal or moral obligation" to pay doesn't "establish (a sum) is a gift," the Tax Court observed. And the law firm hadn't acted out of "disinterested generosity," the court said.

The firm anticipated economic benefit from retaining Ruestow's good will and from "creating the impression (it) was a good firm for which to work," the court remarked. So Ruestow owed tax on the entire $30,000.

Ruestow v. Commissioner, T.C. Memo 1978-147
5/3/78

⌒

Baby sitters: The IRS says they aren't deductible, but it isn't the last word.

If you use your car for a charity and aren't paid for it, the expense normally is deductible. But the IRS contends that baby sitters paid so a taxpayer can help out a charity aren't deductible. A New York City couple took the issue into Tax Court. They had deducted $180 for baby sitters so they could do volunteer work for charities; the IRS barred the deduction.

The IRS argued that a baby sitter is a personal expense and thus nondeductible. But the couple argued that a car also is a personal expense, but is deductible when used on behalf of a charity. So it should follow logically that baby sitters that free a taxpayer to do un-

paid charity work also should be deductible, they asserted. The Small Tax Case division of the Tax Court
agreed with the couple.

*However, their victory doesn't bind the IRS
except in their case, and the agency will bar the
deduction for other taxpayers, a spokesman said.*

T.C. Summary Opinion 1978-74
4/5/78

～

Motives do count when it comes to gifts, a fallen
union leader found.

Charges he misused union funds led to Milton
Weihrauch's being ousted as head of District 3 of the
International Union of Electrical, Radio and Machine
Workers. Yet, union officials solicited contributions for
him and honored him at a testimonial dinner. He received $13,900, figured it was a gift and didn't report it.
But the IRS figured it was taxable income. In determin-
ing if a gift has been made, the motives of the givers
often are crucial.

Weihrauch said his contributors didn't expect anything in return, nor look to be repaid, so the money was
a gift. However, forgoing repayment only meant the
sums weren't loans, the Tax Court said, and that didn't
make the money a gift. There must be "disinterested
generosity" resulting from "affection, respect, admira-
tion, charity or like impulses," the court asserted. The
contributions for Weihrauch didn't result from such
motives, the court concluded, but appeared to result
from "a sense of duty" to help a fellow union official.
So, Weihrauch owed tax on the $13,900.

*About 16 months after the testimonial in his
honor, Weihrauch pleaded guilty to embezzling
union funds.*

Weihrauch v. Commissioner, T.C. Memo 1978-9
1/25/78

Ski patrollers liked skiing, so the IRS wanted to ice their deduction.

Volunteers usually can deduct expenses linked to work for charitable organizations. The National Ski Patrol is one of those organizations; its 38,000 members police ski areas without pay, rendering aid to skiers. Marilyn and Charles McCollum and their two children were patrol members. At least one ski weekend a month they worked 12 hours a day without pay. The Huntington Beach, Calif., couple deducted $4,200 as a contribution to the ski patrol for expenses connected with their patrol work.

The IRS challenged the deduction. Among other things, the IRS argued that the couple enjoyed skiing, the patrol work and the camaraderie of other patrol members. That got an icy reception in the Tax Court. Many volunteers are enthusiastic about their work and enjoy it, but that isn't grounds for denying them a deduction, the court said.

Yet the court cut the deduction to $2,400. The couple couldn't deduct the value of their motor home as lodging as they didn't pay it out of pocket, the court said, though they could deduct motels when they stayed in them. Also, they couldn't write off their ski equipment but could deduct the cost of ski repairs.

McCollum v. Commissioner, T.C. Memo 1978-435
1/8/78

⌣

"A resurrected corpse" and Tastee Freez stock figure in this banking tale.

Tastee Freez settled a debt to a bank by giving it debentures in an arrangement under the Bankruptcy Act's Chapter 11. The bank valued the debentures at $3 and took a $594,000 bad debt deduction. Four years later, the bank exchanged the debentures for Tastee Freez stock valued at $660,000, donated the stock to a foundation and took a charitable deduction. Hold on, the tax code bars that kind of double tax break, the IRS complained.

The IRS argued that in effect the bank had "recovered" the bad debt it had written off and couldn't get another tax benefit from donating the stock. The bank argued that the original debt had been "fully satisfied" when it accepted the then-worthless debentures. The later gain in their value was a separate transaction and shouldn't be linked with the written-off debt.

When the once-worthless debentures gained value, "the corpse was resurrected," the Tax Court noted. But the court sided with the bank, though declaring it was "hardly free from doubt" about its decision.

Continental Illinois National Bank v. Commissioner, 69 T.C. 27
12/14/77

‿

A bundle of joy. An adopted baby is that, but she isn't an economic benefit.

Or so argued a couple who adopted an infant through a Catholic agency, which charged them $475 when they qualified to adopt the girl. The pair deducted the payment as a charitable contribution. But the IRS barred the deduction. The law permits a deduction only if it's made without a benefit in return.

The IRS contended that the couple got a benefit: the child. But the couple said it was "unrealistic to envision the adoption of a child" as being economically benefiting to them, though it was emotionally and spiritually beneficial. That wasn't the point, however, the Tax Court said.

*The $475 had to be paid by all parents the
agency served. The payment wasn't a contribution,
but an adoption fee, which wasn't deductible, the
court determined.*

Arceneaux v. Commissioner, T.C. Memo 1977-363
10/26/77

⌐⌐

Cytospora canker disease and expert opinions went
with this sylvan gift.

A generous fellow gave the Boys' Club of Minneapolis 266,000 uncut Christmas trees, and took himself a
generous $232,000 charitable deduction. But the IRS
said $21,000 was more like it, for the trees weren't in
such great shape: Two diseases, spruce needle miner
and cytospora canker, infected many of them. Too
much weedkiller discolored many trees, yet weeds flour-
ished and had to be killed before a required state inspection was possible.

An IRS-paid expert valued the evergreens at
$21,000, but experts for the taxpayer set much higher
values; one $107,000, the other, $232,000. So, the Tax
Court had to weigh the differing appraisals. It discount-
ed the IRS expert as he had tried unsuccessfully to buy
the trees and "had a proprietary interest" in a low value, the court said. The taxpayer's most generous ap-
praiser also was faulted. He had said he saw no weed
problem—but conceded in court he looked when two
feet of snow was on the ground.

*The court declared the trees were worth
$52,000.*

Estate of Stanley L. Wasie v. Commissioner, T.C. Memo 1977-323
9/28/77

⌐⌐

A "slumlord" learns that his slum has some value
—for tax purposes.

A Virginia man owned 47 units of low-income housing in a black area of Richmond. The buildings were half a century old, hadn't any indoor plumbing and provided little more than minimal shelter. The owner became the focus of press criticism and was labeled a "slumlord." He tried to donate the buildings to a charity but none would take them. So he created a tax-exempt foundation and gave the housing to it.

On his tax returns, the man deducted $60,120 as the value of the gift. The IRS contended that the property was worthless and barred the deduction. The Tax Court, however, decided that the buildings were worth something, but not as much as the owner claimed. His evaluation didn't take into account rent lost as vacancies developed, or such costs as taxes and maintenance. The court set the value at $25,000.

Pearsall v. Commissioner, T.C. Memo 1977-230
8/24/77

～

A humbling lesson? Two college profs had a high opinion of their worth.

They were husband and wife, both full-time college professors, working part time in a "Project Upward Bound" program to help deprived students. The project paid them for giving classroom instruction to the students, but not for other time devoted to the program. The couple worked 219 hours without pay. They deducted as charitable contributions nearly $5,500 based on $25 an hour for their time.

The IRS barred the deduction. Volunteers can't deduct contributions of their time, the agency said. The couple contended that rule shouldn't apply to them. They were different from ordinary volunteers, they donated "purely professional" services, so they should get a deduction for giving away something so valuable. That thesis got an "F" from the Tax Court. The law treats all volunteers alike, the court observed.

Etheridge v. Commissioner, T.C. Memo 1977-175
6/22/77

⌒

Painting nudes. Fouace and Morisot weren't known to. Was that a Clouet?

If the IRS challenges the value of a gift, the taxpayer must prove its worth. Robert E. Peters, of Scottsdale, Ariz., gave five paintings to the Minnesota Museum of Art and took a $100,000 charitable deduction, the art works' value according to his appraisers. The IRS, though, said $8,150 was more like it.

His art experts attributed one oil to Francois Clouet, whose works they conceded were hard to document, and valued it at $26,500. They valued two pictures of nudes at a total of $22,000. One was by Guillaume Fouace, the other by Berthe Morisot, Peters' appraisers said. But IRS experts said the alleged Clouet was by a lesser painter and worth only $2,000—if it were a Clouet it could be worth as much as $1 million. As for the nudes, Fouace and Morisot weren't known to have painted any; rather than $22,000, together they were worth only $150.

The Tax Court declined to rule on the art's authenticity, but not its value: It was worth only $8,700.

Peters v. Commissioner, T.C. Memo 1977-128
5/11/77

⌒

The IRS mind: Someone gave securities to a needy person and paid gift tax. During an audit, the IRS said the gift actually was income taxable to the needy person. So the gift giver asked the IRS to refund the gift tax. But the agency said that though there wasn't a gift for the recipient, there was a gift for the giver, and the IRS was keeping the gift tax.

IRS private letter ruling 7921017
6/6/79

∽

Back in 1970 an ex-Congressman, James H. Morrison, gave a bunch of his congressional papers to Southeastern Louisiana University and took a deduction based on the gift being worth $61,000. Eight years later, he learned in a Tax Court decision that such deductions have been outlawed since July 25, 1969, thanks to legislation designed to halt deductions such as the ones ex-President Nixon took for his official papers. The decision means Morrison will owe some $8,000 in tax.

Morrison v. Commissioner, 71 T.C. 64
2/7/79

∽

A vow of poverty meant he had to assign income from a trust to his religious order. But the trust papers barred any assignments. So he was liable for income tax on the money but could take a charitable deduction for giving it to his religious order, the IRS ruled.

Rev. Rul. 77-436
12/7/77

∽

Share my riches: A supervisor is getting added pay because his employer had a good year. He wants to share a third of his windfall with workers under him, but wants to deduct his gift. He can't, the IRS told him, as such sharing doesn't produce a deductible expense.

IRS private ruling, 7737002 and 7737014
9/21/77

∽

Bar associations in 32 states are so-called "integrated" bars, created by law to police legal practice for the states. For many years, the IRS considered donations to integrated bars deductible as contributions to a state entity. But no more: Noting that the bars serve both public and private purposes, the IRS ruled that donations after July 5, in most instances, won't qualify as charitable contributions.

Rev. Rul. 77-232
7/13/77

⌒

Hanging a judge. If you contribute to a trust set up to have a portrait painted of a certain federal district court judge, you get a deduction. The IRS ruled the donations are gifts to the U.S. for a public purpose. The painting is to be given to the court for display in the courthouse.

IRS private ruling 7723008
6/22/77

Travel and Convention Expenses

For business, a banker went to London and Rio with a bunch of builders.

Dallas-area contractors took trips set up by such suppliers as General Electric. James B. Walliser went along to promote loan business for his employer, First Federal Savings & Loan Association, in Dallas. His wife, Carol Sue, went. She said she didn't relax much as they socialized so much for business. The bank approved of their going, but didn't pay their way.

He deducted his costs as a business expense. (He didn't deduct Carol Sue's.) He didn't work on any specific deals on the trips, but he created a lot of good will, which resulted in deals later. Still, he couldn't deduct the trips. Costs to promote "good will in a social setting" aren't deductible, the Tax Court said.

Walliser v. Commissioner, 72 T.C. 40
6/20/79

◠

His job was working for a Ph.D., but that kind of work didn't move the IRS.

To meet his military obligation some years ago, Benjamin Taylor Jr. took a leave from the University of Pennsylvania, where he had been working toward a Ph.D. in bio-chemistry. He returned two years later. He deducted the $1,482 it cost to move back to the school in Philadelphia, but the IRS barred the deduction. The agency recently said he wasn't a school employe so he wasn't entitled to a moving-expense deduction.

Was he an employe? He did research in the school lab to complete his doctoral thesis. He didn't pay the school any tuition, nor did it pay him any money. Sometimes he did projects for a faculty member supervising his doctoral program. Usually an employer-employe relationship doesn't exist between a university and its students unless they are paid for certain services, the Tax Court observed.

Benjamin Taylor's relationship to the school founded by Benjamin Franklin wasn't that of an employe, and he wasn't entitled to deduct his moving expenses, the court concluded.

Taylor V. Commissioner, 71 T.C. 12
11/15/78

⌒

The uneven hand of the IRS raises the hackles of a retired postal employe.

He's James W. Keough of Springfield, Mass., who was elected a delegate to the national convention of the National Association of Retired Federal Employes. He deducted the $538 it cost him to attend the convention in Salt Lake City. Such expenses usually are deductible if the organization qualifies for tax exemption. However, the IRS said NARFE doesn't qualify.

Indeed, it doesn't because of its lobbying activities, says John F. McClelland, the association's out-going president. Still, NARFE delegates get the deduction from some IRS offices, McClelland notes. The retired U.S. employes group hasn't made any fuss over this. "We thought we would knock it out for those who got away with it."

But Keough, who took his case to Tax Court

and lost it (he owes the IRS $93.16), is steamed about "this discrimination." In the course of his research for his case, he says, he learned that the National Roller Hockey League qualified for the exemption.

T.C. Summary Opinion 1978-297
9/20/78

◠

Twisting his arm: He had to come home and take a month off.

Foreign Service employes are required to return to the U.S. every three years for home leave. David I. Hitchcock came back from Japan on a month's home leave. He toured America, doing what millions of vacationing Americans do each summer. However, he deducted nearly $600 for his food, lodging and transportation as expenses while away from home for business reasons. The IRS barred the deductions.

The outlays were for personal nondeductible expenses, the IRS argued, and the Tax Court agreed a few years ago. But an appeals court overturned the Tax Court's decision. Congress wanted Foreign Service employes to be brought home every three years to renew their feeling for the American way of life; mandatory home leave was part of the job, the appeals court observed.

Home leave "is an unavoidable expense" for such employes, the court asserted. Thus Hitchcock's travel, food and lodging while on home leave "relate primarily to his trade or business as a foreign service officer," and are deductible, the court declared.

Hitchcock v. Commissioner, U.S. Ct. of Appeals, 4th Circ., 1978
6/28/78

Home, sweet home: A traveling portrait salesman argued he had one.

Joram Rauchweger lived in Tulsa, Okla., for 16 years before he took a job as a photo-portrait sales consultant with a St. Louis, Mo., firm. The year he took the job, he spent a week in St. Louis training, then embarked on sales trips to 44 cities in 15 states before year-end. He deducted $4,300 for expenses while on business away from home.

The IRS barred the entire amount, contending Rauchweger hadn't a home to be away from. But he argued that Tulsa was his home. His father and step-mother were there, his mail went to them there and he kept most of his belongings in their home. However, he drove through Tulsa only once that year, maintained "no continuing abode" and "indeed ... had the trappings of an itinerant," the Tax Court said. So he couldn't take the deduction.

The away-from-home business deduction, among other things, is for taxpayers who incur duplicate expenses because of business travel, the court observed. Rauchweger hadn't these duplicate expenses, the court noted.

Rauchweger v. Commissioner, T.C. Memo 1978-177
5/24/78

⌒

A cabin in Montana is my home, he claimed, though he spent little time there.

After a divorce some years ago, Charles W. Rambo moved into a cabin in Beehive, Mont. He worked nearby for five years. But then his employer, a bridge-building outfit, assigned him to job sites in Florida, Puerto Rico and Utah. No assignment lasted more than a year, but he returned to his cabin only for a few weeks each year when he was on vacation. Yet, he considered it his home.

And he deducted $7,700 for food and lodging while "away from home" in pursuit of his trade. But the IRS contended he was an itinerant worker who carried his "tax home" on his back from work site to work site, and thus wasn't "away from home" and couldn't take the deductions. However, all his assignments since leaving Beehive were temporary ones, he returned to the cabin as often as he could—never vacationing anywhere else —and he had family in the area, the Tax Court noted.

It was "a close one," the court said, but the decision went to Rambo: His cabin was his home and he could deduct meals and lodging while working away from home.

Rambo v. Commissioner, 69 T.C. 79
3/29/78

⌒

Off to Florida and a deduction, too, was their wish.

Basil and Barbara Halkides spent 11 days in the sunshine state with their kids. They earlier signed to buy land there, and could cancel the contract only if they personally looked at the property. They did during the trip and canceled. They also met with someone from International House of Pancakes about acquiring a franchise in Florida. They deducted nearly $1,000 for the trip.

The IRS barred the deduction. The trip wasn't for business, it was a vacation, the IRS said. Indeed, "pursuits which could conceivably qualify" as business-related took up only 2½ hours of their time in Florida, the Tax Court noted with disapproval.

However, if the pair had "substantiated" expenses connected directly to the land deal or the franchise discussions, they might be deductible, the court said. But they hadn't and could deduct nothing, the court concluded.

Halkides v. Commissioner, T.C. Memo 1977-420
12/28/77

⌒

Expense money: A Disabled American Veterans' chief must account for it.

When Cecil W. Stevenson, a rural mailman from Jonesboro, Ark., was named national commander of the DAV, he took a leave of absence from the Post Office. He wasn't paid a salary, but the DAV gave him a monthly expense allowance that added up to about $41,000 while he was its chief; the DAV also paid about $11,000 of travel costs for Stevenson and his wife, Lillian, who often traveled with him. The couple reported as miscellaneous income about $5,200 from the DAV that they said exceeded their expenses while traveling extensively on behalf of the veterans' organization.

But the IRS said the Stevensons had to account for about $41,000 from the DAV. The couple didn't give the IRS any records, so the agency estimated their deductible DAV-related expenses and figured they had to pay tax on some $35,000. The Stevensons protested that the IRS was being arbitrary and unreasonable. But the Tax Court said it was the couple who had "forced (the IRS) to make" estimates.

The court did adjust the figures a bit: The Stevensons had to pay tax on nearly $32,000 and were liable for a 5% negligence penalty, the court concluded.

Stevenson v. Commissioner T.C. Memo 1977-260
9/7/77

An out-of-work writer swung a hammer far from home to make a buck.

James M. Waldrop was a South Carolinian whose home was on land owned by his family since 1772. He was primarily a writer (news, speeches, ads), but he couldn't find a writing job and took a carpenter's job at an atomic power plant site in North Carolina many miles from home. His employer offered to pay relocation expenses. But Waldrop regarded the job as temporary and didn't move his home. He rented a trailer at the job site and went back to South Carolina a lot. He deducted $3,200 for meals, travel and lodging while working "away from home."

But the IRS said he wasn't away from home. His home for tax purposes was where he worked, as it wasn't a temporary job for the project would take at least seven years, the IRS argued. The Tax Court rejected the IRS's argument. The job was temporary, and Waldrop considered it temporary, the court said. And his home remained South Carolina: His family had been there for generations, he went back every weekend and when a writing job there came along later he returned, the court noted.

"It is immaterial that the construction" project might go on for seven years, the court declared.

Waldrop v. Commissioner, T.C. Memo 1977-190
7/20/77

⌒

A hard-working guy trekked between Maryland and North Carolina.

Expenses while "away from home" in pursuit of business or a trade normally are deductible. But the "tax home" of construction workers is constantly contested by the IRS. A pipefitter-welder could find work only at an atomic power plant construction project in Lusby, Md. But he kept looking for work nearer his family in Creswell, N.C. He and his wife owned and rented out eight trailers in Creswell. The water supply there was acidic and eroded the pipes, causing a lot of repairs. He returned to Creswell almost every weekend to work on the trailers.

He deducted $8,000 for his meals and lodging in Lusby and for travel between Lusby and Creswell. The IRS barred the deductions, arguing his tax home was Maryland. But he said his Lusby job was temporary, Creswell had been his home for over 40 years and he had to return to care for the trailer-rental business there. The Tax Court agreed. It wasn't reasonable for him to move his family to Lusby, the court determined.

It wouldn't suggest he "forgo one business that's secure and producing steady income to move his tax home to a tandem job that's less stable" and could end "at any time," the court declared.

Patrick v. Commissioner, T.C. Memo 1977-15
6/1/77

〜

A year or two? That mattered a lot to a man in a temporary job location.

David M. Hummell moved to New York City from Ohio to do a job that took two years. He rented a house and brought his family with him. But he kept their Ohio home, his Ohio car registration and his right to vote in Ohio. When the job was done, he and the family returned to Ohio. Hummell figured he was "away from home" while in New York and entitled to deductions for lodging and some other expenses.

But the IRS said New York had become his tax

home for the two years. That time span was too long to be considered temporary, the IRS argued. The Tax Court noted that it had ruled that a one-year assignment was temporary. But in Hummell's case, two years was too much. Two years "can't be considered sufficiently temporary to justify" the deductions, the court asserted.

In Hummell's circumstances, "a two-year span is sufficient to justify the conclusion that Hummell could reasonably have been expected to move his residence" to New York, the court declared.

Hummell v. Commissioner, T.C. Memo 1977-135
5/18/77

◇

A diabetic's wife traveled with him. Could his business deduct her expenses?

Robert L. Quinn was the driving force responsible for the success of the athletic-playing-surface business he founded. He had to travel a lot for business reasons. However, Quinn had diabetes and his doctor advised him to take along someone who could assist in taking care of his illness. So, his late wife traveled with him, and the company picked up her expenses. But the IRS barred the deduction for her travel expenses and said the outlays were taxable income to Mrs. Quinn.

The IRS argued that there wasn't any business purpose for her to go on the trips, and suggested she went to get a vacation paid for by the business. The Tax Court noted that some places they visited were desirable vacation spots, but most weren't. Mrs. Quinn had been trained by her father, a prominent doctor, to care for her husband, the court observed. Her travel expenses were deductible by the business and not income taxable to her, the court concluded.

She was best qualified to care for Quinn and wouldn't have gone "had it not been essential" for business purposes, the court asserted.

Quinn v. U.S., U.S. Dist. Ct. Maryland, 1977
5/11/77

⌒

Submarine crew members often count the sub as their "tax home," and deduct their living expenses while on shore duty. The IRS has been trying to decide what to do about this situation since 1974. Finally, it recently decided to permit the deductions for all years up to 1979. But the agency says it's still pondering how it will treat the matter in 1979 and future years.

IRS Manual, MT 4500-273
3/14/79

⌒

Boat owners can take a tax credit for federal tax paid on gasoline and oil for their boats, Prentice Hall tax publisher advises. Boats qualify as "vehicles" that aren't registered for highway use. The credit is computed on Form 4136. But it is available only if a tax return is filed on time.

4/12/78

⌒

You gotta rest or sleep, it seems, to deduct a meal eaten alone after a long work day. When some sales people worked a 16-hour day, they stopped to eat on the way home. The IRS says their meals aren't deductible. If they had been away from home overnight, or had to stop to "sleep or rest" during the long work day, the meals may have been deductible, the IRS indicated.

IRS private ruling 7803046
2/22/78

News costs: Associated Press Washington reporter Peggy Simpson figures her job "required her to make contact with newsworthy individuals, news sources and fellow correspondents." So she spent $5,000 on business travel, entertainment, office space, telephone and wire service fees one year and the AP didn't reimburse her, Tax Court papers disclose. The IRS barred her deductions and says she owes $3,426 more tax for 1975.

T.C. Wash., D.C. Docket 3765-77
5/4/77

Education Expenses

Was it like this in the days of the one-room schoolhouse?

Teachers sometimes can deduct travel costs. But the travel must be related to their teaching duties. John A. and Marie C. Reilly taught in Los Angeles schools. The couple took a sabbatical, during which they took many trips, including four cruises. They deducted $10,400 of their travel costs as education expenses related to their teaching jobs.

However, the Tax Court barred the deduction, exclaiming: "There was nothing about (the travel) that was any more suited for a teacher than for some widow who was traveling on the proceeds of her deceased husband's life insurance." The court also barred a $2,400 deduction the Reillys claimed for a temporary move to Massachusetts near their parents' homes.

"Careful study of the record . . . convinces us that petitioners are attempting to abuse the educational expenses deduction," the court asserted.

Reilly v. Commissioner, T.C. Memo 1979-253
7/25/79

⌒

Two doctors won a rare victory in a dispute over their pay as residents.

Educational fellowships up to $300 a month often aren't taxed. Doctors in residency training programs sometimes get fellowship money and salaries for hospital work. The IRS says all the money is taxable because even though some is called a fellowship, it actually is pay for their hospital work. The IRS has won more than 50 Tax Court cases on this issue.

But Drs. Jerome and Rochelle Burstein, husband and wife, beat the IRS on this issue in the Court of Claims. A "definite part" of their activities at the Bernalillo County, New Mexico hospital "was entirely educational," a trial judge said. They were paid $300 a month as a fellowship plus $437 salary. The $300 was a nontaxable education grant, the trial judge concluded.

"The result is no more difficult to accept than that a college should give a cash scholarship grant to a student (which would be tax-free) and also employ him, for wages (subject to taxes) to serve in the college dining hall," the trial judge asserted.

Burstein v. U.S., U.S. Ct. of Claims, 1979
5/16/79

〜

He taught air safety, but couldn't fly a plane until he was forced to learn.

Yvan Roussel was a flight engineer and safety instructor to pilots at Flight Safety International, in Long Beach, Calif. His teaching was favorably reviewed by his students, except they complained that he couldn't teach from a pilot's point of view. After being threatened with dismissal because of this criticism, Roussel began taking flying lessons. He got a limited commercial license: He could fly passengers for hire only during daylight and then not beyond 50 miles.

The lessons cost $6,300, which he deducted for education to improve his job skills. But the IRS rejected the deduction, arguing that the lessons qualified him for a new trade: commercial pilot. Roussel said he didn't intend to be a commercial pilot. Besides, his limited license made it unlikely that he could make a living at it. Still, the law is clear: Education that qualifies an employe for a new trade isn't deductible.

The fact is that "he could take passengers for short joy rides on sunny days and be compensated," the Tax Court said, and it denied the deduction.

Roussel v. Commissioner, T.C. Memo 1975-125
4/25/79

A parochial school teacher went back to college and flunked a tax test.

The cost of education to "maintain or improve" job skills usually is deductible, but when education qualifies a taxpayer for a different job, it isn't deductible. Linda Liberi Toner, of Broomall, Pa., got a job as an elementary teacher in a Philadelphia Catholic school. The public schools required elementary teachers to have a college degree, but the Catholic schools required only a high school diploma, though they required teachers to take six college credits a year until they got a degree.

Toner had two years of college already; by taking more than six credits a year, she got her degree in two years. She deducted the cost of her college courses. But she wasn't entitled to a deduction, a Tax Court majority declared. She had qualified herself for a different job, *public school teacher*, so she couldn't take the deduction.

But seven of the court's 15 judges dissented. The tax code says teaching duties entail the "same general type of work," the dissenters noted, and that means she hadn't qualified for a different job; she had merely improved her job skills.

Toner v. Commissioner, 71 T.C. 72
2/21/79

The real godfather is a family business that pays a son's college expenses.

Salvatore M. Taormina went into the family trash business after high school; eventually he made vice president. He took some college courses, but to get his degree he took off nine months (with full pay) to go to college full time. The business reimbursed him $8,900 for his expenses while at college and deducted the entire amount. He didn't report it. But the IRS said the sum wasn't deductible by the business and was taxable income to Taormina.

College enhanced Taormina's job skills, was directly linked to his job and thus was deductible, the firm argued. And if it wasn't deductible for that reason, then it was deductible as compensation. But the Tax Court took a different course: Taormina's studies were general in nature and thus weren't linked to his job; there wasn't an intention for the money to be compensation. So the court found the business made a nondeductible gift to Taormina, who didn't have to count it as income.

"We see no reason why a 'corporate father' should fare any differently than a natural father (who of course, can't deduct a son's college costs)," the court said.

Anaheim Paper Mill Supplies Inc. v. Commissioner and
Taormina v. Commissioner, T.C. Memo 1978-86
3/22/78

⌒

Here's an apple for a teacher that the IRS didn't want to polish.

Margaret Laurano taught school in Canada. When she moved to New Jersey, she had to take a course to be certified to teach there. She deducted the cost of the course. But the IRS barred the deduction. The agency argued the course was required for her to meet "the minimum requirements" for a job and thus wasn't deductible.

However, the law gives teachers a special break, the Tax Court noted. In effect, it considers all teaching jobs as the same type of work. That meant Mrs. Laurano already had met "the minimum requirements" to be a teacher. So she could deduct the course because it was taken to "maintain or improve" her job skills, the court ruled.

The court noted that it had denied a New York lawyer a deduction for a bar review course he took for the California bar exam, ruling that the course helped him qualify for a new job, a licensed California attorney. Mrs. Laurano's case was different, the court said, and the law gives teachers a break denied lawyers.

Laurano v. Commissioner, 69 T.C. 60
3/1/78

⌒

His 'n' hers: The court divorced the costs of a teaching couple's trip.

He was a high school reading specialist, she a junior high school librarian. They motored through France, Spain and Morocco. They deducted $2,700 as job-related travel. The IRS nixed the entire amount, contending they hadn't shown the travel was for education directly related to their professions.

Because he was a reading specialist, the Tax Court couldn't find a direct link to his job. But she spent more than half her time lecturing or working with students and was more involved in teaching students than with traditional librarian duties. "Travel as a form of education would more likely be of direct benefit" to her job, the court said.

He didn't get any deduction. But she could

deduct the entire $796 of their car rentals and gasoline and half their other expenses, a total of $1,800, the court concluded.

Gibbons v. Commissioner, T.C. Memo 1978-75
3/8/78

〜

How smart? Two IRS agents passed CPA exams, but did they pass a tax test?

Each one paid about $400 for a Certified Public Accountant's review course to prepare for the Colorado state CPA License examinations. Both passed and were certified. They deducted the course costs as education expense to improve their job skills as IRS agents. But the IRS barred the deductions.

Becoming CPAs enhanced their job skills, the IRS agreed, but the law says expenses for education that prepares you "for a new trade or business" aren't deductible, regardless of whether it improves skills for your current job. The agents argued that they haven't left the IRS and don't intend to, so they hadn't acquired a new trade.

That wasn't the point, the Tax Court said. It didn't matter if they actually went into another trade. The fact the courses qualified them for a new trade denied them the deduction.

Sevier and Imbornone v. Commissioner, T.C. Memo 1977-346
10/12/77

〜

Travel lesson: The IRS learned about a "new breed" of educator.

Gladys L. Haynie, an assistant high school principal in Los Angeles's Watts area, worked to make the school responsive to students of differing racial and cultural backgrounds. After some years on the job, she took a two-year sabbatical to visit 44 countries. By talking with foreign educators, students and officials, she learned new ways to deal with problems she faced in her work. She deducted $10,700 of her travel costs as job-related expenses.

But the IRS said most of her activity abroad didn't relate directly to a skill needed for her job, so most of the costs weren't deductible. True, her travel often didn't relate directly to a specific skill in the way visits to historic sites relate to teaching history, the Tax Court noted. But that didn't deprive her of a full deduction, the court determined.

Miss Haynie is one of a "new breed" of school administrators using new methods to cope with problems of "troubled schools ... in racially and culturally diverse neighborhoods," the court asserted, and her trip enhanced her ability to do her job.

> *Haynie v. Commissioner, T.C. Memo 1977-330*
> *10/5/77*

⌒

The IRS is reminded that its rules aren't always law.

Education costs usually are deductible if the schooling improves skills required by the taxpayer's job. The IRS didn't deny that graduate courses improved Robert John Picknally's skills as a school administrator, but barred his deduction, contending he wasn't employed in education while taking the courses.

He wasn't: He had worked about 10 years in school jobs, but resigned to go full-time to grad school, and was out of work for three years. The IRS said its regulations permit only a "temporary" suspension from work and defines "temporary" as a year or less—any more and the deduction is lost. However, the Tax Court admon-

ished the IRS that in other cases the court had told the
agency its rule on this wasn't the final word; each case
would be judged on the facts.

*Picknally "actively sought" a job in educa-
tion after finishing his courses: He wrote schools
for employment, he listed himself with two college
job-finding offices, the court noted. So, he "wasn't
an inactive" member of the teaching profession
and was entitled to the deduction, the court said.*

Picknally v. Commissioner, T.C. Memo 197 -321
9/28/77

⌒

A deductible way to travel. Teachers angle for that
every summer.

Two teachers who were husband and wife spent 54
days in Europe. They deducted $2,700 of the cost as em-
ploye business travel. But the IRS challenged them. To
be deductible, the trip had to relate directly to their
jobs, and had to directly maintain or improve skills
their employment required.

Their high school classes "only peripherally related to" what they learned in Europe, the IRS argued, as
neither taught European history, art or culture. But the
couple had letters from their principals saying the trip
would be valuable to their jobs. And they argued that
they hadn't gone as tourists, they had collected abun-
dant information in Europe and compiled a slide show
used in their schools. But the Tax Court denied them
the deduction.

*The court said it couldn't find that the main
result of the trip was "to develop or improve a specific skill or area of knowledge which is of central
importance to accomplishing" their jobs.*

Allison v. Commissioner, T.C. Memo 1977-277
8/31/77

Entertainment Outlays

All is not lost: Deductions may survive for yachts and hunting lodges.

"Entertainment facilities" such as yachts, hunting lodges and fishing camps aren't deductible anymore, thanks to 1978 tax legislation. But the new rules seem to be less severe than originally believed, says Paul A. Schecter, partner at Coopers & Lybrand, a CPA firm. Businesses can't deduct expenses to keep a yacht, but the cost of "business entertainment" on the boat—food, drink, waiters and so forth—should be deductible, he says.

And Randall Snowling, a Coopers & Lybrand tax manager, suggests that when a facility is used for both entertainment and business purposes other than entertaining, then depreciation, maintenance and operating costs allocable to the other business use should be deductible. It might be hard to prove a hunting lodge is used for a business purpose other than entertainment, but fairly easy to show an airplane had dual uses, Snowling says.

Taxes and interest on entertainment facilities are still deductible, as are casualty losses, according to an official congressional explanation of the 1978 legislation.

7/18/79

⌣

A Bar Mitzvah was a blessed event, then the IRS came around.

To celebrate his son David's Bar Mitzvah, Arthur I. Fixler threw a party that cost $4,200. Of the 150 or so people who attended, most were relatives or friends, but 67 were business associates of Fixler, a principal in the accounting firm of Laventhol & Horwath, in Providence, R.I.

The proud father deducted $1,800 of the party expense as business entertainment. But the IRS barred the deduction. There wasn't any substantial business activity or discussion before, during or immediately after the party, the IRS said. Indeed, Fixler failed to show the party was directly related business entertainment or entertainment associated with business activities, the Tax Court decided.

The court chided the accounting firm executive for "gross carelessness" in preparing his return because of a lack of records to support charitable deductions.

Fixler v. Commissioner, T.C. Memo 1978-423
11/1/78

⌒

The IRS tells Congressmen what entertainment they can deduct.

Like other folks, members of Congress can deduct ordinary and necessary business expenses connected with their job. They can deduct the cost of taking a constituent to lunch. That's neither a campaign nor a personal expense, the IRS says, and thus is deductible.

But a party for staffers who are paid out of a lawmaker's annual congressional allowance isn't deductible. The employe-employer relationship necessary for a deduction doesn't exist; the staffers are employes of the U.S. rather than the member of Congress, the IRS observes.

Finally, a cocktail party and buffet to enable constituents and a member of Congress to exchange views and discuss government affairs and policy aren't deductible. The "surroundings" at such a party "aren't conducive to the discussion of business," the IRS asserts.

Rev. Rul. 78-373
11/1/78

⌒

Bending elbows, rather than twisting arms, was how he sold whisky.

Charles Diller was a successful, veteran liquor salesman with 114 accounts in San Francisco. When he called on a bar he was expected to buy drinks for the owner, bartender and their customers. Diller wasn't reimbursed by his employer and he deducted $5,900 he spent for drinks one year (when his income was $27,500.) The IRS barred the deduction, claiming he hadn't shown a business reason for the outlay.

In his daily diary each year he listed the names of owners and bartenders in his January entries. But the other months he noted only the name of the bar and the amount spent each day. Because he didn't list the names of everyone he bought drinks for, he failed to meet rules for substantiating business entertainment deductions, the IRS argued. However, the tax rules require only enough data to show a business relationship, the Tax Court noted.

Diller provided sufficient information to "clearly reflect" the business relationships involved in his drink buying, and he could deduct the $5,900, the court said.

Diller v. Commissioner, T.C. Memo 1978-321
8/30/78

A public defender is denied a tax break given lawyers in private practice.

Kenneth Wells, the public defender of Sacramento County, Calif., since 1963, took some of his staff to lunch about once a month, sometimes to his golf club. He deducted $1,200 for the meals and $408 of his $624 club dues. The IRS barred the deductions, contending they weren't "ordinary and necessary" expenses. One element of "ordinary and necessary" is whether an activity is reasonable.

It was reasonable for him to take key staff people to lunch to discuss the office, Wells argued. His job was akin to a law firm senior partner's, the Tax Court agreed, and a private firm could deduct such expenses. But the public defender couldn't, the court said. The county didn't provide funds for such activity, nor was it something the "usual civil servant" could afford, the court noted. (Wells had income in addition to his county salary.) Also, the meals might have benefited the defender's office, but Wells individually couldn't deduct them, the court asserted.

Wells says he will appeal to the Ninth Circuit. About $800 of tax is at stake.

Wells v. Commissioner, T.C. Memo 1977-419
1/4/78

⌒

Can shop talk fortify an island retreat against an IRS assault?

Entertaining customers merely to create good will isn't deductible, some courts have ruled; entertainment must relate directly to the "active conduct of business." A castings and forgings maker kept a fishing and hunting lodge on Ocracoke Island, off North Carolina's shore. The company took up to 30 customers at a time there for relaxed recreational weekends, but its executives pressed business discussions.

The IRS challenged nearly $300,000 the concern deducted for its Ocracoke retreat. The lodge "furthered business," the IRS agreed. But it wasn't directly related to the active conduct of business, for business was only a byproduct of these pleasure excursions, the IRS claimed. Not so, the company said: Substantial business discussions took place: Customers brought plans and discussed specific jobs.

The lodge was deductible. There was a "strong showing of substantive business purpose (to the) Ocracoke entertainment," the Tax Court declared.

Berkley Machine Works & Foundry Co. v. Commissioner, T.C. Memo 1977-
177
6/29/77

Other Business Expenses

Fee. Fie! A broker became an IRS foe over a modest sum—a mere $7,500.

The $7,500 was the fee Richard S. Harman had to pay to be a member of the New York Stock Exchange after he paid $80,500 for an exchange seat. The self-employed New York City broker deducted the fee.

The IRS contended he had made a capital outlay for a "business benefit," trading on the Big Board, and it extended past the year of payment and had an "indefinite" useful life, and thus was nondeductible. Harman argued that the fee was an "ordinary and necessary" business expense, thus deductible. The IRS was correct, the Tax Court said.

Fees to join a real estate multiple listing service, to join the bar to practice law or for staff privileges at a hospital aren't deductible, the court observed.

Harman v. Commissioner, 72 T.C. 32
5/30/79

∽

It may seem like slavery to fill out your tax return, but it really isn't.

Or so a court determined in a case that might have special meaning for people feeling sorry for themselves for having to do their own tax returns. Alexander Dean Walter Jr., Redlands, Calif., did his own return and deducted $309 as "income tax costs." He figured 61.8 hours of his time at $5 an hour for doing his tax forms.

If he had paid that $309 to a tax accountant or return preparer, he could deduct it without question. But he didn't, and the IRS barred the deduction, reminding Walter that you can't deduct your own labor. He argued that denying the deduction meant he was in "involuntary servitude" for the government and that's outlawed by the 13th Amendment's abolition of slavery. However, the work to fill out a return is "a necessary corollary to the requirement that a return be filed," the Tax Court said. While there isn't a deduction for doing it yourself, there is a reward, the court declared:

"His reward is the privilege of living in a civilized society. ...." Next case.

Walter v. Commissioner, T.C. Memo 1979-132
4/18/79

⌒

She saw her poems in print, but that cost her $3,000.

Fannie B. Hawkins, a legal secretary, had 43 of her poems published in a 56-page book, "Within the Heart of a Woman." But the Los Angeles writer had to pay $3,000 to have the book published by Vantage Press Inc. Vantage is the largest "vanity" publisher; it publishes at the author's expense, the reverse of the usual process: Most publishers pay authors. Mrs. Hawkins was to get back $1.98 for each of the first 4,000 books sold.

The first year only 350 to 400 were sold. Still she deducted $3,000 for expenses to publish her book. But the IRS blue-penciled her write-off, arguing that she hadn't intended to make a profit from her poems and thus could deduct expenses only to the extent of her writing income. Mrs. Hawkins failed to refute the IRS's contentions. She didn't say how much revenue she got from the books that were sold, and she didn't show whether she intended to continue writing "with substantial regularity" and "with the purpose of producing income and a livelihood," the Tax Court said.

The court said it couldn't "distinguish Mrs. Hawkins from someone who writes for a hobby and pays to have the book published for reasons of personal satisfaction" rather than profit.

Hawkins v. Commissioner, T.C. Memo 1979-101
3/28/79

⌒

A good scout? He paid some expenses that the company might have paid.

But Leon D. Horowitz was a major shareholder and president of the company, Camp Skylemar Inc., which owned and operated a boys' camp in Naples, Maine. Most of his income was from his job as a coach and teacher in Baltimore. He worked full-time for the camp only in the summer.

But the rest of the year he traveled, recruiting campers and doing other camp business. The camp wasn't a smashing financial success: Some years it could pay Horowitz only $1,000 or $2,000 salary, though he was supposed to get $5,000. Sometimes it reimbursed him for his travel expenses, sometimes it didn't. One year he deducted $4,000 of unreimbursed camp expenses. But the Tax Court axed the deduction.

"We have held on numerous occasions that a shareholder isn't entitled to deduct from his personal income payment of expenses made on behalf of the corporation," the court asserted.

Horowitz v. Commissioner, T.C. Memo 1979-27
2/7/79

A sorry doc went to court to stay out of the Navy, and the IRS sailed into view.

William P. West agreed to serve two years' active duty with the Navy in exchange for the Navy waiting for him to finish his residency training. The agreement assured the Minneapolis physician of completing his residency training without interruption for military service. His residency ended in 1974, and soon he got orders to report for duty. But the doctor regretted the deal and sought to have it rescinded.

He spent $1,200 on legal fees fighting to stay out of the service—but didn't succeed. He deducted the legal fees as a business related expense. But the IRS barred the deduction. The IRS argued that it was a nondeductible personal expense. He argued that it was connected to his medical practice: Winning the battle would have allowed him to begin practice sooner. But the origin of a legal skirmish determines its deductibility, the Tax Court noted.

And the origin of his legal contest was the doctor's personal decision to defer his military service. So the legal fees weren't deductible, the court concluded.

West v. Commissioner, 71 T.C. 48
1/31/79

⌒

Polo was his game, but he had to play this chukker with the IRS.

Custom-home builder Robert J. Sieber played polo for years. He introduced his sons to the game. Sieber's championship team, the Queen City Polo Club, in Cincinnati, was composed of him and his three boys. His daughter helped by walking the horses, his wife by fixing food for them.

But it was more than a family pursuit; it got him

lots of business, Sieber thought. So he deducted $8,500 it cost him to play the game one year. But the IRS said neigh to that. The builder argued that several jobs resulted from his polo-playing contacts, publicity about his play helped business and polo "enabled him to meet wealthy people" who might become customers. That didn't score in Tax Court.

Polo was a personal and definitely nondeductible pursuit in this instance, the court said.

Sieber v. Commissioner, T.C. Memo 1979-15
1/24/79

⌒

Death of a "Salesman." A man claimed to be one to save some tax.

Richard A. Lovern was responsible for ship loading and unloading for a stevedoring firm in Seattle, Wash. He worked away from the firm's premises and ran up expenses for which he wasn't reimbursed. He deducted auto, phone, office and utility costs on his tax return even though he took the standard deduction rather than itemizing.

Outside salesmen get special treatment in the tax code and can deduct such costs even when they use the standard deduction. But the IRS said Lovern wasn't a salesman. He countered that his job involved "selling" stevedoring services. But the Tax Court said his work didn't come close to filling the description of a salesman, and went on to recite this passage from Arthur Miller's play, "Death of a Salesman":

"He don't put a bolt to a nut, he don't tell you the law, or give you medicine. He's a man way out there in the blue, riding on a smile and a shoeshine."

Lovern v. Commissioner, T.C. Memo 1978-479
1/3/79

What the kids had to wear to work at the super-markets wasn't chic at all.

White dress shirts (gold blouses for the girls), dark slacks and leather shoes "capable of holding a polish" were required for employes at Knowlan's Supermarket, in St. Paul, Minn. Eileen and Robert Harrison's three children worked at the market and had to have the outfits. Their parents bought the clothes and deducted the $200 they cost, But the IRS barred the deduction.

The Harrisons argued in Tax Court that special clothing for a job is deductible. The kids' work clothes normally wouldn't be uniforms, but they refused to be seen in the outfits outside work because the clothes were so unfashionable. Thus the outfits were special-purpose clothing and deductible, the parents urged. Even if the clothes were deductible, it wouldn't be a deduction for the parents, the Tax Court said.

When parents incur an expense connected to their children's employment, it is treated as if paid by the children. But the Harrison kids didn't make enough for the deduction to be worthwhile to them. Their parents owe the IRS $50, the court concluded.

Harrison v. Commissioner, T.C. Memo 1978-476
12/6/78

⌣

Someone killed his wife. The cops said he did it, and that cost him plenty.

After Vernon L. Johnson was indicted for the murder of his wife, he was dismissed from his job. He owned a small tavern, however, that brought him some income. About a year after the indictment, the charges were dropped, and he got back his job. He figured he had lost $19,500 in wages during his layoff; his legal defense cost nearly $3,000.

Johnson deducted the lost wages as a casualty loss, the legal costs as a business expense. The lost wages were a casualty loss that resulted from his being charged with murder, he argued. Defending himself against the charge was a business expense because a successful defense was important to the solvency of his tavern. Legal theory, however, doesn't support a casualty-loss deduction for money that might have been earned but isn't, the Tax Court said.

His defense might have been important to the solvency of the tavern, but the murder charge wasn't connected to his business, the court said, so the cost of his defense was a personal, nondeductible expense.

Johnson v. Commissioner, T.C. Memo 1978-395
10/25/78

⌒

Some angry heirs got $121,000 from an attorney worried about his reputation.

A widow changed her will to cut out relatives and leave her assets to William J. McDonald, a Geneva, N.Y., lawyer and his wife Elizabeth. They had befriended the woman, who noted in her will that they were "consistently faithful" to her. McDonald didn't prepare the will. Yet, when she died, angry relatives challenged the will, alleging the McDonalds had unduly influenced the widow.

Alarmed by the potentially damaging allegations, the attorney paid the relatives $121,000 to withdraw their litigation and deducted the payment as a business expense to maintain his lawyerly reputation. A while ago, the Tax Court upheld the deduction. But recently an appeals court said the Tax Court erred. His reasons for settling didn't determine if the payment was deductible, but the origin of the litigation did, the appeals court said.

The litigation resulted from a personal relationship with the dead woman—the relatives alleged an abuse of her friendship. The legal action didn't result from his activities as an attorney, so the $121,000 to settle the lawsuit was a personal, nondeductible cost, the court said.

McDonald v. Commissioner, U.S. Ct. of Appeals, 2nd Circ., 1978
8/30/78

He called it "fantastic." The authorities called it "novel."

But it wasn't deductible. An Atherton, Calif., tax-shelter annuity salesman, Carl R. Johnson, claimed to be conducting research in economics. He was on the verge, he said, of evolving a theory that would result in a new form of economics, "which would be a fantastic thing, profitable for me and also for the country." Johnson wasn't able to explain the precise nature of the research to the Tax Court, but it had something to do with gross national product.

Johnson deducted all of his and his wife's living expenses—food, shelter, clothing and transportation—as "research and experimental" expenses. After all, he argued, the expenditures all contributed to the GNP, the subject of the research. While many types of research costs are deductible, the Tax Court said the Johnsons' expenses clearly were personal and nondeductible, despite the "purported" research.

"We question whether (the Johnsons) are proceeding in good faith," the court said.

Johnson v. Commissioner, T.C. Memo 1978-293
8/23/78

He served a Senator at great cost to himself and without thanks from the IRS.

Gerald W. Frank is an aide to Sen. Mark O. Hatfield of Oregon. In his first four years on the job, Frank spent $117,000 of his own money doing things for the Senator. He traveled widely to report to Hatfield on various areas of the world. None of his expenses were reimbursed. Frank deducted the $117,000. The IRS barred the deductions.

The IRS didn't dispute the amounts deducted, but claimed they weren't deductible because Frank hadn't taken the Senate post for a profit. The agency argued that without a profit-making motive he wasn't entitled to deduct the outlays as business expenses. But expenses of bona fide public employes usually are deductible, an appeals court declared. Frank could take the deductions.

The Salem, Ore., businessman could afford such hefty expenses even though the Senate paid him only $1,200 a year. His business provided him an income of $88,000 a year.

Frank v. U.S., U.S. Ct. of Appeals, 9th Circ., 1978
8/2/78

          ◇

If you're evicted for nonpayment of rent, can you still tell the truth?

The IRS doesn't seem to think so. Jack H. Barry deducted $12,500 of business expenses connected with his job, selling life insurance. The IRS barred the entire sum because he didn't have any records to prove the deductions. Barry said his records got lost when he moved from one apartment to another.

When taxpayers haven't any records, the Tax Court must rely on their testimony. And the IRS attacked Barry's credibility because he was evicted from his apartment apparently for nonpayment of rent. But this ploy backfired. "Rather than undermining (his) credibility, eviction for nonpayment supports (his) testimony that he incurred substantial expenses in earning the income (the IRS) now seeks to tax," the court observed. Barry's inability to pay his rent "doesn't detract from his credibility," the court asserted.

But without records to substantiate business, travel and entertainment deductions, the court allowed him only $3,900 of the $12,500 of deductions he had listed.

Barry v. Commissioner, T.C. Memo 1978-250
7/19/78

〜

An experimenter said he worked for himself, but the IRS said he didn't.

Edwin T. Lumb was a merchant seaman. While ashore, he worked on developing machines that he hoped to patent and sell. He bought equipment for his experiments under the name Safire Products Co., a sole proprietorship. But he also set up a corporation with a similar name, Safire Products Inc., which he planned to have produce his successful experiments. There weren't any.

On his personal return, Lumb deducted $10,000 of losses from the proprietorship. But the IRS barred the deductions. Lumb was an unpaid employe of the corporation doing experimental work, the IRS argued. His outlays for the experiments were nondeductible contributions to the corporation's capital account, the agency said. Lumb said the development work was done by him personally as a sole proprietor, not as an employe of the corporation.

Lumb intended to develop promising new machines personally and only bring the corporation

in to produce his successes, the Tax Court ob-
served. So he could deduct the losses incurred in
the development effort, the court concluded.

Lumb v. Commissioner, T.C. Memo 1978-245
7/12/78

∽

They sailed round the world, but deducting the
cost wasn't such a breeze.

Charles H. Carter, a rich lawyer, chucked his practice, bought a yacht, took his wife, Virgie Ann, and their
three kids and sailed away from California to roam the
world. They sold some articles about their ventures, but
books and films they made went unsold. They also oc-
casionally chartered the yacht. Charters and writing together provided $4,800 of income over three years.

Expenses, however, ran $38,000; the couple deduct-
ed that amount as business expenses for their writing
and chartering. But the IRS torpedoed the entire sum,
saying they hadn't intended to make a profit from
either pursuit. Carter conceded he wanted to begin a
new way of life to get away from the pressures of his law
career. So the trip mainly was for personal purposes,
the Tax Court ruled.

The couple couldn't convert personal expen-
ses "into business expenses simply by writing
about their personal experiences," the court as-
serted. However, they could deduct expenses up to
the amount of the gross income from their writings
and the charters, the court said.

Carter v. Commissioner, T.C. Memo 1978-202
6/14/78

∽

A lead foot in a midget racer is an accountant
trying to outrun the IRS.

Raymond K. Burrous owned and piloted a midget

race car with "Burrous Accounting Special" on it. He gave business cards to fans who swarmed to the pits after races, and he got a lot of publicity for winning a lot of races. That was good for his accounting practice, which increased markedly in the years he raced. So he wrote off the car as an advertising expense. But the IRS didn't allow the deduction.

There wasn't a close link between his racing and the business's growth, the IRS argued. The car's costs were 25% of his accounting practice receipts, and that was "unreasonably high when compared to the calculated benefits," the Tax Court said, noting that deducting the expenses would leave Burrous's business in the red with no taxable income.

"Any publicity resulting from his racing tended to promote (him) as a sportsman rather than as an accountant," the court averred.

Burrous v. Commissioner, T.C. Memo 1977-364
10/26/77

～

It isn't cheap to run for elected office, even in a union local.

James L. Easley spent about $6,400 trying to win votes to be secretary-treasurer of a Teamsters local. He didn't make it, but he deducted his campaign costs. The IRS barred the deduction, contending campaign expenses aren't deductible.

That applies only to elections for public office, Easley claimed, and shouldn't apply to private elective positions. He argued that the post he sought paid a good salary and his campaign costs were similar to employment-agency fees paid to get a new job, which are deductible. But the Tax Court didn't buy his argument. There isn't a specific law permitting such deductions, the court observed.

If a deduction is to be allowed, "Congress should unequivocally so provide," the court declared.

> *Easley v. Commissioner, T.C. Memo 1977-341*
> *10/19/77*

〜

A dam site better: So much better the owner has to fight for a deduction.

After Sam C. Evans acquired a farm, the earthen dam on the place began to leak. A contractor stopped the leak by draining the reservoir behind the dam and sealing it with 10,000 cubic yards of clay. That cost Evans $50,000, which he deducted as an ordinary and necessary expense of the farm. But the IRS said the $50,000 was a capital expenditure; it couldn't be deducted all at once, but over a number of years.

The IRS argued that the repairs materially added to the value and prolonged the life of Evans's dam, and thus the expense was a capital outlay. The Tax Court earlier had sided with the IRS. But later a federal appeals court sided with Evans, and reversed the Tax Court. The work was done to keep the dam in "ordinary operating condition," the appeals court said.

Fixing a leaky dam involves ordinary and necessary expenses "in the conduct of the business of farming," the court suggested.

> *Evans v. Commissioner, U.S. Ct. of Appeals, 5th Circ., 1977*
> *8/31/77*

〜

Being published was a row a seed expert felt compelled to hoe.

Robert E. Drury was a research associate studying the dormancy and germination of seeds for a state agricultural station. Publishing results of his work was important to keeping his job and getting promoted. He often had two articles a year published in scientific journals without cost to him. But an article on calculus in plant research was rejected several times, largely because it criticized work by another researcher connected with a scientific journal.

So, Drury published the work himself, paying $1,400 to have 1,000 copies printed. He deducted the printing bill. But the IRS barred the deduction. The outlay was neither an "ordinary" nor a "necessary" business expense and thus wasn't deductible, the IRS argued. That contention didn't flourish in Tax Court. The court noted that Drury's "employer expected (although it didn't require) its research associates to communicate the results of their research." Cut off from free publication in a scientific journal, Drury's "only viable alternative" was to pay for publication himself, the court concluded.

He was in a position somewhat like "a handicapped person who ... is required to incur an expense" others usually wouldn't incur, the court said.

Drury v. Commissioner, T.C. Memo 1977-199
7/20/77

⌒

Chancy practice? A law firm was paid expenses only when it won a case.

It raked in over $1 million a year prosecuting personal injury cases on a contingency basis. As many firms do, it advanced litigation costs, with the agreement its expenses would be recovered only out of sums won for clients. If it got a client nothing, the client paid nothing. The firm deducted its litigation costs as business expenses. But the IRS said a large amount of the outlays were actually loans to clients. Amounts lent to someone, of course, aren't deductible.

The firm paid the expenses under a written agreement that it would be reimbursed, and that meant it was making loans to its clients, the IRS argued. Yes, but the firm is paid only when it wins a client enough money to cover the costs, the firm said, and that contingency means it wasn't making loans. However, the Tax Court asserted that repayment wasn't "so uncertain," for the firm screened cases and took only those it figured could be won.

Litigation "costs were advanced with good hopes and/or reasonable expectation of recovery," the court determined, and "were in the nature of loans" and thus weren't deductible.

Silverton v. Commissioner, T.C. Memo 1977-198
7/20/77

～

The IRS howled at dog-and-cat records having depreciable lives.

Patents, copyrights and some other "intangible" assets have limited useful lives and can be depreciated, but goodwill acquired in buying a going business cannot be written off. A Los Angeles veterinarian bought an animal hospital for some $250,000. He obtained 12,000 medical records of former pet patients, mostly dogs and cats. He valued the records at $120,000 and figured their useful life at five years.

But the IRS balked. The medical records couldn't be depreciated; they were a part of the goodwill he had acquired, the agency growled. The vet said the records were a separate asset used to contact owners to return pets for periodic immunizations. The records had a limited useful life that could be determined, and thus were depreciable, the animal doctor contended. The IRS was barking up the wrong tree in this case, the Tax Court indicated.

The pets' records could be depreciated, but they were worth only $85,000 and had a useful life of seven years, the court concluded.

Los Angeles Central Animal Hospital v. Commissioner, 68 T.C. 23
6/8/77

Vida Blue tried to blaze one by the IRS, but the agency struck back. The San Francisco Giants' pitcher claimed a $1.1 million investment in a movie deal and deducted $111,000 for picture-distribution expenses. But the IRS balked, contending he can claim only a $30,000 investment, and thus is entitled to much smaller deductions. The IRS says Blue owes $26,439 in added tax, Tax Court papers show.

T.C. Docket 3908-79
4/25/79

Holy water test? Even though an ordained minister used his boat as much as 50% of the time for excursions on which he counseled parishioners or discussed church matters, the IRS denied him a business deduction for its operating costs.

IRS private ruling 7843129
11/15/78

Kiwanis Club dues and weekly luncheon charges at Kiwanis meetings couldn't be deducted by an assistant school principal, the Tax Court decided. "The relationship between his job and his membership in the club is just too tenuous to justify a deduction" as a business expense, the court asserted.

Wilhelm v. Commissioner, T.C. Memo 1978-327
8/30/78

⌇

An antique desk and chair are worthless as a tax write-off. A teacher who said he used them for business gave the furniture a five-year useful life. But the Tax Court denied a depreciation deduction. "We cannot say whether it has a useful life of five, 10 or perhaps even another 100 years."

Gudmundsson v. Commissioner, T.C. Memo 1978-299
8/23/78

⌇

Away a lot: A federal law enforcer bought his own copy of his agency's manual because he was away from the office so much. The IRS ruled that he can deduct the cost of the manual. (Yet the agency earlier disapproved a deduction for an IRS employe who bought his own IRS manual because the office copy wasn't kept neatly enough to suit him.)

Rev. Rul. 78-265
7/19/78

⌇

A classic T-bird cost $4,700 to restore. The owner bought the 1957 Ford two-seater sportscar for $400, paid more than 10 times that to put it in good shape and deducted the cost. But the Tax Court barred the deduction as the owner didn't prove he intended to profit from the restoration.

Smith v. Commissioner, T.C. Memo 1978-64
3/15/78

⌇

"Generally obnoxious" traffic in New York City

and the fact that a firm's clients included "wealthy Europeans" helped persuade the Tax Court that the company's chauffeur-driven Cadillac was an "ordinary and necessary" expense that it could deduct.

Baker v. Commissioner, T.C. Memo 1977-430
1/18/78

⌣

Sorry, teach: The IRS ruled a room set aside exclusively by teachers to do job-related work in their home didn't qualify for a deduction. It wasn't a "principal place of business," wasn't used by "clients or customers" and "wasn't a separate structure" unattached "to your dwelling unit," the IRS noted in ruling that they couldn't take an office-in-the-home deduction.

IRS letter ruling 7734023
10/12/77

⌣

A handicapped salesman confined to a wheelchair takes an attendant on trips to help him wash, dress and get in and out of bed. The IRS ruled that the cost of the attendant isn't a deductible business expense, and amounts paid him are subject to Social Security tax. However, the expense is a nursing cost and qualifies for the limited medical-expense deduction.

IRS Docu. 7733069
8/31/77

Medical Deductions

Birth costs are deductible, so adoption costs should be, too, a couple argued.

The couple, Lawrence and Barbara Kozlowski, of Redlands, Calif., deducted $560 paid to adopt their son Matthew. The IRS barred the deduction. The Kozlowskis said that wasn't fair; medical expenses for childbirth, which is similar to adoption, are deductible. Denying them the deduction violated their right to "equal protection under the law," they claimed.

But the Tax Court noted that childbirth expenses "involve the physical welfare of the woman," and a deduction for those expenses "advances the congressional effort to enhance public health." Adoption fees "aren't in the nature of medical expenses," they aren't "unexpected" or "catastrophic" and haven't any "direct bearing on the public's health," the court asserted. The couple's rights wouldn't be violated if they were denied the deduction.

"Deductibility isn't controlled by a sense of what is fair or equitable," the court remarked—a remark with which many taxpayers would agree.
Kozlowski v. Commissioner, T.C. Memo 1979-176
5/16/79

❧

Pulverized vegetables—lots of them—were the key to health, she believed.

Using two costly devices called triturators (pulverizers), the Alfred E. Ford family of Cinnaminson, N.J., reduced heaps of vegetables to liquid. It took nine hours, and Alfred's wife, Emilie, paid people to run the machines. Ford's weekly grocery list included 50 pounds of carrots, half a case of celery, four to six packs of spinach, some cukes, beets and parsley.

Emilie said the special preparation controlled "mucolysis, hypertension, sluggish bowel (she also took colonics four times a month), allergies, post-nasal drip and capillary fragility." The IRS was unimpressed and barred "medical" deductions that included $1,500 for piles of vegetables and $1,200 for the triturators, their upkeep and the people paid to run them nine hours weekly. Emilie went to Tax Court as her own lawyer. But the court congratulated the IRS for its action, including "wisely" barring "amounts paid to a certain chiropractor," whose payment system worked like this:

The court said it is "a voluntary system. 'Payment is made into a box . . . if the payment is made by check, she has a record of payment. If she paid cash (sic), we don't have a record of the amount.' "

Ford v. Commissioner, T.C. Memo 1979-109
4/4/79

⌣

A child's lead poisoning was laid to the paint in an old house.

And the parents were told to remove the toxic paint from anywhere their three-year-old could easily reach (surfaces within four feet of the floor) and from spots where the paint was coming off and could drop within the child's grasp. A contractor was hired to scrape the lead-based paint from the woodwork, repaint it with unleaded paint and to cover the lead-painted walls with wallboard or paneling.

Some of the cost was deductible as a medical expense, the IRS ruled. Scraping easily reached or peeling areas was deductible. But the cost to paint them with unleaded paint wasn't deductible, the IRS said. Nor was a deduction allowed for scraping surfaces that didn't pose any threat (areas unreachable by the child or where paint wasn't coming off or if it did the three-year-old couldn't get it).

Installing the wallboard and paneling was deductible only to the extent the cost exceeded the value that the installation added to the house.

Rev. Rul. 79-66
3/7/79

∽

Her hypoglycemia was stilled by a special diet that made the IRS gag.

Leona Von Kalb had a low-blood-sugar condition known as hypoglycemia. Her doctor told her to eat high-quality protein six to eight times a day and avoid processed foods and carbohydrates. Comparing her $3,100 annual food bill with her friends' bills, she concluded that the special diet added 30% to her food costs. So she deducted 30% of her grocery bill as a medical expense.

The IRS found that totally unpalatable. The special foods "satisfied her nutritional needs," were "substitutes for food normally consumed," and thus weren't deductible, the IRS argued. However, the Tax Court declared that "an average person doesn't include six to eight feedings of protein a day or exclude all processed foods and carbohydrates." Food or beverages prescribed for medicinal purposes and consumed in addition to normal diet usually qualify as a deductible medical cost, the court said.

Leona could deduct the added expense of

*"high-quality protein foods used as treatment for
her disease," the court concluded.*
Von Kalb v. Commissioner, T.C. Memo 1978-366
9/27/78

⌢

Her $195,000 pool was good medicine, but an ap-
peals court won't swallow it.

Because Bonnie Bach Ferris had to swim daily to
prevent paralysis from a back ailment, the Ferrises added an indoor pool to their home. It cost $195,000, largely
because it matched the expensive cut-stone architec-
ture of their Tudor-style home in Madison, Wis. The
couple deducted as a medical expense $86,000, the bal-
ance after subtracting the cost of nonessential items in
the addition and the value the pool added to their
home.

The IRS argued that much of the outlay was
caused by luxurious construction and shouldn't be deductible. But the Tax Court in 1977 said the law didn't
require "bare-bone" spending for medical care. Still, the
entire outlay for the pool can't be considered "for medical care," an appeals court asserted. "Only the minimum reasonable cost of a functionally adequate pool
and housing structure" will count as spent "for medical
care," the appeals court said.

*The Ferris-pool case should surface again in
Tax Court, where the appeals court sent it for de-
termination of "minimum reasonable cost."*
Ferris v. Commissioner, U.S. Ct. of Appeals, 7th Circ., 1978
9/13/78

⌢

"Foolish Pleasure" won the Kentucky Derby. Will
its owner whip the IRS?

John L. Greer's late wife, Russell, was flown for
medical treatment in a Greer company airplane. The

owners of the 1975 Kentucky Derby winner didn't pay for the flights. But the IRS said they should have and assessed them tax of $13,500 of income, the estimated value of the plane trips.

Medical-plan benefits aren't taxable income. Greer argued that the plane trips were a benefit of his company's medical insurance plan because the aircraft was available to any employes or their families needing it for medical purposes. However, there wasn't any written commitment that they could use it, the IRS argued.

Nothing was written, but there was a "policy or custom" of such use; other employes had been taken in the plane for medical reasons, the Tax Court observed. So the flights to take the late Mrs. Greer for treatment weren't taxable, the court said.

John L. Greer and Estate of Russell Z. Greer v. Commissioner, 70 T.C. 26
6/7/78

⌒

Can a savings account cost a dutiful son deductions for his parents' care?

William C. Hewell's ailing parents were in a nursing home. Their expenses exceeded their income, and they worried about using up their savings. So Hewell paid $8,000 of their medical bills. The sum exceeded half their support. He deducted the outlays, claimed his mother as a dependent (his father's income prevented him from being William's dependent) and filed as head of a household. The IRS barred his deductions, his mother as a dependent and his filing as head of a household, meaning William owed $4,400 of added tax.

Years earlier the father opened a joint account that included his son's name so the money would go to William without going through probate. The IRS argued that William's share of the $63,000 savings account reimbursed him for what he paid on his parents' behalf. The fact his parents had the money to pay their medical costs wouldn't bar William's deductions, the Tax Court noted, but his having an immediate right to the money would.

However, his parents didn't intend to give him an interest in the money until both of them were dead, the court determined. So he could take the deductions, claim his mother as a dependent and file as head of a household.

Hewell v. Commissioner, 69 T.C. 66
3/8/78

⌒

Can adopting parents deduct medical bills paid for the natural mother?

As many adoptive parents do, Benny and Judy G. Kilpatrick paid the medical bills of the woman whose son they adopted. They deducted the outlay as a medical expense. But the IRS barred the deduction. The IRS argued that only medical bills paid for a dependent are deductible. The woman wasn't their dependent, so they couldn't take the deduction.

However, the couple argued that medical care for a pregnant woman is medical care for their unborn child. The child, of course, was Benny's and Judy's dependent when they paid the bills, so they should get the deduction, the couple insisted. The Tax Court agreed that "under certain circumstances" care for an expectant mother was "intimately connected with the health of the (unborn) child" and might be deductible by the adopting parents.

Unhappily, though, the couple didn't show "which services rendered to the mother were so proximately or directly related to" the child's health "as to constitute medical care for the child," the court noted in denying them the deduction. More detailed evidence might gain a couple a deduction under like circumstances, the court indicated.

Kilpatrick v. Commissioner, 68 T.C. 40
7/27/77

∽

The Rx for a doctor's boy was boarding school. Was it deductible?

Eric was a problem in school: He was hyperactive, childishly selfish and threw tantrums. His behavior was a reaction to his father's "perfectionistic overcoercion" and his mother's "irritable oversubmission," a psychiatrist said. Though Eric's dad was a doctor, his parents weren't able to change the atmosphere in their home to help the boy, so the psychiatrist recommended boarding school for Eric.

Eric's father deducted the boarding school costs as medical expenses, figuring the school was treatment recommended by the psychiatrist. But the IRS said that was an ill-gotten diagnosis. The school didn't cater to problem children and didn't provide Eric any special treatment; a psychiatrist's recommendation wasn't enough to make the school costs deductible, the IRS contended. A U.S. district court agreed with the IRS, even though the boy improved.

". . . merely because a child flourishes in a particular environment doesn't mean that child is receiving medical treatment for tax purposes," the court concluded.

Newkirk v. U.S., U.S. Dist. Ct., S. Dist. Ohio 1977
6/15/77

Bad news, fat smokers: You can't deduct the cost of either weight-reduction or smoke-ending programs, the IRS says in two recent public rulings. In the examples the IRS uses, taxpayers were advised by a physician to join a weight-reduction or a smoke-ending program. Yet, the costs weren't deductible because the programs didn't treat "any specific ailment or disease." Costs to maintain or improve "general health" normally aren't deductible, the IRS observed. (Earlier, a private ruling barred a deduction for a smoke-ending course, but public rulings carry more weight.)

Rev. Ruls. 79-151 and 79-162
5/30/79

⌒

Laetrile is a "quack" substance to some federal regulators, but that doesn't affect the IRS. The cost of the controversial apricot-pit derivative, a purported cancer cure, is deductible as a medical expense when prescribed by a physician and used as prescribed in a locale where its sale and use are legal, the IRS ruled. Some states permit its use despite a federal ban.

Rev. Rul. 78-325
9/13/78

⌒

Small comfort: A Minnesota electrician's statement that a new mattress was more comfortable than an old one didn't convince a court that he deserved a medical deduction for the $248 cost of the mattress. The man had had a back operation years earlier but hadn't had his back examined by a doctor in the year for which he took the deduction.

Powers v. Commissioner, T.C. Memo 1978-311
8/23/78

If the folks pay: A man's parents paid his medical bills. But he intended to pay them back and signed a note with interest payable to his folks. He can deduct the medical expenses the year they were paid, even though his folks paid the bills, and even if he doesn't repay them until a year or so later, the IRS ruled.

Rev. Rul. 78-171
5/10/78

A cop can't deduct the use of a health spa to keep in shape, even though his job requires him to be in excellent physical condition. Many expenses necessitated by employment, such as extra haircuts for military men, aren't deductible, the IRS noted in barring the police officer's deduction.

Rev. Rul. 78-128
5/3/78

The babysitter watched the kids so mother could go to the doctor for treatment. But the sitter's pay isn't deductible, the IRS ruled. Babysitter expenses are non-deductible personal expenses, it said.

Rev. Rul. 7809004
3/15/78

Kojak, take note: Bald may be beautiful. But covering it may get you a deduction. At least a bald guy tells us he was allowed to deduct his hair pieces. The IRS nixed the toupees as a business deduction, but "let me take them as a medical deduction," relates the fellow who wishes anonymity. When he met with the IRS, he had a psychiatrist's letter that stated camouflaging his baldness "was extremely important for my mental health."

3/1/78

Retirement and Taxes

At the New Yorker, life was swell until you-know-who looked in.

The magazine keeps some 105 artists and writers under contract. They give The New Yorker first refusal for their art, fiction and poetry or do nonfiction articles on assignment. They get paid a small sum for being under contract; most of their pay is based on what they produce. The magazine doesn't control how they work, doesn't consider them employes, and thus doesn't pay or withhold employment taxes on them.

But it has funded retirement and profit-sharing plans for these contract artists and writers since 1944. The IRS, though, said they couldn't be in the plans. "We're trying to cover more people," says George Green, The New Yorker Inc.'s president, "but the government said we must cover fewer people." Not to worry: A special bill in the Senate would make these creative people "employes" for the magazine's retirement and profit-sharing plans and subject them to payroll and withholding taxes.

The Treasury told a Senate panel it supported the special legislation, which would affect, among others, writers Renata Adler, John McPhee, Calvin Trillin and John Updike, as well as cartoonists George Booth, Charles Saxon and Saul Steinberg.

5/30/79

Does a loan to buy securities mean a profit-sharing plan can be taxed?

Profit-sharing plans usually don't pay tax on income from their investments. Elliot Knitwear Corp.'s profit-sharing fund bought some securities by borrowing through a margin account. The IRS said income from the debt-financed securities was "unrelated income" on which the otherwise tax-exempt fund owed $20,700 in tax.

The fund's trustee argued that borrowing to acquire securities was "related" to the fund's main function: to provide retirement income for its participants. But the Tax Court said Congress meant income from debt-financed assets to be taxed unless the debt was incurred in the performance of the tax-exempt entity's main function, such as a credit union incurring debt in accepting members' deposits.

"It isn't necessary for a profit-sharing plan to buy securities on margin," the court asserted; the plan must pay the tax.

Elliot Knitwear Profit Sharing Plan v. Commissioner, 71 T.C. 71
2/21/79

⌒

An old judge claimed there wasn't any retirement age for him.

Judge Ross F. Jones, of the Arizona Superior Court, left the bench in the midst of a four-year elected term due to a physical disability some years ago. He was aged 70 then, and the disability got him a fatter pension than if he had retired in good health. Normally up to $100 a week of "sick pay" isn't taxed. Judge Jones excluded $5,200 a year of his pension as sick pay, but the IRS said all of it was taxable as retirement income.

Usually people forced to "retire" early due to disability get the sick pay exclusion. The IRS argued that at age 70, Jones wasn't retiring early. But he argued that Arizona hadn't any mandatory retirement age for its judges, that he left before his term was up and that he probably would have been elected again as he had run unopposed for years. Thus, he insisted, he was retired early due to his disability.

But a Tax Court judge saw it differently. If an employer hasn't a mandatory retirement age, the tax code says age 65 shall be considered the mandatory age, the court said, rejecting Jones's attack on that part of the tax code.

Jones v. Commissioner, 71 T.C. 13
11/22/78

One day can mess up a whole year's deduction, an employe found out.

Robert H. Pervier was a machinist in 3M Co.'s Northboro, Mass., plant. He opened an individual retirement account, or IRA, in June a few years ago; during the year he put $1,000 in it. At the time he wasn't eligible for 3M's profit-sharing plan. But on the last day of the year 3M enrolled him in the plan due to a change in eligibility rules.

The IRS barred his deduction for the $1,000 contribution to his IRA and levied a $60 excise penalty, too. Poor Pervier, he was eligible for an IRA when he paid into it, but he became a participant in his employer's plan, and thus wasn't entitled to deduct the $1,000 and was subject to the 6% levy on excess contributions, the Tax Court ruled. So he owed the IRS $320.

The law bars a deduction for an IRA contribution if an employe participates "for any part of a year in an employer's plan," the court observed.

Pervier v. Commissioner, T.C. Memo 1978-410
10/25/78

Dropouts from some company retirement plans can set up their own.

People who participate in pension plans at work usually are barred from individual retirement accounts, or IRAs. Congress intended IRAs for taxpayers who hadn't another retirement plan. However, it isn't always clear when the IRS will consider someone a participant in a retirement plan: Sometimes, employes are participants even though their employers don't pay into the plan for them during the year.

Yet, the IRS ruled favorably for employes who stop contributing to a company plan that requires them to contribute in order to continue participating in the pension plan. In a private ruling, the IRS says employes who don't pay into the plan for a full year won't be considered active participants, even though previously accrued benefits continue to increase and earn interest. Thus, they can make and deduct payments to an IRA, the IRS says.

IRS letter ruling 7806044
5/31/78

⌒

A man who got money from one pension plan was barred from another.

Donald E. Ziegler was a lawyer who had a retirement plan for himself when he practiced alone. But he became a partner in a new law firm and took all the money, $2,800, from his pension plan. He paid the penalty imposed for this early withdrawal. The partnership set up a retirement plan, and the IRS denied a deduction for contributions on Ziegler's behalf.

Owner-employes like Ziegler are barred from retirement plans for five years if they get premature distributions from a retirement plan, the IRS asserted.

"That rule applied only if I took money from the partnership plan," he argued; "I didn't, I took it from another plan." The law isn't clear on this point, the Tax Court conceded. But Congress clearly intended to discourage early distributions from such plans, the court said.

Congressional intent would be thwarted if taxpayers like Ziegler could readily withdraw from one plan and get into another, the court said. He was barred from the partnership plan for five years, the court concluded.

Ziegler v. Commissioner, 70 T.C. 13
5/17/78

⌒

The IRS didn't like the way a firm invested pension and profit-sharing funds.

Businesses can lose all or part of a deduction for payments into pension or profit-sharing trusts if the funds are invested improperly. A building company's pension and profit-sharing trusts were controlled by theowner and his son. They had the trusts buy from a bank a $56,000 note owed by the firm. The IRS barred about $53,000 of the $67,000 the company deducted for contributions to its pension and profit-sharing plans.

The IRS claimed the trusts weren't organized "for the exclusive benefit" of employes because of the way some of the trust money had been invested. However, the firm was financially solid and didn't need the trust to finance its needs. The note the trust bought was paid off on time and earned the trust more interest than some other investments, the Tax Court noted.

The court rejected the IRS's argument, asserting that the law doesn't prevent investment in "securities or obligations of the employer."

Bing Management Co. v. Commissioner, T.C. Memo 1977-403
12/7/77

A clever pathologist cut everyone but himself out of a pension.

He formed a one-man professional corporation and had it form a 50-50 partnership with another doctor's one-man corporation. The partnership employed everyone else in the pathology lab the doctors ran. The pathologist's corporation deducted pension contributions to a plan that only covered him. But the IRS barred the deductions. The agency argued that the pension plan didn't qualify for favorable tax treatment because it discriminated against the lab employes.

The IRS said the pathologist's corporation controlled the partnership so the pension plan must cover the partnership's employes. However, the Tax Court observed that the corporation didn't control the partnership, it owned only 50%. The court concluded that the pension plan didn't discriminate and the contributions to the plan were deductible.

The decision upholds a tax device for professionals who want pension plans to only cover themselves, William Raby, national director, tax services at Touche Ross & Co., a CPA firm, says.

Thomas Kiddie MD Inc. v. Commissioner, 69 T.C. 94
4/12/78

〜

A retired airman figured one disability was as good as another.

John J. Johnson retired from the Air Force after 20 years without any disability. But after retiring, he applied for and got a disability rating from the Veterans Administration. The VA found he was 40% disabled due to prostatitis, back strain and a bone disease. But the Air Force refused to change Johnson's retirement status. The VA pay was exempt from tax, and Johnson figured he could exempt 40% of the Air Force pay, too.

But the IRS said he couldn't because the Air Force paid him taxable retirement benefits. Johnson argued that he should be treated as if he had retired from the Air Force due to disability because the VA considered him disabled. But similar arguments haven't swayed the Tax Court before and didn't this time, either. The VA's view of him as disabled didn't change the character of the Air Force benefits, which were paid for length of service and weren't for disability, the court said.

Johnson v. Commissioner, T.C. Memo 1977-367
11/9/77

⌣

This Paul Newman retired from a New York State job.

And he received an annuity based on his payments to the state's retirement fund, plus interest the state paid while it held his money. Annuities pay a fixed amount, usually monthly, for the beneficiaries' lifetimes. Proceeds are taxable. But an amount equal to the investment in the annuity usually is excluded from tax. Newman, of Brooklyn, N.Y., figured he could exclude both the $16,000 he paid into the state annuity fund over the years, and the $18,000 interest the state paid while holding his money.

However, the IRS said he couldn't exclude the interest; it wasn't part of his investment in the annuity. Newman argued that the interest was akin to interest on state bonds, and thus tax-exempt. The IRS said the tax exemption was intended to aid sales of government securities and applied to state or city bonds. It didn't apply to interest on money held in retirement accounts. The Tax Court sided with the IRS.

New York hadn't paid interest on a debt: It got Newman's money "principally to hold for (his) own benefit," the court concluded.

Newman v. Commissioner, 68 T.C. 37
7/13/77

⌒

Eye wash didn't keep this employment scheme afloat.

An optometrist and ophthalmologist shared office space but had separate professional corporations, each of which had pension and profit-sharing plans. An accounting service "employed" some of the doctors' staff and was reimbursed for keeping them on its payroll. The doctors didn't consider these staffers eligible for pension or profit-sharing as they were employes of the accounting service.

But the IRS did and disqualified the retirement plans for excluding them. The IRS argued that the staffers actually weren't employes of the accounting firm because it had no power over them. The doctors hired them, set their pay and could fire them. So they were the doctors' employes and should have been included in the retirement plans. The Tax Court saw it that way, too. The plans didn't qualify for favorable tax treatment, the court asserted. The doctors must pay tax on sums paid to the plans for their benefits, but their corporations can deduct the payments, the court said.

Burnetta P.A. v. Commissioner, 68 T.C. 13
5/4/77

⌒

Pension plans can cut benefits to retired workers who get workmen's compensation. Some plans reduce benefits a dollar for each dollar a retiree receives from workmen's compensation. But can plans do the same to retirees getting unemployment compensation? They can't. Unemployment benefits can't be used to offset retirement plan benefits, the IRS said.

Rev. Rul. 78-178
5/31/78

⌒

Retired military people often get retirement pay, which is taxable, but later are ruled to have been eligible all the time for disability pay, which isn't taxed. Pay received during the retroactive period, on which tax probably was paid at the time, won't be considered taxable income, the IRS ruled. The ruling reverses an IRS position, which a court had overruled.

Rev. Rul. 78-161
4/12/78

⌒

"Outside" directors get a tax break if they fund a Keogh retirement plan with their director fees, which are considered self-employment income. Price Waterhouse advises that as much as $7,500 a year put into a plan can be deducted, even if the director is covered by the corporation's retirement plan. The benefit isn't available to "inside" directors, those who are employes of the company.

11/2/77

⌒

Betty White and Allen Ludden lost a $27,000 contest in Tax Court. The husband and wife TV stars' corporation paid $53,000 to pension and profit-sharing plans for them, but left out an eligible worker. That disqualified the plans, so the $53,000 was taxable income to the performers, the IRS figured; the court agreed.

Ludden v. Commissioner, 68 T.C. 71
9/21/77

Retired clergy's boon. The portion of a minister's pension designated "housing allowance" by the church can be exempt from tax, the IRS told a national church body in a private ruling. However, the agency warned the pension must conform with IRS regulations.

IRS letter ruling 7734028
10/12/77

Accidents and Various Mishaps

Don't let the kids fool around in a company car—
one family's nightmare.

Earl E. Kopp owned Kopp's Co., a Lineboro, Md.,
firm. He knew his son Wayne had 10 speeding convictions and two license suspensions. Yet Earl let Wayne,
then aged 23, use a company car while he was home on
a military furlough. Wayne had an accident that left the
other driver, Warren T. Danner, paralyzed from the
neck down. Danner sued the firm and the family for
$4.2 million.

The suit scared the firm's bank and suppliers as insurance covered only $100,000 for such a claim. Some
suppliers froze the firm's credit line; the bank demanded collateral for an unsecured $114,000 loan. Eventual-
ly, the Kopps settled with the victim for $152,000. Insur-
ance paid $102,000, the firm paid $50,000, which it deducted as a business expense to protect its financial in-
tegrity. However, the settlement isn't deductible
because the accident didn't arise from company business, a U.S. district court concluded.

*Kopp was lucky he owned the firm; else he
could have had to pay for exposing it to such a
liability by letting his son with his driving record
use a company car, the court added.*
Kopp's Co. v. U.S., U.S. Dist. Ct., Maryland, 1979
7/11/79

If disaster hits, be able to show it happened, and the damage it did.

Winter brings natural disasters like the ice storm that glazed Dallas at the beginning of 1979. Taxpayers usually can take a casualty loss deduction for damage to their property. But they must be able to prove the loss. The IRS often reduces or bars casualty deductions because the taxpayer can't adequately substantiate the amount of the loss, warns Peat, Marwick, Mitchell & Co., a CPA firm.

Peat Marwick advises taxpayers to be prepared to prove that the disaster occurred and caused the damage claimed. Photos and newspaper accounts can help with that. Also, proof is needed to show that the taxpayer owns the damaged property, how much it cost and how much it was worth immediately before and after the destruction. Often the IRS accepts repair costs as the measure of a property's decrease in value. If insurance pays, it, of course, reduces the amount that can be deducted.

And if the property cost less than the insurance proceeds (that's possible if a home has been owned for a long time), the owner ends up with a taxable gain rather than a casualty loss deduction.

1/10/79

⌒

If you don't file an insurance claim, you can lose several ways.

Casualty losses normally are deductible to the extent they aren't covered by insurance proceeds. But what happens when someone chooses to absorb a loss and forgo insurance payment for fear premiums will be increased or the policy canceled? The loss isn't deductible, the IRS ruled.

The IRS ruling involves a lawyer who gave a client erroneous advice that cost the client money. The lawyer reimbursed his client. But the attorney didn't file a claim under his malpractice policy because he feared cancellation or a premium increase. The lawyer can't deduct the sum paid the client, the IRS ruled. The agency cited court decisions that say taxpayers who absorb losses, forgoing insurance proceeds, can't deduct their losses.

Applying similar reasoning, courts have barred a deduction for business use of an auto by an executive who could have been reimbursed by his employer but didn't seek reimbursement.

Rev. Rul. 78-141
4/26/78

⌒

Killer bugs. They do in trees faster than disease. Fast enough for a tax break?

A Georgia physician lost 30 trees to infestations of Southern pine beetles, "one of the most destructive enemies of pine." Thousands often bore into a tree, killing it off in 30 days or less. The value of his property was cut by $3,000 due to the dead trees, the doctor figured, and he wrote that amount off as a casualty loss. But the IRS axed the deduction; the destruction wasn't quick enough to qualify as a casualty loss.

The loss of trees to Dutch Elm disease doesn't qualify as a casualty, the agency noted, and it contended losing trees to beetles was similar. But the Tax Court said a casualty includes "some sudden invasion by a hostile agency."

"Infestation . . . by Southern pine beetles is a

sufficiently sudden event to be classed as a casualty," the court asserted. It did, though, whittle the doctor's loss to $1,000.

Black v. Commissioner, T.C. Memo 1977-337
10/12/77

～

Oh, my Porsche engine blew up, so I can deduct the loss, a Little Rock, Ark., car buff figured. But the sudden destruction of the engine because of an oil leak wasn't a "casualty loss," for the engine hadn't been "struck or invaded by any external force," the IRS said. Then the Tax Court cleared the road for the IRS to collect $1,400 from the Porsche owner.

Smith v. Commissioner, T.C. Memo 1979-82
3/28/79

Gambling

Oh, "Calcutta." A tale of golf clubs, bets and traps.

We're talking about tax traps and sand traps. Many private golf clubs hold "calcuttas," in which each player in a tournament is "sold" at auction. The club often keeps 10% to 15% of the calcutta pool, the rest is prize money for the "owners" of winning players and the players. Clearly this is gambling. But the IRS said in 1974 that calcuttas for members and guests normally are exempt from wagering taxes.

However, the IRS recently considered a calcutta in which members of other clubs could participate. The members of the other clubs "aren't guests of the members of the host club," the IRS noted, as the host club members didn't pay for them. So they're "members of the general public," and their participation means the calcutta is subject to gambling taxes, the IRS said.

So the host club must pay $500 for an occupational gambling stamp, plus 2% tax on the amount wagered on the calcutta players.

Rev. Rul. 79-145
5/16/79

〰

Horse sense: His led him to take a plunge on a system for playing the ponies.

He is Milton O. Brown, a Portland, Ore., attorney, who sent away for John A. Reppert's $100 blackjack "strategy." Reppert told Brown about a system for winning on the horses. The lawyer was impressed: He formed Gold Pot Inc., paid $21,000 for all its stock and gave $20,000 of the corporate kitty to Reppert, who was to keep 75% of the winnings and hand over 25% to Brown.

A hand-over didn't come: Two months later Reppert reported losing the entire $20,000. In a creative attempt to deduct gambling losses that normally wouldn't be deductible, Brown dissolved Gold Pot and deducted the $20,000 as a loss from investing in the stock of a small business. When the IRS got wind of the deduction, the agency charged that the lawyer set up Gold Pot to try to avoid taxes. (Presumably, if Reppert had succeeded at the track, Gold Pot rather than Brown would have counted the winnings as taxable income.)

"The corporation was merely a sham," the Tax Court concluded. Brown couldn't take the deduction; as a result he owed the IRS $5,700.

> *Brown v. Commissioner, T.C. Memo 1979-24*
> *2/7/79*

◇

A poker parlor kept the action going by using shills it bankrolled to play.

Once upon a time you could play "lo-ball" draw poker (worst hand wins) legally at the Avalon Club in Emeryville, Calif. Players didn't gamble against the house, but played against one another, and the club collected an hourly table charge. To assure a game would be going on, the club gave chips to shills to play in the games. Shills had to give 50% of their winnings to the club. But shills' poker losses cost the club $15,000.

The club deducted the money as promotional expense. But the IRS argued that the $15,000 was lost gambling; wagering losses are deductible only to the extent of gambling winnings, which for the club were zero, so the money wasn't deductible. The club owners contended that the club itself wasn't gambling.

However, an appeals court said that "the shill, in placing a bet, was acting for the club." So the club couldn't deduct the $15,000.

Nitzberg et al. v. Commissioner, U.S. Ct. of Appeals, 9th Circ., 1978
9/13/78

⌒

Alas, Alvin: A racetrack teller made errors on the job and on his tax return.

Clerks who handle bets at the tracks usually must make up shortages due to their mistakes, but they get to keep overages. Alvin Butcko, however, was short $358 one year, and the track deducted it from his paycheck. So Butcko reduced his income by $358 when he filed his return. He couldn't do that, the IRS said. Shortages can't be offset against gross income.

If he couldn't offset it, Butcko argued, he should be able to take it off "above the line," for his shortage was similar to above-the-line deductions for employe auto expenses or salesman's expenses. He was wrong, the Tax Court said. The tax code spells out above-the-line deductions; his shortage couldn't be considered like any of them. Thus it was only deductible "below the line" as an itemized deduction.

But that didn't help poor Alvin: He used the standard deduction instead of itemizing. Thus he couldn't deduct his shortage and owed the IRS $105 more, the court said.

Butcko v. Commissioner, T.C. Memo 1978-209
7/5/78

⌒

A horse player hoped to nose out the IRS in a contest over betting losses.

Ahmed Salem was an admitted racetrack addict who lived but four blocks from Hazel Park Raceway. He earned only $6,000 at a Michigan auto plant, but reported winning $12,600 on the ponies, from which sum he deducted $12,500 of wagering losses. Actually he had $19,000 of losing tickets, but reported less to avoid "repercussions" from the IRS. But the IRS disputed all his losses and told him to ante up $2,300 tax on his winnings.

The losing parimutuel tickets that Salem showed the Tax Court were clean and untorn, and most were sequentially numbered. Still, some weren't sequential, and the IRS said someone else could have bought them. The court acknowledged its skepticism about clean sequentially numbered tickets as evidence of betting losses. But the court said Salem's testimony was "credible for the most part," though not wholly. He could deduct $8,000 of wagering losses from his winnings, the court concluded.

This equestrian tax case was pursued for the IRS by a lawyer fittingly named Hack. (Which, of course, means, among other things, a horse for hire.)

Salem v. Commissioner, T.C. Memo 1978-142
4/26/78

⌒

The winner of a state lottery gets $1 million tax-free but in installments over a number of years. The state pays interest on the installments and wanted it declared tax-exempt like interest on state bonds. But the IRS said the "interest" wasn't interest—it was part of the cash prize and thus taxable income to the winner.

IRS letter ruling 7745023
12/28/77

Questionable Gains—
and Losses

A menace to society. That's how a judge viewed a convicted tax evader.

Courts almost routinely grant bail so most convicted tax-law violators don't go to jail pending an appeal of their convictions. Terrence J. Karmann worked as a driver for Times Mirror Co., publisher of the Los Angeles Times. He stated on withholding forms that he didn't owe any tax and wouldn't owe any so that the company wouldn't withhold income tax from his pay. But that was held to be a lie, and he was convicted of filing false withholding statements and of willful failure to file tax returns for two years.

Karmann, acting as his own attorney, is appealing his conviction and sought to stay free on bail during the appeal. But U.S. District Judge A. Andrew Hauck noted that Karmann "made a mockery of the income tax laws," indicated "he will continue to do so," and "thereby constitutes a menace and a danger" not only to himself, but also to society. So the judge refused to free Karmann on bail while he appeals his tax conviction.

U.S. v. Karmann, U.S. Dist. Ct., Cent. Dist. Calif., 1979
7/11/79

⌒

Her husband cheated, but the IRS told her to pay for the crime, too.

Jerry E. Johnson, of El Paso, Texas, and John T. Fraley cheated the IRS by filing false refund claims. Fraley's sister, Cora Fraley Baggett, an IRS employe, helped the scam work. Before they were caught, Jerry pocketed $60,000. Most of the refund checks were in other people's names, but $6,000 was in four checks to Jerry and his wife, Mary Helen.

Texas is a community property state, so half of Jerry's income was Mary Helen's. Yet, she counted a small part of his loot as hers when she filed a separate tax return. The IRS said 50% of the $60,000 was taxable to her. It was only if Jerry "acquired title" to the money, and that depended on whether the IRS "intended to pass title" to the money to Jerry, the Tax Court said. Title was meant to pass to him only with respect to the $6,000 in checks made out to the couple, so Mary Helen owed tax on only half that sum, the court said.

She also can deduct part of Jerry's $7,000 legal costs, the court ruled, as the expense was incurred "in connection with the . . . production of income."

Johnson v. Commissioner, 72 T.C. 29
5/23/79

◝◞

A "church" involved in a $3.3 million marijuana bust cursed an IRS levy.

Zion Coptic Church Inc. isn't your usual Sunday-go-to-meetin' kind of church. Marijuana use is a tenet of its religion, it says. There's evidence it "has been engaged in illegal activities," uses shell corporations, aliases and false identities to disguise its activities and to hide its assets. The IRS denied the "church" tax exemption as a religious organization some years ago and told it to file tax returns. The "church" didn't.

The IRS figured that about $2 million passed through the Miami Beach, Fla., "church" in six months. Some "church" members were implicated with 33 tons of marijuana valued at roughly $3.3 million seized by authorities. The IRS slapped a $2.1 million assessment for taxes, penalties and interest on the "church" and attached $91,000 in cash that Miami Beach police found in a raid on the "church." The outfit argued in court that the assessment was unreasonable.

But after ticking off a list of the "church's" unchurchly involvements, a U.S. district court determined that the IRS had acted properly.

Zion Coptic Church Inc. v. U.S., U.S. Dist. Ct., So. Dist. of Florida, 1979
5/9/79

⌢

The owner of the Red Sauce and her brother got burned by her lover.

Lucille Barrie owned the Red Sauce Restaurant in New York City. Salvatore Pisello was the manager, who, though wed to Assunata, lived with Lucille. Lucille's brother, Jay Starr, handed $150,000 to his sister's lover, who apparently said he would invest it. He did: In the ponies, losing the entire bundle in fast bets on slow horses.

Jay pressed Pisello and eventually got $12,000. But Lucille paid Pisello only $200 a week and he couldn't pay Jay any more. Later, the Red Sauce borrowed $80,000, which the lender paid out in several checks. One check for $20,000 fell into the hands of Pisello, who got a bank to cash the check, even though his name wasn't on it. A few years later, the IRS peppered the Red Sauce manager with $102,500 of assessments.

The lover-manager argued that the money was the proceeds of loans, and thus nontaxable.

*But he hadn't a prayer of paying back so much,
and, in fact, he obtained the money fraudulently,
and thus owed the tax and penalties, the Tax
Court said.*

Pisello v. Commissioner, T.C. Memo 1979-143
4/25/79

⌣

A welfare cheater admitted his guilt, but proved
hard for the IRS to nail.

Robert Fulp was a caseworker in New York City's
Welfare Department. He had unauthorized emergency
assistance checks issued to welfare clients who kicked
back part of the money to him. He pleaded guilty to
grand larceny, got five years probation on condition he
make restitution of $14,300. Fulp didn't report the
kickbacks.

Eventually, the IRS assessed him nearly $4,000 in
tax on his illicit earnings plus $2,000 in tax-fraud penal-
ties. He put up virtually no defense in Tax Court. Still,
the burden of proving fraud was on the IRS. Among
other things, a consistent pattern of understating a substantial amount of income over a period of years is persuasive evidence of fraud. But, the IRS failed to submit
evidence showing how much he didn't report.

*And "since the (IRS) failed to show the
amounts omitted, we can't find that they were substantial," the Tax Court asserted, and it ruled
that Fulp didn't have to pay the $2,000.*

Fulp v. Commissioner, T.C. Memo 1978-382
10/4/78

⌣

A man of convictions knew he would enjoy his day
in court—even Tax Court.

An IRS lawyer had summed up the agency's case

for the Tax Court: Gary Frederick Ayers kidnaped a woman, robbed two banks, in Zephyr Cove and Sparks, Nev., collected $78,100, yet unrecovered, and went to jail. He failed to pay income tax on the loot and owes $37,000 of tax and a $9,000 failure-to-file penalty. The court asked Ayers, who acted as his own lawyer, what he had to say. Said the convict:

"I have no defense. I'd like to get just one thing straight. I come (sic) up here only for the ride. I'm doing life and 25. That mess, what he said, is exactly what happened. I just come for the ride. I'm in a U.S. penitentiary doing 25 years. When I finish that, I go to Nevada to do a life sentence. All I wanted to do was come up here for a ride. What that man says is exactly true. Now, it's back to you, friend."

"Friend" ruled that Ayers owes the tax and penalty. (Collecting it will be another story.)

Ayers v. Commissioner, T.C. Memo 1978-341
9/13/78

⌒

Hindsight: An embezzler says his loot should be treated as a loan.

The treasurer of a Midwestern amusement park lifted a total of $89,304 from his employer over a four-year period. When the thefts were discovered, after he resigned, he readily admitted taking the money and promised to repay it. Eventually he reimbursed the company, with interest. Even if stolen money is repaid, however, it is taxable in the year it is stolen. The man didn't report the money on his tax returns, and the IRS tried to collect back taxes, plus a 50% fraud penalty.

In arguing that the money should be treated as a loan—normally nontaxable—the man said there was an "implied recognition, at the time of the misappropriation, of an obligation to repay." But the Tax Court would have none of that. It said the thefts didn't resemble loans in any way, despite the company's eventual accepting of promissory notes and charging of interest.

"Such acts reflect the employer's realistic appraisal of the situation, once discovered, and its decision to minimize its financial losses," the court concluded.

Tirre v. Commissioner, T.C. Memo 1978-298
8/23/78

〜

Two Tennessee brokers lose a tax tussle in an insider-trading case.

J. C. Bradford & Co. of Nashville and its two principals, James C. Bradford Sr. and Jr., are well known in Southern financial circles. Some time back, the SEC accused them of profiting illegally by buying stock on favorable information before it was announced publicly. The Bradfords were enjoined against securities law violations and suspended from the brokerage business for brief periods. They also agreed to deposit their profits from the stock transactions in an escrow account for investors who had valid claims against the ill-gotten gains.

On their tax returns the Bradfords deducted the payments to the escrow account as ordinary business expenses, contending that the purpose of the payments was to avoid embarrassing litigation, protect their business reputations and create good will. However, the Tax Court decided that the tax treatment of the payments wasn't governed by their purpose but instead by the type of transaction from which they stemmed—an investment in stock.

For tax purposes, of course, stock investments

generate capital gains or losses rather than ordinary income or loss. Thus, payments like the Bradfords' must be treated as capital expenditures, the court said. That means a less favorable tax result than a straight business-expense deduction.

Bradford v. Commissioner, 70 T.C. 58
8/16/78

⌒

To sell life insurance, he unlawfully rebated part of his commissions.

The year his commissions ran $130,000, his kickbacks to customers exceeded $88,000. The IRS wanted to tax him on the entire $130,000. The agency said he couldn't reduce his gross income "above the line" by the amount of the rebates, and he couldn't deduct them "below the line" as a business expense because illegal kickbacks can't be deducted.

However, businesses that make unlawful rebates usually can reduce gross income "above the line" by the amount of their rebates, so he could, too, he argued. Indeed, the Tax Court had ruled in favor of an insurance agent in a similar case. But a court majority overruled the earlier decision and said the agent must pay tax on the entire $130,000. A seller is entitled to make an "above-the-line" adjustment to cut income by the amount of illegal rebates, but the agent wasn't the seller, his insurance company, which condemned rebating, was. And the rebates violated state law, so he couldn't deduct them "below the line."

The majority's opinion meant taxing the salesman on "phantom income," money he never had the use of, a dissenting judge said.

Alex v. Commissioner, 70 T.C. 29
8/9/78

Behind her skirts: A roofer hoped his wife could shield him from the tax man.

The year E. L. Scott married Joy he was indicted for willfully attempting to evade income tax owed by his roofing business and himself. He pleaded guilty and conceded he owed the IRS $98,450. But he didn't pay. And it seemed he had nothing the IRS could attach to satisfy the debt. Scott terminated his roofing company, and Joy began a new roofing business with a $500 investment.

He managed the concern for Joy, who knew nothing about the roofing business. The company prospered. She paid herself about $68,000 over four years, while Scott got much less. Finally, the IRS went after Joy for her husband's tax debts. The agency claimed she must pay because the business profit that she had taken actually belonged to Scott as he was responsible for the firm's prosperity. The Tax Court agreed; she must pay what he owed.

Having Joy own the new firm was "a device to keep from (her) husband's creditors" income that actually was his, the court concluded.

Scott v. Commissioner, 70 T.C. 10
5/10/78

〜

Selling marijuana was his trade; getting "busted" caused a business loss.

Bill Doug Holt lived in El Paso, Texas, bought marijuana a ton at a time on the Mexican border and trucked it to Atlanta. The law caught up with Holt, seized his truck, horse trailer, $4,575 cash and a ton of illegal weed. And the IRS figured he and wife Gail owed income taxes of about $137,000.

That was based on Holt's grossing $780,000 from

"pot" sales and the IRS allowing him deductions of about $682,000, including $280,000 "cost-of-goods" (the weed), $320,000 "sales commissions" and $40,000 "driver's expense." Holt figured he would deduct the value of the marijuana the authorities seized. It clearly was a business loss. The Tax Court agreed it was, but even more clearly it would be "contrary to public policy" to allow such a deduction, the court said.

He and the wife would have to bear the loss from his illicit doings, which got him a $30,000 fine and five years in jail. The government won't bear part "through a tax benefit" for a wrong-doer, the court declared.

Holt v. Commissioner, 69 T.C. 6
11/2/77

∾

A thief avoids jail by paying $5,000 but says he wasn't fined.

Fines paid for breaking the law aren't deductible. Russell W. Spitz misappropriated $5,000 that a man paid Spitz's employer, Odin Inc., a Wisconsin firm. Spitz was convicted of theft in a state court, but avoided jail. He was put on probation on condition he pay back the $5,000. Spitz did and deducted the payment. But the IRS barred the deduction.

The IRS argued that the $5,000 was a nondeductible fine because it had been imposed by a court and paid to a state agency. (The agency then passed it on to the victim.) The IRS also contended that permitting the deduction would "frustrate state policy." However, a federal district court sided with the thief. Spitz hadn't paid a fine, the court said, he had made restitution. The money wasn't paid to the state, merely funneled through it, the court noted.

The IRS hadn't shown "in what way a restitution of stolen funds frustrates . . . state policy," the court asserted and awarded Spitz a $9,900 tax refund and $500 for attorney's fees.

Spitz v. U.S., U.S. Dist. Ct., East. Dist. Wisc., 1977
8/10/77

∽

Illegal payments. Did a price fixer, or a dairy-price violator make them?

Illegal payments usually can't be used to reduce taxable income. The IRS recently made two rulings about illicit payments. One involved a firm convicted of a price-fixing conspiracy. The firm conspired with other companies to keep prices high. But it paid rebates to customers who got lower price quotes from non-conspiring competitors. Could the firm reduce gross sales by the amount of the rebates, and thus cut taxable income? Yes, the IRS ruled. Price-fixing was an illegal act, but the rebates paid "to remain competitive with nonconspiring companies" didn't violate the law, and thus were deductible.

The other case involved a wholesale dairy concern that sold milk below minimum prices set by the state, an illegal act. The firm billed customers at the legal prices, and rebated a portion of the price. The payments themselves violated state law. Because they were illegal, the payments couldn't be used to reduce taxable income, the IRS ruled.

The dairy firm had to figure gross income "without subtraction of such payments," the IRS asserted.

Rev. Ruls. 77-244 and 77-243
8/3/77

Sure I cheated a client, but you can't disbar me for that, a CPA insisted.

The certified public accountant was charged with bribing and conspiring to bribe an IRS agent. During his criminal trial, he admitted he told a client an IRS agent demanded $2,000, but he paid the agent only $1,250 and pocketed $750 for himself. Still, a jury acquitted him. The CPA claimed he was entrapped by the IRS. Later, the Treasury disbarred him from representing taxpayers before the IRS.

His acquittal blocked the Treasury from disbarring him, he argued. But he was "clearly wrong," a U.S. appeals court said. More proof is required in a criminal trial to establish guilt than in administrative actions like Treasury disbarment proceedings, the court said. A jury wasn't convinced "beyond a reasonable doubt" of the CPA's guilt, the court noted, but that didn't stop the Treasury from finding the accountant guilty.

Moreover, "every professional knows or should know that cheating a client can lead to disbarment," the court asserted.

Harary v. Blumenthal, U.S. Ct. of Appeals, 2nd Circ. 1977
6/29/77

⁓

"Sam the plumber," also known as Simone De Cavalcante, a New Jersey felon convicted of conspiring to run a numbers operation, split a Tax Court decision with the IRS. He owed $3 million in tax and penalties on five years of unreported numbers profits, the IRS alleged. But the Tax Court said the evidence only showed his involvement in the racket for 1½ years, indicating he owes about $900,000.

DeCavalcante v. Commissioner, T.C. Memo 1978-432
11/15/78

Crime's fruits: A search of a drug dealer's car yielded $27,000 cash. Hudson County, N.J., claimed the bundle as "fruits of a crime." But the IRS wanted to seize $17,000 of the dough to satisfy the convicted heroin peddler's tax bill. A federal appeals court declared that the IRS must be paid out of the seized cash. And what's left must be returned to the narcotics pusher because Hudson County didn't show that the money was linked to the specific crime for which he was convicted.

Hudson County v. Morales, Jorge et al., U.S. Ct. of Appeals, 3rd Circ., 1978
9/6/78

Living in Another Land

The IRS as art critic: Did it know a sculptor from a brain surgeon?

Expatriate American sculptor Robert H. Cook lived in Rome, but most of his works were sold in the U.S. As an American overseas, he figured his earnings qualified for the $25,000 exclusion afforded U.S. citizens abroad. But the IRS said his income came from sales in the U.S. of foreign-made "products," his sculptures, and thus didn't qualify for the tax break.

However, the Court of Claims rejected the IRS's argument. Cook's income resulted from his personal labor in his Rome studio, not from selling products, and qualified for the $25,000 exclusion. Quoting from an earlier Tax Court decision involving expatriate artist Mark Tobey, who also beat the IRS on this issue, the Court of Claims observed:

> Artists' incomes result from their "personal efforts, skill and creativity" and shouldn't be treated differently from the income of "a confidence man, a brain surgeon, a movie star, or, for that matter, a tax attorney."

> Cook v. U.S., U.S. Ct. of Claims, 1979
> 6/6/79

～

Foreigners working in the U.S. can get hit by double Social Security taxes.

Many times a foreigner working here for a few years will pay the equivalent of Social Security taxes to his native land and have to pay them to Uncle Sam, too. Accountants say foreign Social Security taxes are deductible on alien workers' U.S. tax returns.

But treatment of the deduction is "inconsistent" from one IRS district to another; some accept the deduction, some don't, Peat, Marwick, Mitchell & Co., CPAs, found. "These foreign Social Security payments should be deductible as a foreign income tax," asserts Robert Decelles, a national tax partner at Peat Marwick. The U.S. has an accord with Italy that lets Italian citizens working here choose which Social Security tax they want to pay.

Such accords are being negotiated with other countries.

5/30/79

⌢

The Islands are under Uncle Sam's thumb, the IRS said, but he pressed on.

When John D. McComish, a U.S. citizen, was the district attorney of the Trust Territory of the Pacific Islands, he figured his salary was excluded from U.S. tax as foreign income. But the IRS said the territory, also known as Micronesia, was an agency of the U.S., so McComish didn't qualify for the foreign-income exclusion.

The U.S. administers the trust territory under a United Nations mandate, and provides most of the government's funds. The IRS insists that the U.S. "controls" the Micronesian government, making it a U.S. agency. But McComish convinced the Ninth Circuit Court of Appeals the IRS was wrong. Control doesn't always accompany funding, the court said. The U.S. can't alter the trusteeship without United Nations approval, so it doesn't control Micronesia, the court asserted.

The Ninth Circuit's recent decision is at odds with decisions concerning Micronesia by the Tax Court and the Fifth Circuit.

McComish v. Commissioner, U.S. Ct. of Appeals, 5th Circ., 1978
9/20/78

⌒

A quien el dinero? Half a Navy man's pay was hers, his Spanish wife said.

Mr. West was in Spain with the U.S. Navy and married a woman there. His income earned in Spain was subject to U.S. tax because he was a U.S. citizen. But hers wasn't. And she contended that half his Navy pay was hers under Spain's community property law and thus was free from U.S. income tax.

However, the IRS claimed that a wage earner's domicile determines who owns his earnings. His legal domicile was Kansas, which wasn't a community-property state, so she didn't own any of his income, the IRS argued. Kansas law has nothing to do with this, the Court of Claims said: Spain's law determined who owned whose earnings.

"Since (she's) a nonresident alien, she is entitled to exclude . . . her share of the income" he earned in Spain, the court concluded.

West v. U.S., U.S. Ct. of Claims, 1978
8/9/78

⌒

A job and classes work a hardship on a student from Pakistan.

Amirali Budhwani, a Pakistani, was here on an F-1 visa, which admitted him to the U.S. as a full-time student. He took enough classes to be a full-time student, but he also had a full-time job and went to classes at night. On his U.S. tax return, he excluded $5,000 of his income, claiming an exemption granted under a tax treaty between the U.S. and Pakistan.

But the IRS said he didn't qualify because he had become a "resident alien" and the exemption applied only to nonresident aliens. Budhwani argued that he wasn't a resident: He paid the nonresident tuition at his college and had nonresident status with U.S. immigration. Neither his status with his school nor with the immigration agency established his status for tax purposes, the Tax Court said.

Even if he qualified as a nonresident alien, his job violated his student visa and disqualified him for the $5,000 exemption under the treaty's provisions, for he was supposed to be here "temporarily . . . solely as a student," the court asserted.

> *Budhwani v. Commissioner, 70 T.C. 25*
> *5/31/78*

⌒

He trusted pay from a trust territory was exempt from U.S. tax.

Income earned abroad often is exempt from U.S. tax, but it isn't when paid by "an agency of the U.S." Robert J. Toothman was budget director of the Congress of Micronesia, the legislative branch of the Trust Territory of the Pacific Islands. Often referred to as Micronesia, the area embraces some 2,000 islands and atolls, including the Mariana, Caroline and Marshall islands.

The U.S. administers the territory under a trust agreement with the United Nations. Washington set up Micronesia's congress, courts and executive branch. Toothman figured the $17,400 the congress paid him was exempt from tax as foreign income. But the IRS said the Congress of Micronesia was an agency of the U.S. Toothman countered that it wasn't; the U.S. couldn't force the congress to act, though it can veto any legislation the congress enacts.

The Tax Court observed that this issue has been decided before: Micronesia's congress is an agency of the U.S. Thus, Toothman's salary didn't qualify as foreign income exempt from U.S. tax, the court concluded.

Toothman, T.C. Memo 1978-140
4/19/78

⌒

About "face," and why a house is much more than a home in Japan:

Social status means a lot there: An executive must possess suitable "face" to be accepted by Japanese business people. A man's home is a measure of his standing. However, real estate is dear, so many U.S. firms own homes in Japan occupied by their chief executives. A Mobil Oil unit owned the house its president occupied. The place would rent in the U.S. for about $4,400, but in Tokyo it was valued at $20,000 a year. The executive counted as income and paid tax on the U.S. rental value.

But the IRS said the entire $20,000 rental value was taxable income to him. The Court of Claims found it wasn't. The court, in effect, found a legitimate business reason for the housing arrangement, and allowed the executive to exclude the excess rental value. The home's "prestige value" gave the executive social standing that was "extremely important to his employer," the court declared.

The case was a close one, the court noted. The taxpayer won "due in vital respects to busi-

ness and social mores peculiar to Japan," where
" 'face' is an almost tangible reality," the court
asserted.

Adams v. U.S., U.S. Ct. of Claims, 1977
9/14/77

∽

Britannia rules these waves, a tugboat captain told the U.S.

Lester A. Plaisance was an American who wanted to apply the foreign-income exclusion to his overseas earnings and cut his U.S. income taxes. To do that he had to be "within a foreign country" for at least 510 days out of a minimum 18 consecutive months. He qualified only if weeks spent captaining a tug in the North Sea counted as being "within a foreign country." The boat operated beyond Britain's three-mile limit, normally international waters that don't count as a "foreign country" for U.S. tax purposes.

However, the captain argued that the tax code defines a foreign country as "territory under the sovereignty of (another) government," and this North Sea area was under British "sovereignty" because an international pact gave Britain "sovereign rights" to exploit resources there. A seaworthy argument? Well, it didn't hold water in court. The pact didn't give Britain "total or absolute sovereignty" over the sea where the tug worked, merely the right to resources, a U.S. District Court noted.

The tug worked on the high seas, which
aren't "conceded by modern nations to be subject
to the exclusive sovereignty" of any single nation,
the court concluded, scuttling the captain's hope
for a $5,600 tax refund.

Plaisance v. U.S., U.S. Dist. Ct., East. Dist. Louisiana, 1977
7/13/77

These Chileans can stay as long as Dad works. Are they U.S. residents?

The Escobars were citizens of Chile. Carmen R. Escobar worked in Washington, D.C. The whole family had U.S. G-4 visas, allowing them to stay only as long as he held his job. After five years here, the couple filed a joint return, claiming their children as dependents. The IRS said they were nonresident aliens, so they couldn't file jointly, nor claim any nonresident-alien relatives, even their children, as dependents.

Their stay was limited to a "definite period," the duration of his job, and that made the Escobars nonresident aliens, the IRS argued. But Mrs. Escobar said her husband's job was secure and he intended to keep it many years until he retired. They considered themselves residents: They had been in the U.S. five years, owned a home in Maryland, licensed three cars there and were involved in the community.

Immigration status alone doesn't set whether aliens are residents or not, the Tax Court said; the facts in each case will. In the Escobars' case, "there is really no question" they're residents, the court said.

Escobar v. Commissioner, 68 T.C. 26
6/15/77

⌒

Whither thou goest: A dutiful wife can find kowtowing taxing.

Kazuko S. Marsh married Wesley in Tokyo. He was a U.S. Air Force officer; she was Japanese. She came with him to the U.S., declaring to immigration officials her intention to stay permanently. While they were living in Louisiana, Wesley was ordered to Vietnam. She was barred from going with him and went to stay with her mother in Japan for several years. Later, Wesley took her back to the U.S. When she first was in the U.S., Kazuko was a resident alien, taxed like a U.S. citizen. Louisiana law entitled her to half her husband's income wherever earned.

The IRS wanted to tax her on Wesley's overseas military pay. But Wesley, a lawyer, argued that Kazuko abandoned her resident-alien status when she returned to Japan. As a nonresident alien she couldn't be taxed on overseas earnings. However, staying away for several years wasn't enough to erase her resident-alien status, the Tax Court said. There must be evidence she intended to abandon it.

Kazuko intended to follow Wesley wherever he went and eventually returned to the U.S. with him. That didn't indicate an intent to give up her resident-alien status, the court said.

Marsh v. Commissioner, 68 T.C. 7
5/4/77

⌒

A resident nonresident: An American in Belgium is considered a "noninhabitant" by that country and files a nonresident Belgian tax return. Yet he's a Belgian resident as far as the IRS is concerned, the agency affirmed.

Rev. Rul. 78-254
7/5/78

⌒

It's rough in the foreign service: High embassy officials can't deduct expenses for servants or keeping households clean, the IRS ruled in two separate private opinions.

IRS Dockets 7814006 and 7814009
4/12/78

A British professor visited some U.S. colleges for only a few months each year. He wanted to exclude the fees he earned from these trips as provided by a U.S.-British tax treaty. The pact says the first two years of U.S. income are tax-free, so even though he was here only a short time each year, his third year's earnings were taxable by the U.S., the IRS informed him.

Rev. Rul. 77-242
7/20/77

⌒

Legal logic: Foreigners who take temporary farm jobs and their employers needn't pay Social Security taxes. And the workers—most come from Mexico—aren't eligible for Social Security benefits. But temporary farm workers who enter the U.S. (mostly from Mexico) *illegally* aren't exempt, the IRS ruled. The law exempts only "lawfully admitted" temporary farm labor, the IRS noted. So, illegal workers and their employers should pay Social Security taxes, even though most of the workers can't qualify for the benefits for which they're taxed.

Rev. Rul. 77-140
5/11/77